우루과이라운드

서비스 협상 3

우루과이라운드

서비스 협상 3

| 머리말

   우루과이라운드는 국제적 교역 질서를 수립하려는 다각적 무역 교섭으로서, 각국의 보호무역 추세를 보다 완화하고 다자무역체제를 강화하기 위해 출범되었다. 1986년 9월 개시가 선언되었으며, 15개 분야의 교섭을 1990년 말까지 진행하기로 했다. 그러나 각 분야의 중간 교섭이 이루어진 1989년 이후에도 농산물, 지적소유권, 서비스무역, 섬유, 긴급수입제한 등 많은 분야에서 대립하며 1992년이 돼서야 타결에 이를 수 있었다. 한국은 특히 농산물 분야에서 기존 수입 제한 품목 대부분을 개방해야 했기에 큰 경쟁력 하락을 겪었고, 관세와 기술 장벽 완화, 보조금 및 수입 규제 정책의 변화로 제조업 수출입에도 많은 변화가 있었다.

   본 총서는 우루과이라운드 협상이 막바지에 다다랐던 1991~1992년 사이 외교부에서 작성한 관련 자료를 담고 있다. 관련 협상의 치열했던 후반기 동향과 관계부처회의, 무역협상위원회 회의, 실무대책회의, 규범 및 제도, 투자회의, 특히나 가장 많은 논란이 있었던 농산물과 서비스 분야 협상 등의 자료를 포함해 총 28권으로 구성되었다. 전체 분량은 약 1만 3천여 쪽에 이른다.

2024년 3월
한국학술정보(주)

| 일러두기

· 본 총서에 실린 자료는 2022년 4월과 2023년 4월에 각각 공개한 외교문서 4,827권, 76만여 쪽 가운데 일부를 발췌한 것이다.

· 각 권의 제목과 순서는 공개된 원본을 최대한 반영하였으나, 주제에 따라 일부는 적절히 변경하였다.

· 원본 자료는 A4 판형에 맞게 축소하거나 원본 비율을 유지한 채 A4 페이지 안에 삽입하였다. 또한 현재 시점에선 공개되지 않아 '공란'이란 표기만 있는 페이지 역시 그대로 실었다.

· 외교부가 공개한 문서 각 권의 첫 페이지에는 '정리 보존 문서 목록'이란 이름으로 기록물 종류, 일자, 명칭, 간단한 내용 등의 정보가 수록되어 있으며, 이를 기준으로 0001번부터 번호가 매겨져 있다. 이는 삭제하지 않고 총서에 그대로 수록하였다.

· 보고서 내용에 관한 더 자세한 정보가 필요하다면, 외교부가 온라인상에 제공하는 『대한민국 외교사료요약집』 1991년과 1992년 자료를 참조할 수 있다.

| 차례

정 리 보 존 문 서 목 록

기록물종류	일반공문서철	등록번호	2019080105	등록일자	2019-08-14
분류번호	764.51	국가코드		보존기간	영구
명 칭	UR(우루과이라운드) / GNS(서비스협상그룹) 회의, 1991. 전5권				
생 산 과	통상기구과	생산년도	1991~1991	담당그룹	
권 차 명	V.4 9-10월				
내용목차					

0001

외 무 부

종 별 :

번 호 : GVW-1889   일 시 : 91 1002 1730

수 신 : 장관(봉기, 경기원, 재무부, 법무부, 농림수산부, 문화부, 상공부, 건설부,

발 신 : 주제네바대사   보사부, 노동부, 교통부, 체신부, 과기처,

제 목 : UR/서비스 협상   공보처, 항만청)

　　10.2(수) 당관에 전달된 호주의 대아국 서비스분야 REQUEST-LIST 를 별첨 송부함.
동 LIST 중 불명확한 사항은 추후 파악 보고 계획임.

　　첨부: 호주의 REQUEST-LIST 1부.(GVW(F)-0381).끝

　　(대사 박수길-국장)

통상국	차관	안기부	법무부	보사부	문화부	교통부	체신부	경기원
재무부	농수부	상공부	건설부	노동부	과기처	해항청	공보처	

PAGE 1   91.10.03   09:43 CG

외신 1과 통제관

0114

GVW(开)-038/   //002 1730   7경제2소-222
  " GVW-1889 첨부 "   (사본 경기세)

26 September 1991

H.E. Mr Soo Gil Park,
Ambassador,
Permanent Representative
 to GATT,
Permanent Mission of the
 Republic of Korea,
20 route de Pre-Bois,
1216   COINTRIN

Dear Colleague,

In accordance with procedures agreed to by the GNS, I have
attached, for your consideration, an initial list of requests
by Australia with respect to your country.

In addition to the specific requests on the attached list,
Australia would also appreciate clarification of all laws,
regulations, policies and other measures governing foreign
investment which affect foreign service providers.

Australia would appreciate the opportunity to discuss, at an
appropriate time, the attached requests and would be pleased to
provide clarification or background details. We do, of course,
reserve the right to modify (including through the addition of
further requests) the request list for your country.

Yours sincerely,

DAVID HAWES
Ambassador and Permanent Representative
to GATT

0115

ROK	ACCOUNTANCY	Remove regulations that deem audit corporations with financial links to foreign firms as lacking professional independence and therefore ineligible to practice in Korea. Eliminate current prohibition on non-nationals sitting local tests to qualify as certified public accountants.
ROK	ADVERTISING	Liberalise qualifying criteria of the Korean Broadcasting Advertising Corporation, that commissions will only paid if agencies are accredited to it.
		Remove requirement that an advertising agency must be accredited to the Korean Newspapers Association in order to receive commissions on advertisements placed in local daily newspapers.
		Rationalize regulations for the preview of advertising material.
		Remove time limits applying to advertising time.
ROK	AVIATION	Match Australian offer on Computer Reservation Systems and repair and maintenance.
ROK	CONSTRUCTION	Allow non-Korean firms to be prime contractors. Grant foreign firms market access in government projects by revising qualificational requirements to enable foreign firms to bid for projects awarded by government owned agencies.
ROK	ENGINEERING	Allow non-Korean firms to act as prime contractors.
		Revise qualification requirements in that foreign companies can bid for projects awarded by government owned agencies.
		Liberalise and bind requirements for registration of foreign engineering firms with Dept. of S & T.
ROK	FINANCIAL	Grant national treatment to all foreign banks with respect to limitations on capital plus retained earnings and surplus for each branch.
		Raise ceiling on maximum holdings limit of foreign securities firms in Korean securities brokerages.

0116

Permit foreign banks to establish subsidiaries, both banking and non-banking.

Abolish "top 500 banks in the world on an assets basis" criteria for the establishment of foreign banks.

Cease discriminatory basis for calculating ceilings on insurance of certificates of deposit.

Remove criteria for establishment that a bank must have existed in Korea for several years.

Extend forms of ownership of non-bank financial institutions beyond joint ventures and partnership arrangements.

Specify and bind regulations governing access to the securities market.

Remove restrictions on where foreign banks must place surplus funds.

Remove restrictions on foreign banks' access to swaps transactions.

Remove discrimination between foreign and domestic operators with respect to capital solvency requirements.

ROK   INSURANCE   Liberalise market access (on MFN basis) giving Australian firms the same market access that US firms receive.

Remove restriction on acquisition of equity in existing firms.

Cease practice of offical price fixing for insurance products.

Specify and bind MOF criteria for issue of new insurance licences.

Specify and bind procedures to ensure transparency in the establishment of returns granted holdings in Statuatory Guarantee fund.

0117

Remove restriction on the establishment of local
subsidiaries. (ISC)

ROK   LEGAL   Specify and bind measures to permit foreign lawyers to practice
                                foreign law as members of a foreign firm in Korea.

ROK   SHIPPING   Schedule commodities that are considered "strategic".

ROK   TELECOMMUNICATIONS   Expand an offer on telecommunications services including basic
                                and value-added services.

                                Remove foreign ownership limits on general and specialised
                                carrier licences.

                                Liberalise and bind access for provision of value-added services,
                                including all relevant testing and certification standards and
                                permissible foreign ownership levels.

0118

외 무 부

종 별 :

번 호 : GVW-1986   일 시 : 91 1014 1500

수 신 : 장관(통기)

발 신 : 주 제네바 대사

제 목 : UR/GNS 협상

(사본:경기원,재무부,법무부,농수부,문화부,상공부,건설부,보사부,노동부,교통부,체신부,과기처,공보처,항만청)

10.14(월) 당관에 전달된 캐나다의 대아국 서비스분야 REQUEST-LIST 를 별첨송부함.

첨부: 캐나다의 REQUEST-LIST 1 부

(GVW(F)-0410). 끝

(대사 박수길-국장)

예고:91.12.31. 까지

통상국 문화부 과기처	장관 교통부 해항청	차관 체신부	1차보 경기원	2차보 재무부	청와대 농수부	안기부 상공부	법무부 건설부	보사부 노동부

PAGE 1   91.10.15   05:15

외신 2과 통제관 CH

0119

GVW(A)-0410   11014 1500
                                      " 첨 부 "

The Permanent Mission of Canada   La Mission Permanente du Canada
    to the United Nations   auprès des Nations Unies

                                    7~6장 서~L

                            1, rue du Pré-de-la-Bichette
                            1202 Geneva

                            October 8, 1991

H.E. Mr. Soo Gil Park
Ambassador
Permanent Representative to GATT
Permanent Mission of
the Republic of Korea
20, route de Pré-Bois
1216 Geneva

            MTN: Group for Negotiations on Services
            S. G7

Dear Ambassador Lee:

        I have the honour to attach the detailed requests
which Canada is making to Korea with respect to initial
commitments to be entered into as part of the overall
Services Agreement in the Uruguay Round.

        Our services negotiator will be in touch with
yours to pursue these matters in the near future.

                            Yours sincerely,

                            Gerald E. Shannon
                            Ambassador
                            Permanent Representative

                                                    0120

                        6-1

October 7,1991

TRADE IN SERVICES: CANADIAN REQUEST LIST

The requests which Canada is making at this stage in the services negotiations are set out below. Canada reserves the right to modify, add to, or correct the list.

1. COMMON REQUESTS

Canada requests commitments from all participants for the elimination of (a) all quantitative limitations as per Article XVI of the draft Framework, and (b) all discriminatory measures as per Article XVII of the draft Framework, for the modes of supply and in the sectors and sub-sectors described in Attachment A.

An elaboration of the general requests set out in the CPC format will follow shortly.

A copy of these common requests is also being provided to the Secretariat.

On international shipping and on port and auxilliary services, Canada is strongly supportive of the common removal of all quantitative limitations and all discriminatory measures, including with respect to users of such services.

2. TEMPORARY MOVEMENT OF SERVICES PROVIDERS

With respect to the temporary movement of natural persons performing services, Canada is making a common request of all participants as presented in the Attachment B.

A copy of these common requests is also being provided to the Secretariat.

3. FINANCIAL SERVICES

On Financial Services as many participants as possible should take on the enhanced obligations and commitments elaborated in Part III of document MTN.TNC/W/50 of 3 December, 1990. Common requests to this effect are being made by Canada to a number of participants. Specific requests regarding particular financial services items are also put forward to individual participants; where applicable, these are listed in Attachment C.

4. SPECIFIC REQUESTS

Canada has additional specific requests of Korea which are set out in Attachment C.

0121

6-2

Attachment "A"

SECTORS COVERED BY COMMON REQUESTS

Mining

    Metal mining and processing services
    Coal mining and processing services
    Oil and gas field and processing services
    Non-metallic minerals (except fuels) services

Construction Services

    Capital project and feasibility studies and project planning
    Project Design
    Project Management
    Construction Management
    Urban Planning

Commercial Business and Technical Services

    Stenographic, reproduction and mailing services
    Telephone answering services
    Personnel services
    Equipment rental and leasing services without crew
    Automotive rental and leasing services
    Engineering, architectural, surveying and mapping services, including all types of
        geoscientific surveys, whether carried out by land, air or remote sensing
    Agrology services
    Agricultural consulting services
    Training services, including commercial educational correspondence services
    Commercial physical and biological research services
    Commercial economic, marketing, sociological, statistical and educational research
        services
    Commercial testing laboratory services
    Environmental (e.g. potable water supply and distribution, sewage collection and
        treatment, non-hazardous solid waste disposal and processing)
    Quality control and inspection consulting services
    Linguistic services
    Translation services
    Fairs and exhibitions services
    Farm management services
    Forestry management services
    Management consulting services

0122

6-3

Computer and Software Services

Computer Programming
Prepackaged software
Custom software development*
Computer integrated systems design
Computer processing and data preparation
Information retrieval services
Computer Facilities management
Computer leasing and rental
Computer maintenance and repair, and
other computer-related services, including consulting* services and those integral to
the provision of other covered services

Telecommunications Services

Enhanced telecom services
(as defined)

Tourism Services

Travel agencies services and tour operator services
Restaurant and catering
Business convention services

Transport Services

Freight forwarding

MODES OF DELIVERY

For the purposes of this request, the designated modes of delivery include the supply of a service

(i)   from the territory of one Party into the territory of another Party;

(ii) in the territory or from the territory of one Party to the service consumer of another Party, including infrastructural services and technology e.g. access by foreign ships to marine port services or the ability of nationals of one party to consume tourism services in the territory of another party);

(iii) by natural persons of one party temporarily in the territory of another Party viz sellers, intra-corporate transfers (managers, executives and specialists);

(iv) through the initial establishment in its territory by a juridical person. Initial establishment is limited to the new implantation of a juridical person through incorporation, the creation of wholly or partially owned subsidiaries, partnerships, branches or representative offices.

0123

6-4

GENERAL COMMITMENT ON
TEMPORARY MOVEMENT OF NATURAL PERSONS PERFORMING SERVICES
UNDER THE AGREEMENT

Canada requests each participant to undertake to provide market access for services covered by the Agreement, to the services suppliers listed below:

1.   Services sellers

2.   The following intra-corporate transferees:
         executive
         managers
         specialists

In granting such access the following conditions will apply:

Access means that Parties will not require labour market tests or procedures of similar effect for those services suppliers of other Parties to whom access has been granted in accordance with this Request.

Parties granting access will ensure that any balance of payments restrictions imposed under Article XII of the Agreement will not frustrate the return of services suppliers and their personal belongings to their country of origin.

This Request assumes that a mutually satisfactory Annex on this subject is achieved.

Definitions

Service Sellers:
         are representatives of business carrying on activities in a party seeking temporary entry to another party for the purpose of selling or negotiating for the sale of services, or entering into agreements to sell services for that business, where those representatives will not be engaged in making direct sales to the general public:
         length of temporary entry - 90 days

Intra-corporate transferees:
         are people who have been employed by their firm for a period of not less than one year and who seek temporary entry in order to render services to the same employer or a subsidiary or affiliate thereof. More specifically:
         executives - are persons within an organization who primarily direct the management of the organization or establish goals and policies for the organization or a major component or function of the organization, exercise wide latitude in decision-making, and receive only general supervision or direction from higher-level executives, the board of directors, or stockholders of the business.
         managers - are persons within an organization who direct the organization, or department or subdivision of the organization, supervise and control the work of other supervisory, professional or managerial employees, have the authority to hire and fire or recommend hiring, firing, or other personnel actions and exercise discretionary authority over day-to-day operations at a senior level.
         specialists - are persons within an organization who possess knowledge at an advanced level of expertise and who possess proprietary knowledge of the organization's product, service, research equipment, techniques, or management.

0124

6-5

Attachment C

CANADIAN REQUEST LIST: KOREA

1. <u>Financial Services</u>

    Canada

    o Requests the removal of restrictions as described:

    - Banking -- Limits on operations. Unequal access to local currency financing as result of restrictions on foreign banks' acceptance of won deposits and on their money market operations.

    - Banking -- establishment. Retail banking and branch operations have been restricted to largest (ie US and Japanese) banks through minimum requirements for capital, assets, duration of operations.

    - Banking -- limits on operations. Banks are required to make 35% of their incremental loans to small and medium sized companies.

    - Insurance. The insurance sector is on the negative list of the Foreign Capital Inducement Law (see 2. below). It has been largely closed to new entrants except for specified in U.S. firms.

    - Reinsurance. Foreign reinsurers are prohibited from offering direct reinsurance to local insurers.

    - General: Permit the use of Canadian personnel in branches and subsidiaries of Canadian financial institutions as provided for in TNC/W/50.

2. <u>Various Service Sectors</u>

    Canada

    o Requests the right of commercial presence in insurance, telecommunications, computers, freight forwarding and aviation services:

    - The Foreign Capital Inducement Law gives broad discretion to the Korean government to authorize inward foreign investments. This is exercised through a negative list, used to prohibit or restrict establishment.

0125

6-6

경 제 기 획 원

봉조삼 10502-*/>/*   503~9149   1991. 10. 16

수 신 수신처참조

제 목 UR/해운분야 부속서 협상대책 회의결과 통보

1. 봉조삼 10502-709(´91.10.9)와 관련입니다.

2. 표제회의결과를 별첨과 같이 통보하니 회의결과이행에 만전을
기해 주시기 바랍니다.

첨부 : UR/해운분야부속서 협상대책 회의결과 1부.   끝.

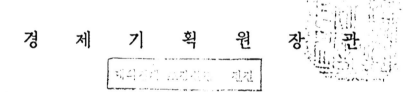

경 제 기 획 원 장   관

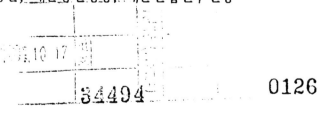

수신처 : 외무부장관, 교통부장관, 해운항만청장, 해운산업연구원장

34494   0126

UR/海運分野附屬書 協商對策 會議結果

Ⅰ. 會議槪要

- 日時 및 場所 : '91. 10.14(月), 16:00～18:00, 第2協力官室

- 參席範圍

  ○ 經濟企劃院 第2協力官(會議主宰), 通商調整3課長
  ○ 港 灣 廳 海運局 振興課長
  ○ 交 通 部 輸送政策局 國際協力課 事務官(황성연)
  ○ 海運産業研究院 研究員(최동현)

- 會議議題 : UR/海運分野附屬書 協商對策

Ⅱ. 主要會議結果

1. 附屬書協商에서의 我國立場

① 沿岸海運과 UN Liner Code와 관련없이 맺어진 既存兩者協定下의
   화물분할 및 유보조치에 대해서는 MFN原則 적용상의 예외를 주장
   하되 既存兩者協定에 대한 MFN逸脫 適用時限에 있어서는 5년이상이
   反映되도록 함.

   다만, 沿岸海運分野의 MFN逸脫問題에 있어서는 대부분 나라의
   입장이 MFN을 逸脫하자는 것이기 때문에 대세를 감안 我國으로
   서는 적극적인 意思表明은 자제토록 함.

0127

② 北歐가 제안한 Common Approach에 대해서 긍정적으로 대응하되 상기 아국의 입장이 반영되는 것을 전제로 하며 國際海運서비스 분야 規制事項撤廢의 경우 5년이상의 履行期間이 필요함을 주장 토록 함.

③ 상기이외의 爭點에 대해서는 '91.9.12 UR對策 實務委員會의 결정 사항을 중심으로 대처토록 함.

2. 現地協商 參加問題

- 금번 10.22 개최 예정인 海運分野附屬書 협상회의는 主要爭點에 대한 最終實務會議가 될 것으로 예상되므로 現地協商에 本部代表의 참가를 推進토록 함.

0128

외　무　부

종　별 :

번　호 : GVW-2033　　　　　　　　　　일　시 : 91 1017 1800

수　신 : 장관(봉이, 경기원, 재무부, 법무부, 농림수산부, 문화부, 상공부, 건설부, 보사부,

발　신 : 주 제네바 대사　교통부, 체신부,　노동부, 과기부, 해항청, 공보처)

제　목 : UR/GNS비공식 협의

　　　10.16(수) 오후 HAWES 호주 대사 주재로 SCHEDULING에 관한 주요국 비공식 협의(약 20개국 참석)가 있었던바, 주요 내용 하기 보고함.

　　　1. 협의 개요

　　　- 갓트 사무국에서 작성한 제 6조, 16조, 17조등 SCHEDULING 관련 조문(별도 FAX송부)중 제 6조(국내규제) 및 제 17조(내국민 대우)에 대하여 항목별로 토의하였음.

　　　0 제 6조에 대하여는 9월 GNS 회의시 보고한바와같이 무차별적 질적 규제는 그운영(ADNINISTRATION)에 대하여만 REASONABLE,OBJECTIVE AND IMPARTIAL MANNER 하에 운영하여야 한다는 의무를 규정하고 동 규제 자체가 합법적 국내규제가 되기 위한 조건 은 UR 이후에 설정한다는 작업 계획만 규정하는 접근 방법에 대체적 합의가 형성되었으나 북구, 호주, 스위스,뉴질랜드등이 제기하는 일부 사항에 대하여 토의가 진행되었음.

　　　0 제 17조와 관련 동 조문에 포함할 요소에대하여는 거의 합의가 완료된 상태이며 동요소들을 법적 용어로 구체화 하는 작업과 관련 갓트 법률국과 GNS 협상 대표단의 의견교환이 있었음.

　　　2. 주요 토의 내용

　　　가. 제 6조(국내규제).

　　　- 북구등 4개국은 사무국 작성 초안 2항 I)에괄호로 표기된 바와 같이 NATIONAL SCHEDULE 에당재되지 않은 분야에 대해서도 각종 정부조치(MEASURE)를 동 조치 자체가 목적하고 있는 무역장벽의 정도를 증대시키는 결과가 되도록 운영해서는 안된다는의무를 규정할 것을 주장

　　　- 기타 국가들은 시장접근 약속이 없는 서비스분야에 대하여 이와 같은 일반적

통상국 농수부	2차보 상공부	법무부 건설부	보사부 노동부	문화부 과기처	교통부 해항정	체신부 공보처	경기원	재무부

PAGE 1

의무를 규정할 경우 향후 분쟁해결 관련 무슨 의미를 가지는지, PANEL 에서 검토할 사항이 무엇인지 의문을 표시한바

0 북구 및 호주는 시장접근 약속이 없는 분야에도 MFN 은 적용되므로 동 규정이 MFN 을 강화하는 의미를 갖는다고 하였으나 기타 국가들은 MFN 은 본래 정부의 모든조치를 대상으로 하므로 북구등이 주장하는 것과는 별개 문제라고 함.

- 또한 북구등 4개국은 별첨 호주 제안(FAX송부)과 같이 인가기준, 기술적 표준, 자격기준등이 국내규제에 의하여 시장접근 약속을 침해해서는 안되며 동 규제들이 NON MORE BURDENSOME THAN NECESSARY 등 3개 기준에 기초하여야 한다고하여 무차별적질적 규제 자체에 대한 기준 설정을 시도하고 있는바

- 기타 국가들은 다음과 같은 이유에서 반대입장을 견지하였으며, 갓트 법률국도유사한 의견을 표명하였음.

0 동 3개 기준의 실제 해석이 나라마다 사례별로 다르기 때문에 많은 분쟁 발생이 예상되며 분쟁해결 과정에서 PANEL 의 작업도 극히 어려움.

0 동 3개 기준을 규정할 경우 각국이 엄청나게 많은 유보 목록을 제시하는 결과를 초래하게 됨.

0 국내 규제에 의한 시장접근 약속 침해 사례는 NON-VIOLATION 조항에 의하여 해결 가능

나. 제 17조 (내국민 대우)

- 제 17조에 규정할 다음 3개 요소에 대하여는 협상대표간에 합의 되었으나 갓트법률국이 제시한 법적 문안이 동 요소들을 포괄하지 못하고 있다고 각국이 지적하였으 며, 이에 따라 새로운 법적 문안작성이 필요하게 되었음.

0 외국인에게 사실상 동등한 대우를 부여하는 한 어떤 조치가 형식상 내.외국인간 동일한 조치일수도 있고 서로 다른 조치일수도 있음.

0 어떤 경우에는 내.외국인 동등 대우를 부여하기위하여 형식상 서로 다른 조치를 취할 필요가 있을수도 있음.

0 형식상으로는 동일한 조치이나 사실상 외국인에게 불리한 조치도 규율되어야 함.

3. 표제 협의는 10.17(목) 속개될 예정임.

첨부: 1. 사무국 작성 SCHEDULING 관련 조문 초안1부

2. 호주제안 1부. 끝 (대사 〜족장)

(GVW(F)-423)

14.10.91

GWM(33)-42 1101718○○

GWM-2033 첨부

SCHEDULING GROUP OF ARTICLES

This informal note is circulated at the request of Ambassador D. Hawes and will be the basis for further discussion.

P.01   022 791 0525 2   KOREAN MISSION GENEVA   18:39   1991-10-17

UR(우루과이라운드).GNS(서비스협상그룹) 회의, 1991. 전5권(V.4 9-10월) (2)   25

Article VI

Domestic Regulation

[1. Subject to the provisions of this Agreement, the right of Parties to regulate the provision of services within their territories in order to meet national policy objectives is recognized. This includes the right to introduce new regulations. It is recognized that, given the asymmetries existing with respect to the degree of development of services regulations in different countries, developing countries may have a particular need to exercise this right. Such right may include, inter alia, the granting of exclusive rights in certain sectors in order to implement national policy objectives.]*

Proposed new paragraph 2**

2.(i)   [The administration of a measure affecting trade in services shall not increase its degree of trade distortion.]   In sectors or sub-sectors where specific commitments are undertaken, each party shall administer all measures*** in a reasonable, objective and impartial manner.

2.(ii)   [Paragraph on obligation not to frustrate commitments: see Pour Mémoire, second indent.]

---

*See paragraph 5 of the Preamble of the Agreement.
**New paragraph 2 is based on the EC text. All text of Article VI shown in bold reflects ideas suggested during the discussions.
***The word "measures" is used in the sense of draft Article III of the GATS to mean: "relevant laws, regulations, administrative guidelines and all other decisions, rulings or measures of general application".

2.(iii)   With a view to ensuring that measures relating to qualification requirements, technical standards and licensing requirements do not constitute unnecessary barriers to trade, the PARTIES shall, through appropriate bodies they may establish, develop any necessary disciplines. Such disciplines shall aim to ensure that such requirements are, _inter alia_:

> (a)   based on objective and transparent criteria, such as competence and the ability to provide the service;

> (b)   not more burdensome than necessary to maintain the quality of the service;

> (c)   in the case of licensing requirements and procedures, not in themselves a restriction on the supply of the service.

3.   (a)   Each Party shall maintain judicial, arbitral or administrative tribunals or procedures which provide, at the request of an affected service provider or consumer, for the prompt, review of and, where justified, appropriate remedies for administrative decisions relating to the supply of services. Where such procedures are not independent of the agency entrusted with the administrative decision concerned, the Party shall ensure that they do in fact provide for an objective and impartial review.

> (b)   The provisions of sub-paragraph (a) shall not require a Party to institute such tribunals or procedures where this [would be inconsistent with] [is not provided for under] its constitutional structure or legal system.****

****[In the absence of a review procedure the matter may be taken up under Article XXIII (Dispute Settlement).]

4.   Where authorization is required for the provision of a service on which a specific commitment has been made, the competent authorities of a Party shall, within a reasonable period of time after the submission of an application considered complete under domestic laws and regulations, inform the applicant of the decision concerning the application. At the request of the applicant, the competent authorities of the Party shall provide, without undue delay, information concerning the status of the application.

[5.   Where measures of a Party impose obligations on service providers in the territory of another Party, and lead to conflicting requirements or adverse effects, affected Parties shall promote co-operation and, as appropriate, respond promptly and positively to requests for consultations on such matters.]

[6.   Parties shall not, by immigration measures related to the temporary movement of natural persons, frustrate the intent of this Agreement, nor nullify or impair benefits arising from specific commitments set out in their national schedules. Where specific commitments involving the movement of natural persons have been made, each Party shall issue work permits and other permissions needed for the work and stay on a temporary basis in its territory of persons covered by such commitments.]

Pour mémoire

- An issue to be settled is whether the paragraph 2.(i) should relate to "good administration" of regulations in all service sectors or whether it should be limited to sectors or sub-sectors where specific commitments have been undertaken.

- Whilst recognizing the right of Parties to modify or introduce measures relating to technical standards, and licensing and qualifications requirements, there is concern that such requirements could be subsequently varied or made more restrictive so as to

- 4 -

frustrate market access commitments. There appeared to be wide
support for the idea of protecting the extent of access commitments
and for finding the means to express this concern. It has been
suggested that text incorporating this notion could run along the
lines of: "each Party .... shall not frustrate the commitments
accruing to service providers of other Parties by measures relating to
licensing requirements, technical standards and qualification
requirements."

Paragraph 2.(iii)(c): It has been pointed out that the restriction on
the supply of the service relates not so much to the licensing
requirement, but to the licensing procedure in the sense that
procedures should not be unnecessarily complicated or costly, or
entail unreasonable, time-limits or unwarranted delays.

DRAFT
14.10.91

Article XVI

MARKET ACCESS*

1. With respect to market access through the modes of supply identified in Article I, each Party shall accord services and service providers of other Parties treatment no less favourable than that provided for under the terms, limitations and conditions agreed and specified in its schedule.

2. In sectors or sub-sectors where a Party undertakes market access commitments with respect to more than one mode of supply, service providers of other Parties shall be free to choose their preferred mode.

3. In sectors or sub-sectors where market access commitments are undertaken, and unless otherwise specified in its schedule, a Party shall not maintain any of the following measures either on the basis of a regional sub-division or on the basis of its entire territory:

    (a) limitations on the number of service providers whether in the form of numerical quotas, monopolies, exclusive service providers or the requirements of an economic needs test;

    (b) limitations on the total value of services transactions or assets in the form of numerical quotas or the requirement of an economic needs test;

    (c) limitations on the form of commercial presence and on the participation of foreign capital in terms of maximum percentage limit on foreign share holding, or the total value of individual or aggregate investment;

---

*All text in bold reflects ideas suggested during the discussions.

(d) limitations on the total number of service operations or on the total quantity of service output expressed in terms of designated numerical units in the form of quotas or the requirement of an economic needs test**;

(e) limitations on the total number of natural persons necessary for and directly related to the supply of a specific service in the form of numerical quotas or the requirement of an economic needs test.

Pour mémoire

The footnote to para.3(d) is still the subject of disagreement.

**Limitations on the hours of operation or sales floor area need not be scheduled.

Article XVII

NATIONAL TREATMENT

1. In the sectors or sub-sectors inscribed in its Schedule of Commitments, and subject to any conditions and qualifications set out therein, each Party shall accord to services and service providers of any other Party, in respect of all measures affecting the supply of services, treatment no less favourable than that it accords to its own like services and service providers.

2. Paragraph 1 above shall be understood to require each Party to accord conditions of competition to the services and service providers of any other Party no less favourable than those it accords to its own like services and service providers. This requirement may be met by according either formally identical treatment or formally different treatment to the services or service providers of the Party and those of another Party.

Interpretative Notes

The assessment of whether the requirements of Article XVII are met shall not be based on economic performance in the relevant market, including market share achieved.

Commitments assumed under this Article shall not be construed to require any Party to eliminate any competitive disadvantages which result from the foreign character or origin of the relevant services or service providers.

Pour mémoire

The above text has been prepared in consultation with the Legal Division to reflect concerns raised in the discussion that, from a legal point of view, the intention of the text dated 25 July 1991, might be unclear and therefore require revision. In particular, the following concerns should be reflected in a national treatment provision:

- regarding the national treatment standard with respect to measures applying to services listed in national schedules, a Party may accord no less favourable treatment to the services and service providers of other Parties through the application of the same measures as are applied to its own services and service providers, or through different measures as long as they provide equivalent treatment;

- in some cases it has been pointed out that it may be necessary to impose formally different treatment in order to provide equivalent treatment;

- the provision should also address situations where a measure may accord formally identical treatment to national and foreign services or service providers but nevertheless affects competitive conditions to the detriment of foreign services or service providers;

Paragraph 2 defines the national treatment obligation in terms of the granting of conditions of competition and not in terms of economic results arising from the application of internal regulations. It, therefore, does not contain wording which could be interpreted to suggest that the economic results produced by a regulation after its introduction could be relevant in determining whether the national treatment requirement had been met. Hence, from a legal point of view, the first interpretative note does not seem to be relevant.

Article XVIII

ADDITIONAL COMMITMENTS

Parties may negotiate commitments with respect to measures affecting trade in services not subject to scheduling under Articles XVI or XVII, including those regarding qualifications, standards or licensing matters. Such commitments shall be inscribed in [the final column of] a Party's schedule [possible reference to final version of Article XX].

ARTICLE VI: DOMESTIC REGULATION

2(ii)

In sectors or subsectors where specific commitments are undertaken, each Party may apply licensing requirements, technical standards and qualification requirements in order to ensure the quality of the service and the competence and ability of service providers, providing such measures are not inconsistent with Articles XVI or XVII. Such measures shall not be applied so as to nullify or impair benefits arising from specific commitments set out in each Party's schedule. These measures shall not be deemed to frustrate such commitments if they are

(a) based on objective and transparent criteria, such as competence and the ability to provide the service

(b) not more burdensome than necessary to maintain the quality of the service

(c) in the case of licensing requirements, not in themselves a restriction on the supply of the service.

0141

외 무 부

관리
번호 91-682

종 별 :

번 호 : GVW-2042   일 시 : 91 1017 1930

수 신 : 장관(봉기, 경기원, 재무부, 법무부, 농림수산부, 문화부, 상공부, 건설부,

발 신 : 주제네바대사   보사부, 노동부, 교통부, 체신부, 과기처, 공보처, 항만청)

제 목 : UR/GNS 협상

　　10.17(목) 미 USTR 제네바 사무소는 당관에 대 아국 서비스 분야 REQUEST LIST 를 (FAX 송부)보내오는 한편 별첨 서한 (FAX 송부)과 같이 11.1(금) 14:30 에 금융분야를 제외한 모든 서비스 분야(보험 포함)에 대한 한. 미 양자 협상 개최를 제의하여 왔는바, 별도 지침이 없을 경우 미측 요청대로 일정을 확정코자 하니 양지 바람.

　　첨부: 1. USTR 서한 1 부

　　　　 2. 미국의 REQUEST LIST 1 부. 끝

　　(GVW(F)-428)

　　(대사 박수길-국장)

　　예고 91.12.31. 까지

일반문서로 재분류(1981. 12. 31.)

통상국	장관	차관	2차보	정와대	안기부	법무부	보사부	문화부
교통부	체신부	경기원	재무부	농수부	상공부	건설부	노동부	과기처
해항청	공보처							

PAGE 1   91.10.18   05:47

외신 2과 통제관 CD

0142

(UW(五)-0428
11.077.1P30.
"첨부"

UNITED STATES TRADE REPRESENTATIVE

1-3 AVENUE DE LA PAIX
1202 GENEVA, SWITZERLAND
TELEPHONE: 732 09 70

October 16, 1991

Dear Mr. Han:

Ms. Bonnie Richardson from USTR/Washington has requested an
appointment with you on Friday, November 1 at 2:30 p.m. to
discuss initial requests and offers as part of the Group of
Negotiations on Services. She proposes meeting at USTR, 1-3
Avenue de la Paix, in the second floor conference room. She is
prepared to discuss all services sectors, except for banking
and securities. This latter sector is being handled by an
official from the US Treasury Department, who will be
contacting your delegation separately.

Given the necessity of meeting with so many delegations in a
short time period, we would appreciate confirmation from your
mission as soon as possible. You may contact me or Ms. Brita
Lineburger at 749-5280 or 749-5310. Our fax number is
749-4885.

For your information, USTR/Washington has completed its work on
most of the initial services requests, including the banking
and securities sector. You should be receiving your
delegation's confidential request shortly.

Thank you for your consideration. I look forward to hearing
from you.

Sincerely,

Christina Lund
Attache, USTR Geneva

0143

8-1

UNITED STATES TRADE REPRESENTATIVE
1-3 AVENUE DE LA PAIX
1202 GENEVA, SWITZERLAND
TELEPHONE: 732 09 70

October 16, 1991

In accordance with the procedures agreed by the Group of
Negotiations on Services, the United States presents its list of
requests on trade in services with respect to your country. The
list contains both requests for liberalization of specific
barriers to trade in services and general requests for bindings
in sectors not currently covered by your country's initial offer.

Nothing in the attached request list should be understood to
diminish any rights acquired in bilateral or multilateral
agreements.

The United States reserves the right in the course of the
negotiations on specific commitments on services to modify the
request list for your country, including adding requests in
additional sectors.

The United States would appreciate the opportunity to discuss
these requests with your government at the earliest possible
time. The United States would be pleased to provide
clarification with regard to any of the items on its request
list.

0144

8-2

SERVICES BARRIERS TABLED BY THE UNITED STATES
GROUP ON NEGOTIATIONS ON SERVICES

Date 10/16/91

Report to GATT Yes

KR Korea, Republic of

ID #	Sort by Country & Sector / Barrier Category / Sector Code	Detail	Law Policy
362	National Treatment / Accounting	REQUEST THAT FOREIGN CPA'S WHO HAVE RECEIVED KOREAN CERTIFICATION BE PERMITTED TO PROVIDE THE FULL RANGE OF ACCOUNTING AND AUDITING SERVICES IN KOREA WITHOUT RESTRICTIONS OR NATIONALITY OF CUSTOMERS. REQUEST ELIMINATION OF ANY NATIONALITY RESTRICTIONS ON LICENSING.	
1,341	National Treatment / Accounting	REQUEST THE REPUBLIC OF KOREA ELIMINATE THE PROHIBITION ON FINANCIAL LINKS BETWEEN LOCAL AUDIT FIRMS AND INTERNATIONAL FIRMS. FURTHER REQUEST THE ABILITY TO USE INTERNATIONAL FIRM'S NAME.	
125	National Treatment / Advertising	REQUEST LIBERALIZATION OF RESTRICTIONS ON IMPORT AND USE OF FOREIGN MADE ADVERTISING MATERIALS. DEVELOP AND BIND TRANSPARENT STANDARDS FOR SCREENING BY KOBACO AND THE MINISTRY OF CULTURE AND INFORMATION.	INFORMAL GUIDELINES FROM THE MINISTRY OF CULTURE AND INFORMATION; BROADCAST MEDIA ADVERTISING REGULATIONS (MAR).
1,340	Barrier to Movement of Personnel / All Sectors	BIND A ROLLBACK OF EXISTING MEASURES OR PRACTICES AS NECESSARY TO PERMIT THE TEMPORARY ENTRY INTO KOREA OF MANAGERS, EXECUTIVES, AND SPECIALISTS WHO ARE EMPLOYEES OF FIRMS THAT PROVIDE SERVICES WITHIN KOREA THROUGH A BRANCH, SUBSIDIARY, OR AFFILIATED FIRM ESTABLISHED IN KOREA.	
199	Market access / Audio and Visual Works	REQUEST LIBERALIZATION OF LIMITATIONS ON THE SHOWING OF FOREIGN FILMS. FURTHER REQUEST BINDING ON LIBERALIZATION OF RESTRICTIONS ON THE NUMBER OF MOTION PICTURE PRINTS WHICH MAY BE ENTERED.	
1,046	National Treatment / Consulting, Management and Technical	REQUEST THE REPUBLIC OF KOREA INCLUDE A BINDING ON MARKET ACCESS AND NATIONAL TREATMENT, WITH NO LIMITATIONS, FOR THE MANAGEMENT OF HEALTH CARE FACILITIES.	
912	National Treatment / Telecommunications, Data Processing and Info Services	REQUEST PHASE-OUT OF FOREIGN EQUITY RESTRICTIONS ON GROUP VANS, COMPUTER COMMUNICATIONS SERVICES, AND DATA TRANSMISSION SERVICES.	ARTICLE 9 OF THE FOREIGN CAPITAL INDUCEMENT ACT AND ARTICLE 73-2 OF THE PUBLIC TELECOMMUNICATIONS BUSINESS LAW.
916	INS: Mandatory use of government-prescribed standards or pro / Telecommunications, Data Processing and Info Services	REQUEST FOR BINDING TO PERMIT COMPANIES PROVIDING VALUE-ADDED SERVICES TO USE PROPRIETARY OPERATING PROTOCOLS.	Ministry of Communications decrees issued in September 1989.
917	INS: Restriction on resale and shared use / Telecommunications, Data Processing and Info Services	REQUEST A BINDING ON THE ABILITY TO RESELL EXCESS CAPACITY ON LEASED LINES FOR THE PROVISION OF VALUE-ADDED TELECOMMUNICATIONS SERVICES.	FOREIGN CAPITAL INDUCEMENT ACT PUBLIC TELECOM BUISNESS LAW

SERVICES BARRIERS TABLED BY THE UNITED STATES
GROUP ON NEGOTIATIONS ON SERVICES

KR Korea, Republic of

ID #	Barrier Category / Sector Code	Detail	Law Policy
84	National Treatment Construction, Engineering, Architecture	ENGINEERING: REQUEST THE ABILITY TO PROVIDE ENGINEERING SERVICES WITHOUT LOCAL ESTABLISHMENT. REQUEST THE ABILITY TO ESTABLISH WITHOUT REGISTERING WITH THE MINISTRY OF SCIENCE AND TECHNOLOGY, SUBJECT ONLY TO INDIVIDUAL PROFESSIONAL QUALIFICATIONS OF ENGINEERS. FOREIGN ENGINEERS SHOULD BE ABLE TO TAKE ENGINEERING EXAMS AND FOREIGN ENGINEERING FIRMS SHOULD BE ABLE TO HIRE A LOCALLY QUALIFIED ENGINEER.	THE ENGINEERING SERVICES PROMOTION LAW
85	National Treatment Construction, Engineering, Architecture	REQUEST THE REPUBLIC OF KOREA EXTEND A BINDING TO COVER NATIONAL TREATMENT "INTERALIA" ELIMINATION OF LIMITS ON CONTRACT AMOUNTS FOR GENERAL CONSTRUCTION AND SPECIAL CONSTRUCTION BEGINNING IN 1996. NOTE: THE KOREAN OFFER ALREADY PROVIDES ROLLBACK OF THESE RESTRICTIONS THROUGH THE BINDING OF ROLLBACK ON FOREIGN EQUITY RESTRICTIONS.	CONSTRUCTION BUSINESS LAW. TECHNICAL SERVICE DEVELOPMENT LAW.
276	Additional commitments Construction, Engineering, Architecture	REQUEST ELIMINATION OF GOVERNMENT-PROVIDED TAX INCENTIVES, FINANCING, AND INSURANCE OF PRE-BID SURVEYS FOR EXPORT OF CONSTRUCTION SERVICES TO THIRD COUNTRY MARKETS.	
534	Lack of Transparency, Notification or Due Process Franchising	REQUEST THE REPUBLIC OF KOREA ESTABLISH AND BIND SPECIFIC CRITERIA FOR THE APPROVAL OF FRANCHISE LICENSES. REQUEST THE REPUBLIC OF KOREA ESTABLISH AND BIND TIME LIMITATIONS ON EACH STAGE OF THE APPROVAL PROCESS. REQUEST LIMITATIONS ON THE DURATION OF THE LICENSING AGREEMENT BE SIGNIFICANTLY LIBERALIZED.	THE FOREIGN CAPITAL INDUCEMENT ACT.
71	Other Services Barriers, NES Insurance	REQUEST THAT FOREIGN BROKERAGE FIRMS OR AGENTS BE PERMITTED TO REPRESENT NUMEROUS INSURANCE COMPANY.	CRITERIA FOR AUTHORIZATION AGENT OFFICE OF FOREIGN INSURANCE COMPANIES ANNOUN▨ IN DECEMBER 1988
1,345	National Treatment Legal	REQUEST THE REPUBLIC OF KOREA EXPAND ITS OFFER TO INCLUDE A BINDING ON MARKET ACCESS AND NATIONAL TREATMENT WITH NO LIMITS, FOR THE PROVISION OF LEGAL ADVICE ON FOREIGN AND INTERNATIONAL LAW, WITH NO REQUIREMENT TO BE LICENSED IN THE PRACTICE OF KOREAN LAW. REQUEST FOREIGN LEGAL CONSULTANTS BE ALLOWED TO ESTABLISH FIRMS, HIRE KOREAN LAWYERS, AND/OR FORM PARTNERSHIPS WITH KOREAN LAWYERS.	
353	Lack of Transparency, Notification or Due Process Other Sectors	DISTRIBUTION SERVICES: REQUEST THAT THE REPUBLIC OF KOREA EXPAND ITS OFFER TO REFLECT RECENT LIBERALIZATION IN RESTRICTIONS ON RETAIL DISTRIBUTION SERVICES, I.E., THAT FOREIGNERS MAY INVEST IN UP TO 10 SHOPS FOR RETAIL DISTRIBUTION PER INVESTMENT, THE FLOOR AREA OF WHICH MAY BE UP TO 1000 SQUARE METERS PER SHOP.	THE FOREIGN CAPITAL INDUCEMENT ACT

SERVICES BARRIERS TABLED BY THE UNITED STATES
GROUP ON NEGOTIATIONS ON SERVICES

Sort by Country & Sector   Report to GATT Yes

KR Korea, Republic of

ID #	Barrier Category / Sector Code	Detail	Law Policy
496	Market Access Tourism, Hotel/Hotel	REQUEST THAT REPUBLIC OF KOREA EXPANDS ITS OFFER ON TOURISM SERVICES TO INCLUDE A BINDING ON MOVEMENT OF CONSUMERS, INCLUDING ELIMINATION OF ANY LIMITATIONS ON TRAVEL EXPENSES OF OUTWARD BOUND KOREAN TOURISTS. IN PARTICULAR, REQUEST THAT KOREA SPECIFY IN ITS OFFER THAT CREDIT CARD HOLDERS ARE ALLOWED TO CHARGE, WITHOUT LIMIT, ALL EXPENSES DIRECTLY ASSOCIATED WITH OVERSEAS TRAVEL.	ARTICLE 21, FOREIGN EXCHANGE CONTROL LAW.

U.S. REQUEST OF KOREA
BANKING, SECURITIES, AND OTHER FINANCIAL SERVICES
(EXCLUDING INSURANCE)

1. List all financial subsectors as set out in the Services
    Sectoral Classification List. (See MTN.GNS/W/120, 10 July
    1991.)

2. Bind a standstill.

3. Accept with few reservations the commitments, including Part
    III, of a Financial Services Annex.

4. Bind a rollback to eliminate the following measures or
    practices:

    BANKS AND RELATED SERVICES

    a. Foreign banks face discriminatory treatment (higher
        interest rates, limited availability of funds) in the
        interbank call money market.

    b. Banks are subject to a ceiling on the amount of
        certificates of deposit (CDs) they are able to issue.
        There are also restrictions on the minimum denomination
        and maturity of CDs that banks can offer.

    c. Banks are required to use a large percentage of funds
        taken in trust to purchase government monetary
        stabilization bonds at primary issue.

    d. Banks are subject to informal guidance on lending
        rates.

    e. Banks are required to obtain original underlying
        documentation of a commercial transaction before
        entering into any foreign exchange transaction.

    f. A variety of funding and lending limits are tied to
        foreign banks' local branch capital rather than to the
        capital of the entire bank, as is the case for domestic
        banks.

    g. Multiple branches of a foreign bank must be separately
        capitalized and are otherwise considered separate
        entities for legal purposes.

    h. The procedures by which foreign banks obtain approval
        to open additional branches are highly informal,
        opaque, and prone to inconsistency.

    i. Foreign banks are unable to join Korea's automated
        teller machine, GIRO, and other electronic funds
        transfer networks.

0148

8-6

- 2 -

j. Rules and regulations governing the activities of banks
    are often applied in the form of informal guidance, or
    enforced inconsistently, and are not made available for
    public review and comment.

k. Banks are required to seek official permission before
    introducing new products and services.

l. Under Korean law, foreign banks are permitted in
    principle to establish as subsidiaries, but in
    practice, the ROKG has given approval only for
    branches.

m. Foreign banks are not permitted to own shares in a
    Korean bank or to establish or have a controlling
    interest in non-banking finance subsidiaries in Korea.

n. Non-bank financial firms are unable to obtain licenses
    to deal in foreign exchange or access to the electronic
    funds transfer and ATM networks.

SECURITIES FIRMS AND RELATED SERVICES

a. The application process for foreign securities branch
    establishment in Korea is unnecessarily long and
    onerous.
    funds in won and may not hedge the resulting foreign
    exchange risk.

c. Securities firms are subject to restrictions on the
    scope of their business activities in Korea.

d. Foreign firms' brokerage commissions must be divided
    with domestic firms according to set percentages.

e. Foreign securities firms are denied access to Korea's
    over-the-counter capital markets.

f. Foreign securities firms without membership in the
    Korea Stock Exchange are denied direct access to the
    Exchange for dealing on their own account.

g. Foreign securities firms established in Korea are
    treated as foreigners rather than as residents.

h. The bond market, investment trust, and investment
    advisory businesses are closed to foreign
    participation.

0149

8 - 7

- 3 -

i. Foreigners are subject to 10% general and 3% specific
    limits on investment in Korean stocks.

j. Repatriation of profits from portfolio investment in
    Korea is subject to restrictions.

                                            10/11/91

0150

8-8

외 무 부

종   별 :

번   호 : GVW-2034   일   시 : 91 1017 1800

수   신 : 장 관(봉기, 경기원, 재무부, 상공부)

발   신 : 주 제네바대사

제   목 : UR/GNS 협상

　　UR/GNS 금융분야 공동의장 FRANK SWEDLOVE 가작성 배부한 금융부속서 초안을 별첨
송부함.

　　첨부: 금융부속서 초안 1부(GVW(F)-0424).끝

　　(대사 박수길-국장)

통상국　　2차보　　경기원　　재무부　　상공부

PAGE 1   91.10.18   08:31 WH

GVW (규)-0424   11017 /1800

14.10.91

11 GVW—2034 첨부,,

Group of Negotiations on Services

Informal Note by the Co-chairman for Financial Services

This draft text is circulated at the request of the Co-chairman of the discussions on Financial Services in the Group of Negotiations on Services.

The document is divided into two parts: the first contains drafting suggestions for Parts I, II, V and VI of the Articles of Agreement that could be dealt with in an Annex on Financial Services. The second part relates to Part III of the Articles of the Agreement and an attachment. This part of the document will require a decision by the GNS with respect to its placement.

0152

ANNEX ON FINANCIAL SERVICES

PART I: SCOPE AND DEFINITION

Article I: Scope and Definition

1. This Annex applies to measures affecting the provision of financial services. Reference to the provision of a financial service in the Annex shall mean the supply of a service as defined in paragraph 2 of Article I of the Framework.

2. Subparagraph 3(b) of Article I of the Framework shall not apply.

3. Nothing in this agreement requires a Party to permit financial service providers to conduct the following activities:

   a) Activities carried out by central banks or monetary authorities or by any other public institution in pursuit of monetary and exchange rate policies.

   b) Activities conducted by central banks or monetary authorities, government agencies or departments, or public institutions for the account or with the guarantee of the government, except when those activities are permitted to be carried out by financial services providers in competition with such public entities.

   c) Activities forming part of a statutory system of social security or public retirement plans, except when those activities are permitted to be carried out by financial service providers in competition with public entities or private institutions.

PART II: GENERAL OBLIGATIONS AND DISCIPLINES

Article II: Transparency

For the purposes of Article III of the Agreement, transparency shall be limited to laws, regulations, and to administrative guidelines of general application.

Article III: Domestic Regulation

1. Notwithstanding any other provisions in the Agreement, a Party shall not be prevented from taking reasonable measures for prudential reasons, including for the protection of investors, depositors, policy holders or persons to whom a fiduciary duty is owed by a financial service provider, or to ensure the integrity and stability of the financial system.

two track approach

0153

2

or

1. Notwithstanding any other provisions in the Agreement, a Party shall not be prevented from taking measures for prudential reasons, including for the protection of investors, depositors, policy holders or persons to whom a fiduciary duty is owed by a financial service provider, or to ensure the integrity and stability of the financial system. A Party shall not take such measures for the purpose of avoiding any of its commitments and obligations under the Agreement.

2. In addition to the information referred to in paragraph 3 of Article VI of the Framework, the competent authorities of a Party shall provide, without undue delay, information as to what may be necessary to reach a decision concerning an application referred to in that paragraph.

Article IV: Harmonization and Recognition

In lieu of Article VII of the Framework, the following shall apply to financial services:

Each Party may adopt arrangements or enter into agreements that provide for recognition of measures of, harmonization of measures with, or cooperative arrangements with any other Party or any other country relating to the provision of a financial service, provided the Party is willing to adopt comparable arrangements and agreements with any other Party in like circumstances. Such arrangements and agreements shall not be formulated or applied in a manner which would constitute a means of arbitrary or unjustifiable discrimination between Parties. Each Party shall administer these arrangements and agreements in a reasonable, objective and an impartial manner. Each Party shall promptly inform the PARTIES of any such new arrangements and agreements and of any significant changes therein.

Article V: Exceptions

Nothing in the Agreement shall be construed to require a Party to disclose information relating to the affairs and accounts of customers or any confidential or proprietary information. The PARTIES shall not be prevented from concluding procedures under Article XXIII of the Framework with respect to a Party invoking this paragraph.

0154

3

PART V: INSTITUTIONAL PROVISIONS

Article VII: Institutional machinery

1. The Council shall establish a body possessing expertise in financial services and supervisory matters for the effective discharge of its functions under this Agreement with respect to financial services. That body shall be called the Financial Services Body.

2. The Financial Services Body shall exercise responsibility for matters arising from the Annex, for significant matters arising from this Agreement pertaining to the provision of financial services, and for all other matters as may be assigned to it.

3. The Financial Services Body will report annually to the Council regarding the implementation and operation of financial services liberalization under this Agreement. The Financial Services Body will, as appropriate, assess the scope for further liberalization.

4. Where a party undertakes commitments with respect to the financial services sector in its schedule, it shall be a member of the Financial Services Body.

Article VIII: Dispute settlement and enforcement

1. Any measures authorized as a result of a settlement of a dispute, or taken as a compensatory adjustment, shall in principle be confined to the sector which is the subject of the dispute or where the benefits were denied.

2. The Financial Services Body shall exercise the responsibilities of the PARTIES with respect to Article XXIII of the Framework where the matter involves an obligation relating to the provision of financial services. The Council and the Financial Services Body shall establish procedures to deal with areas of joint responsibilities.

3. Unless the Parties to a dispute involving financial services agree otherwise, panels shall consist of at least one member possessing financial services expertise. Any appeals body considering matters involving financial services shall consist of at least one member possessing financial services expertise. In the case of a dispute involving paragraph 1 of Article III of the Annex, a majority of the panel shall consist of members possessing financial services expertise.

0155

4

4.   A Party may have recourse to Article XXIII of the Framework with respect to individual prudential decisions only where the Party considers that the decision violates obligations or commitments under the Agreement.

PART VI: FINAL PROVISIONS

Article IX: Definitions

For the purposes of this Annex:

1.   A financial service is any service of a financial nature offered by a financial service provider of a Party. Financial services include all insurance and insurance-related services, and all banking and other financial services (excluding insurance). Financial services include, inter alia, the following activities:

Insurance and insurance-related services

a)   Direct insurance (including co-insurance);

    i)   life
    ii)   non-life

b)   Reinsurance and retrocession;

c)   Insurance intermediation, such as brokerage and agency;

d)   Services auxiliary to insurance, such as consultancy, actuarial, risk assessment and claim settlement services;

Banking and other financial services (excluding insurance)

e)   Acceptance of deposits and other repayable funds from the public;

f)   Lending of all types, including, inter alia, consumer credit, mortgage credit, factoring and financing of commercial transaction;

g)   Financial leasing;

h)   All payment and money transmission services, including credit, charge and debit cards, travellers checks and bankers drafts;

i)   Guarantees and commitments;

0156

5

j)   Trading for own account or for account of customers, whether on an exchange, in an over-the-counter market or otherwise, the following:

   i)   money market instruments (cheques, bills, certificates of deposits, etc);

   ii)   foreign exchange;

   iii) derivative products including, but not limited to, futures and options;

   iv)   exchange rate and interest rate instruments, including products such as swaps, forward rate agreements, etc;

   v)   transferable securities;

   vi)   other negotiable instruments and financial assets, including bullion;

k)   Participation in issues of all kinds of securities, including underwriting and placement as agent (whether publicly or privately) and provision of services related to such issues;

l)   Money broking;

m)   Asset management, such as cash or portfolio management, all forms of collective investment management, pension fund management, custodial, depository and trust services;

n)   Settlement and clearing services for financial assets, including securities, derivative products, and other negotiable instruments;

o)   Provision and transfer of financial information, and financial data processing and related software by providers of other services;

p)   Advisory, intermediation and other auxiliary financial services on all the activities listed in subparagraphs e) to o), including credit reference and analysis, investment and portfolio research and advice, advice on acquisitions and on corporate restructuring and strategy.

2.   A financial service provider means any natural or juridical person of a Party wishing to provide or providing financial services but the term "financial service provider" does not include a public entity.

3.   "Public entity" means a government or a central bank of a Party, or an entity owned or controlled by a Party, that is principally engaged in carrying out governmental functions or activities for governmental purposes. The term

0157

6

public entity shall not include an entity principally engaged in supplying financial services on commercial terms.

4.   "Agreement" means the Articles of the General Agreement on Trade in Services, this Sectoral Annex on Financial Services, and the schedule of each Party with respect to financial services.

0158

PART III: SPECIFIC COMMITMENTS

Article VI: Manner of Undertaking Commitments

1. A Party may undertake commitments with respect to financial services as set out in the attachment to this Annex by inscribing in its schedule that the Party agrees to undertake the commitments of the attachment. Where a Party undertakes commitments in this manner, such commitments shall be in lieu of Part III of the Framework.

2. Where a Party undertakes commitments pursuant to paragraph 1,

    a) that shall not, in and of itself;

        i) create any presumption as to the degree of liberalization to which that Party is committing itself under the Agreement; or

        ii) affect any rights, benefits, or obligations of that Party under the Agreement, including appropriate consideration being given to modalities of progressive liberalization; and

    b) a Party may undertake additional commitments in its schedule.

0159

14-8

2

ATTACHMENT[1]

<u>Market Access</u>

<u>Monopoly Rights</u>

1. In addition to Article VIII of the Framework, the following shall apply:

    Each Party shall list in its schedule pertaining to financial services existing monopoly rights and shall endeavour to eliminate them or reduce their scope. [This paragraph does not apply to activities forming part of a statutory system of social security or public retirement plans.

<u>Financial Services Purchased by Public Entities</u>

2. Notwithstanding Article XIII of the Framework, each Party shall ensure that financial services providers of any other Party established in its territory are accorded most-favoured-nation treatment and national treatment as regards the purchase of financial services by public entities of the Party in its territory.

<u>Cross-Border Trade</u>

3. Each Party shall permit non-resident providers of financial services to provide, as a principal, as a principal through an intermediary or as an intermediary, and under terms and conditions that accord national treatment, the following services:

    a) Insurance of risks relating to

        i) maritime shipping and commercial aviation with such insurance to cover any or all of the following: the goods being transported, the vehicle transporting the goods, and any liability arising therefrom; and

        ii) goods in international transit;

    b) reinsurance and retrocession and the services auxiliary to insurance as referred to in subparagraph 1(d) of Article XIV of the Annex;

    c) provision and transfer of financial information and financial data processing as referred to in subparagraph 1(o) of Article X of the Annex, and advisory and other auxiliary services, excluding

---

1. The words and phraseology of the attachment were based (a) on the ordinary meaning of the terms, without specific reference to the jurisprudence under the General Agreement on Tariffs and Trade, and (b) where they have special meanings, on their customary usage in the financial services sector.

0160

/ ʋ _ D

3

Intermediation, relating to banking and other financial services as referred to in subparagraph 1(p) of Article X of the Annex.

4. Each Party shall permit its residents to purchase in the territory of another Party the financial services indicated in:

   a) subparagraph 3(a);

   b) subparagraph 3(b); and

   c) subparagraphs 1(e) to (p) of Article IX of the Annex.

Commercial Presence

5. Each Party shall permit financial service providers of any other Party the right to establish or expand within its territory, including through the acquisition of existing enterprises, a commercial presence.

6. A Party may impose terms, conditions and procedures for authorization of the establishment and expansion of a commercial presence in so far as they do not circumvent the Party's obligation under paragraph 5 and they are consistent with the other obligations of this Agreement.

New Financial Services

7. A Party shall permit financial service providers of other Parties established in its territory to offer in its territory any new financial service.

Transfers of Information and Processing of Information

8. No Party shall take measures that prevent transfers of information or the processing of financial information, including transfers of data by electronic means, or that, subject to importation rules consistent with international agreements, prevent transfers of equipment, where such transfers of information, processing of financial information or transfers of equipment are necessary for the conduct of the ordinary business of a financial service provider. Nothing in this paragraph restricts the right of a Party to protect personal data, personal privacy and the confidentiality of individual records and accounts so long as such right is not used to circumvent the provisions of the Agreement.

Temporary Entry of Personnel

9. (a) Each Party shall permit temporary entry into its territory of the following personnel of a financial service provider of any other Party,

0161

4

that is establishing or has established a commercial presence in the territory of the Party:

    i)   senior managerial personnel possessing proprietary information essential to the establishment, control and operation of the services of the financial service provider; and

    ii)   specialists in the operation of the financial service provider.

b)   Each Party shall permit, subject to the availability of qualified personnel in its territory, temporary entry into its territory of the following personnel associated with a commercial presence of a financial service provider of any other Party:

    i)   specialists in computer services, telecommunication services and accounts of the financial service provider; and

    ii)   actuarial and legal specialists.

Non-Discriminatory Measures

10.   Each Party shall endeavour to remove or to limit any significant adverse effects on financial service providers of any other Party of:

a)   non-discriminatory measures that prevent financial service providers from offering in the Party's territory, in the form determined by the Party, all the financial services permitted by the Party;

b)   non-discriminatory measures that limit the expansion of the activities of financial service providers into the entire territory of the Party;

c)   measures of a Party, when such a Party applies the same measures to the provision of both banking and securities services, and a financial service provider of any other Party concentrates its activities in the provision of securities services; and

d)   other measures that, although respecting the provisions of this Agreement, affect adversely the ability of financial service providers of any other Party to operate, compete or enter the Party's market;

provided that any action taken under this paragraph would not unfairly discriminate against financial service providers of the Party taking such action.

1.   With respect to the non-discriminatory measures referred to in subparagraphs 10(a) and (b), a Party shall endeavour not to limit or restrict the present

0162

5

degree of market opportunities nor the benefits already enjoyed by financial service providers of all other Parties as a class in the territory of the Party, provided that this commitment does not result in unfair discrimination against financial service providers of the Party applying such measures.

National Treatment

1. Parties shall grant to financial service providers of other Parties, in the application of all measures, treatment no less favourable than that accorded to its financial service providers in like circumstances.

2. A measure of a Party, whether such measure accords different or identical treatment, shall be consistent with paragraph 1 if it provides to financial service providers of other Parties equal competitive opportunities as are available to financial service providers of the Party in like circumstances. Equal competitive opportunities shall be deemed to exist where a measure does not disadvantage financial service providers of other Parties in their ability to compete as compared with domestic financial service providers in like circumstances. In assessing equal competitive opportunities a principal factor will be the effect of a Party's measures. The absence of a significant market share in a Party by financial service providers of another Party shall not in itself constitute denial of equal competitive opportunities.

3. Terms, conditions and procedures for authorization of a commercial presence shall be no less favourable for a financial services provider of another party than for financial service providers of that Party.

4. Under terms and conditions no less favourable than those applied to financial service providers of a Party in like circumstances, Parties shall grant to financial service providers of other Parties established in a Party access to payment and clearing systems operated by public entities, and to official refinancing facilities available in the normal course of ordinary business. This paragraph is not intended to confer access to the lender of last resort facilities of the Party in which the financial service provider of another party is established.

5. When membership or participation in, or access to, any self-regulatory body, securities or futures exchange or market, clearing agency, or any other organization or association, is required by a Party in order for financial services providers of another Party to provide financial services on an equal basis with financial service providers of such Party, or when such Party provides directly or indirectly such entities, privileges or advantages in providing financial services, the Party shall ensure that such entities accord national treatment to financial service providers of other Parties resident in the Party.

0163

6

DEFINITIONS

For the purposes of this annex:

Option 1

1. A juridical person means any entity legally constituted under the laws applicable in the territory of any Party and includes a sole proprietorship, partnership, corporation, organization or other association organized under such law.

    A juridical person that is ultimately controlled by natural persons of a Party is a juridical person of the Party.

    Where

    a) a financial service provider is a juridical person that is not ultimately controlled by national persons of a Party; and

    b) the juridical person which ultimately controls the financial service provider

        i)   is not controlled by any other person; and

        ii) more than 50 per cent of the ownership interests, however designated, of the juridical person are owned beneficially by natural persons of a Party or juridical persons legally constituted or organized in the territory of a Party

    the financial service provider is a juridical person of the Party.

    A juridical person is controlled by natural or juridical persons of a Party if such persons have the ability to name a majority of the directors, by whatever name called, of the juridical person or otherwise direct its actions.

0164

7

Option 2

1. A financial service provider of a Party is a natural person who is a national of a Party or a juridical person of a Party wishing to provide or providing financial services. A juridical person of a Party is an entity which is incorporated in the territory of that Party, and has its registered office, central administration or principle place of business within the Party, in case it has only the registered office in the territory of that Party; has an effective and continuous link with the economy of that Party. In addition, and for the purposes of the application of the Agreement of the Party in which it is incorporated, a juridical person of a Party is a juridical person of a Party where it is incorporated, but a financial service provider of the Party from whom it is owned or controlled.

2. A non-resident provider of financial services is a financial service provider of a Party which provides a financial service into the territory of another Party from an establishment located in the territory of whatever Party, regardless of whether such a financial service provider has or has not a commercial presence in the territory of the Party in which the financial service is provided.

3. "Commercial presence" means an enterprise within a Party's territory for the provision of financial services and includes wholly-or partly-owned subsidiaries, joint ventures, partnerships, sole proprietorships, franchising operations, branches, agencies, representative offices or other organizations.

4. A new financial service is a service of a financial nature, including services related to existing and new products or the manner in which a product is delivered, that is not provided by any financial service provider in the territory of a particular Party but which is provided in the territory of another Party.

5. "Market access" means, with respect to financial services, the obligations referred to in Article XVI of the Framework, except that, where a Party has made commitments pursuant to subparagraph 1(b) of Article V of the Annex, "market access" means the obligations set out in Article VI of the Annex.

6. "National treatment", means, with respect to financial services, the treatment provided under Article XVII of the Framework, except that, where a Party has made commitments pursuant to subparagraph 1(b) of Article V of the Annex, "national treatment" means the treatment provided under Article VII of the Annex.

0165

외 무 부

종 별 :

번 호 : GVW-2044 일 시 : 91 1017 2000

수 신 : 장관(통기, 경기원, 상공부, 체신부)

발 신 : 주제네바대사

제 목 : UR/GNS 협상

UR/GNS 통신분야 공동의장 ROBERT TRITT 가 갓트법률국과 협의하여 작성 배부한
통신부석서초안을 별첨 송부함.

첨부: 통신부속서 초안 1부(GVW(F)-0429)

(대사 박수길-국장)

통상국   2차보   체신부   경기원   상공부

91.10.18   08:43 DU

외신 1과 통제관

0166

G VW(F)-042p //o/9200

" GVW-2044 첨부

14.10.91

Group of Negotiations on Services

Informal Note by the Co-chairman 개정안 TRITT 案

Attached is an informal note by the Co-chairman for the discussions on
Telecommunications Services in the Group of Negotiations on Services. This
note is intended to assist in preparing a draft text of the Telecommunications Annex for circulation on 21 October 1991.

Any comments should be forwarded to the GATT secretariat for consideration by the Co-Chairman.

The 21-October draft is intended to serve as a basis for open-ended
informal consultations on the Telecommunications Annex to be held on 23
October at 5:00 p.m. at the GATT Secretariat.

1 C —1

0167
18-MISC4

11 October 1991
Page 1

TELECOMMUNICATIONS
Annex

General remarks on revised text:

1.   References to "Parties" have been changed to "each Party" or "a Party" or "any Party" because it is each Party that is responsible for the obligations provided under the Agreement and the Annex, not Parties as a group. References to "service providers" have been changed to "service suppliers" to conform to the scope and definitions of the Agreement text.

2.   The drafting also reflects the overall purpose of this annex, to provide a minimum level of telecommunications "access to and use" whenever a party to the GATS schedules a commitment. It follows from this purpose that parties to the GATS would not be permitted to, for instance, provide a commitment on one service which would be subject to a scheduled restriction on such "access to and use". A party not prepared to offer such "access to and use" as part of some or all of its service commitments would, of course, retain the right to refrain from making commitments.

0168

11 October 1991
Page 2

REVISED TEXT	BRUSSELS TEXT	REMARKS
Article 1 - Objectives	[Objectives]	As a drafting matter, only the Parties can "recognize" such specificities, so the sentence has been clarified accordingly. Further changes reflect negotiators' views that the purpose of this annex is to avoid frustration of commitments on services trade through restrictions on access to and use of telecommunications. However, it is inappropriate legally to use the annex as a means of codifying the meaning of "non-violation" nullification or impairment – once codified, these obligations would be enforceable through dispute settlement cases under Article XXIII:1, not Article XXIII:4.
Recognizing the specificities of the telecommunication services sector and, in particular, its dual role as a distinct sector of economic activity and as the underlying transport means for other economic activities, the Parties have agreed to the following Annex with the objective of elaborating upon the provisions of the Agreement with respect to measures affecting access to and use of public telecommunications transport networks and services. Accordingly, this Annex provides notes and supplementary provisions to the Agreement with respect to access to and use of public telecommunications transport networks and services.	1. Recognizing the specificities of the telecommunication services sector and, in particular, its dual role as a distinct sector of economic activity and as the underlying transport means for other economic activities, the purpose of this Annex is to ensure that [benefits accruing to any Party under the Agreement are not nullified or impaired by the failure of another Party to carry out its obligations or commitments with respect to measures1 affecting] [the general obligations and disciplines of the Agreement and the implementation of specific commitments provided for in Parties' schedules are not nullified or impaired by measures affecting] access to and use of public telecommunications transport networks and services.2	
	1 The use of this term may need to be reviewed in light of the final text of the Agreement.
2 The need for this paragraph may have to be reviewed in light of the final text of the Agreement including provisions on dispute settlement for non-violation nullification or impairment of benefits.	

0163

0170

4-4-1

REVISED TEXT	BRUSSELS TEXT	REMARKS
Article 2 - Scope	Scope	"Measures of a party" is defined in the GATS. As seen in the recent GNS Note on Definitions, while most measures may be acts by parties, an omission by a party can also be a "measure" if the substantive provisions in an agreement establish a duty to act. Because ¶5.1 below establishes a duty for Parties to ensure access to and use of public telecommunications transport networks and services, omissions relative to that duty are "measures". Thus, former ¶2(b)(new ¶2.1.2)in the revised text is in brackets because it is unnecessary.
2.1 This Annex shall apply to:	2. This Annex shall apply], with respect to commitments included in a Party's schedule,] to:	
2.1.1 all measures of a Party that affect access to and use of public telecommunications transport networks and services]; and	(a) all measures of a Party that affect access to and use of public telecommunications transport networks and services; and	
2.1.2 the manner in which such measures are enforced by a Party with respect to providers of public telecommunications transport networks and services under its jurisdiction].	[(b) the manner in which such measures are enforced by a Party with respect to providers of public telecommunications transport networks and services under its jurisdiction.]	
2.2 This Annex shall not apply to measures affecting the cable or broadcast distribution of radio or television programming.	3. For the purposes of this Annex, "access to and use of" public telecommunications transport networks or public telecommunications transport services is limited to such access or use by service providers of other Parties for the provision of a service in the territory of a Party as specified in its schedule.	Bracketed words in the chapeau of ¶2,and all of Brussels ¶3, were deleted because (a) some of the provisions of this annex do apply even where there are no scheduled commitments (for instance, provisions on transparency, or technical cooperation), and (b) the provisions that only apply where there are commitments have been restated in ¶5.1to clarify this point. Also, as a legal drafting change, Brussels paragraph 4 has been restated in the same terms as the rule to which it is an exception.
	4. This Annex shall not apply to the cable or broadcast distribution of radio or television programming.	

0171

REVISED TEXT	BRUSSELS TEXT	REMARKS
23 Nothing in this Annex shall be construed:	5. Notwithstanding the provisions of the Agreement or this Annex:	
23.1 to require a Party to authorize a service supplier of another Party to establish, construct, acquire, lease, operate, or supply telecommunications transport networks or services, other than as provided for in its schedule; or	(a) A Party shall not be required to authorize a service provider of another Party to establish, construct, acquire, lease, operate, or provide telecommunications transport networks or services, unless otherwise provided for in its schedule;	Lawyers advise that the reference to "Agreement" in Brussels ¶5 might be construed as an exception to MFN. Nothing in the Agreement other than MFN would otherwise require a party to take the actions specified, and the negotiating group never intended to confer an MFN exception, so the reference to the Agreement has been deleted. The revised text clarifies this provision to clearly limit the effects of the Annex in these respects. The change in the last sentence ties the obligations of the Annex more closely to the commitments in schedules.
23.2 to require a Party (or to require a Party to oblige service suppliers under its jurisdiction) to establish, construct, acquire, lease, operate or offer telecommunications transport networks or services not offered to the public generally.	(b) A Party shall not be required to establish, construct, acquire, operate, operate or offer public telecommunications transport networks or services not offered to the public generally on the date of entry into force of the Agreement. Access to, and use of, such networks and services offered to the public generally after that date will be subject to the provisions of this Annex.	The revised text adds "lease" to parallel the list in the preceding paragraph. It is understood that "lease" in that paragraph would mean "lease from" and "lease" in this paragraph would mean "lease to". A "Party" would include service suppliers operated by a Party. Since the Annex already defines a public telecommunications transport network or service as offered to the public generally, the word "public" was deleted as redundant.
	[(c) A Party shall not be required to grant market access to service providers, including telecommunications service providers, of other Parties other than as specified in its schedule.]	Under the Brussels text of (b), a PTTN-or-S that was not offered to the public on the date of entry into force would not be subject to the annex but as soon as it were offered to the public it would be subject to the Annex. This is logically equivalent to the statement in new ¶23.2 here.

14-5

0172

14-6

REVISED TEXT	BRUSSELS TEXT	REMARKS
Article 3 - Definitions For the purposes of this Annex 3.1 Telecommunications means the transmission and reception of signals by any electromagnetic means. 3.2 Public telecommunications transport service means any telecommunications transport service required explicitly or in effect by a Party to be offered to the public generally. Such services may include, inter alia, telegraph, telephone, telex, and data transmission typically involving the real-time transmission of customer-supplied information between two or more points without any end-to-end change in the form or content of the customer's information. 3.3 Public telecommunications transport network means the public telecommunications infrastructure which permits the conveyance of telecommunications signals between and among defined network termination points.	Definitions For the purposes of this Annex 6. Telecommunications means the transmission and reception of signals by any electromagnetic means. 7. Public telecommunications transport service means any telecommunications transport service - [offered to the public generally] - [offered to the public generally or required [, directly or indirectly] by a measure of a Party to be offered to the public generally]. Such services may include, inter alia, telegraph, telephone, telex, and data transmission typically [...] 8. Public telecommunications transport network means the public telecommunications infrastructure which permits the conveyance of telecommunications signals between and among defined network termination points.	

0173

REVISED TEXT	BRUSSELS TEXT	REMARKS
3.4 Intra-corporate communications means telecommunications through which a company communicates within the company or with or among its subsidiaries, branches and affiliates. For these purposes, "subsidiaries, branches and affiliates" shall be as defined by each Party. "Intra-corporate communications" in this Annex excludes commercial or non-commercial services supplied to unrelated companies or firms, or offered to customers or potential customers.	[9 Intra-corporate communications means telecommunications [through the public telecommunications transport network] - [by which a service provider supplying services as specified in the schedule of a Party] [which allow companies or firms to] - communicate[s] for internal purposes on a non-commercial basis with or among [its] [their] subsidiaries, branches [and affiliates]. For these purposes, "subsidiaries, branches [and affiliates]" shall be as defined by such Party. "Intra-corporate communications" in this Annex excludes commercial or non-commercial services supplied to unrelated companies or firms, or offered to customers or potential customers.]	
3.5 Any reference to an article, paragraph or subparagraph of this Annex includes all subdivisions thereof.		

REVISED TEXT	BRUSSELS TEXT	REMARKS
Article 4 - Transparency	Transparency	
Each Party shall ensure that relevant information on conditions affecting access to and use of public telecommunications transport networks and services is publicly available, including: tariffs and other terms and conditions of service; specifications of technical interfaces with such networks and services; information on bodies responsible for the preparation and adoption of standards affecting such access and use; conditions applying to attachment of terminal equipment; and notifications, registration or licensing requirements, if any.	10. In the application of Article III of the Agreement, Parties shall ensure that relevant information on conditions affecting access to and use of public telecommunications transport networks and services is publicly available, including: tariffs and other terms and conditions; specifications of technical interfaces with such networks and services; conditions applying to attachment of terminal equipment; information on bodies responsible for the preparation and adoption of standards affecting such access and use; and notifications, registration or licensing requirements, if any.	
Article 5 - Access to and use of Public Telecommunications Transport Networks and Services	Access to and use of Public Telecommunications Transport Networks and Services	
5.1 In any sector or subsector in which it has scheduled a commitment, each Party shall ensure that any service supplier of another Party is accorded access to and use of public telecommunications transport networks and services on reasonable and non-discriminatory terms and conditions, for the purpose of supplying a service as provided for in its schedule. This obligation shall be implemented, inter alia, through the application of paragraphs 5.2 through 5.4 below.	11. Parties shall ensure that access to and use of public telecommunications transport networks and services offered within or across borders for the provision of a service, as provided for in their schedules, is accorded to service providers of other Parties on reasonable and non-discriminatory terms and conditions consistent with Articles II, VI and XVII of the Agreement.3 3 This provision may need to be reviewed in the light of the final text of the Agreement.	This paragraph has been rephrased to clarify its status as an overall obligation which applies only where a party has scheduled a commitment. The reference to Articles II, VI and XVII has been taken out as redundant.
[5.2 Each Party shall endeavour to ensure that pricing of public telecommunications transport services is cost-oriented and does not frustrate the nullify or impair commitments scheduled by it.]	[13. Parties shall [endeavour to] ensure that pricing of public telecommunications transport services is cost-oriented and does not nullify or impair commitments provided for in a Party's schedule.]	

0175

REVISED TEXT	BRUSSELS TEXT	REMARKS
5.3 Each Party shall ensure that service suppliers of other Parties have access to and use of any public telecommunications transport network or service offered within or across the border of that Party, including private leased circuits. [To that end, and subject to the provisions of paragraphs 5.6 and 5.7 below, each Party shall ensure that such suppliers are permitted:	12. Parties shall ensure that service providers of other Parties may have access to and use of public telecommunications transport services they require, including national and international private leased circuits, subject to the provisions of paragraph 5 of this Annex.	
5.3.1 to purchase or lease and attach terminal equipment;		
5.3.2 to interconnect private leased or owned circuits with public telecommunications transport networks and services or with circuits leased by another service supplier; and		
5.3.3 to use proprietary protocols in the provision of any service other than a public telecommunications transport service.]		
[5.4 Each Party shall ensure that service suppliers of other Parties may use public telecommunications transport networks and services for the movement of information within and across borders, including intra-corporate communications of such service suppliers, and for access to information contained in data bases or otherwise stored in machine-readable form in the territory of any Party. Any new or amended measures of a Party affecting such use shall be notified and shall be subject to consultation, in accordance with relevant provisions of the Agreement.]	[14. [In accordance with national legislation [consistent with this Agreement]] Parties shall ensure that service providers of other Parties may use public telecommunications transport networks and services for the movement of information within and across borders, [including intra-corporate communications of such service providers,] and for access to information contained in data bases or otherwise stored in machine-readable form in the territory of any Party.] [Any changes [by a Party] affecting such use shall be notified [in advance] and shall be subject to consultation in accordance with relevant provisions of the Agreement.]	Material in brackets in first sentence deleted as it is not necessary or appropriate to include an obligation that parties abide by their own laws.

0176

REVISED TEXT	BRUSSELS TEXT	REMARKS
5.5 Notwithstanding the preceding paragraph, a Party may take such measures as are necessary to ensure the security, confidentiality and privacy of messages and personal data, subject to the requirement that such measures are not applied in a manner which would constitute a means of arbitrary or unjustifiable discrimination or a disguised restriction on international trade in services.*	15. Notwithstanding the preceding paragraph, a Party may take such measures as are necessary to ensure the security, confidentiality and privacy of messages and personal data, subject to the requirement that such measures are not applied in a manner which would constitute a means of arbitrary or unjustifiable discrimination or a disguised restriction on international trade in services.4	
* The privacy-related aspects of this sentence may need to be reviewed in light of the final text of the provisions of the Agreement related to protection of personal privacy. Even if privacy issues are dealt with elsewhere, the aspects of this provision regarding security and confidentiality of messages, which are specific to telecommunications, may need to remain.	4 The privacy-related aspects of this sentence may need to be reviewed in light of the final text of the provisions of the Agreement related to protection of personal privacy. Even if privacy issues are dealt with elsewhere, the aspects of this provision regarding security and confidentiality of messages, which are specific to telecommunications, may need to remain.	
5.6 Each Party shall ensure that no condition is imposed on access to and use of public telecommunications networks and services other than as necessary:	16. In the application of Article VI of the Agreement, Parties shall ensure that conditions are not imposed on such access and use other than as necessary:	
5.6.1 to safeguard [the ability of the public network operator to carry out its responsibility to make public telecommunications transport networks and services available to the public generally] [the public service responsibilities of telecommunications transport networks and services];	(a) to safeguard the public service responsibilities of telecommunications transport networks and services, including the prevention of bypass of such networks and services unless allowed by a Party;	
5.6.2 to protect the technical integrity of public telecommunications transport networks or services;	(b) to ensure the technical integrity of public telecommunications transport networks and services; and	

0177

REVISED TEXT	BRUSSELS TEXT	REMARKS
5.6.3 to prevent the provision, resale or shared use of public telecommunications transport networks and services when a Party has not scheduled a commitment in respect of such provision or resale; or		
5.6.4 to ensure that service suppliers of other Parties supply only those services that they may supply or are authorized to supply pursuant to commitments in a Party's schedule and its laws and regulations consistent with such commitments.	(c) to ensure that service providers of other Parties provide only those services that they may provide or are authorized to provide pursuant to commitments in a Party's schedule and its laws and regulations consistent with such commitments.	
5.7 Provided that they satisfy the criteria set out in paragraph 5.6 above, conditions for access to and use of public telecommunications transport networks and services may take the form of requirements regarding, inter alia:	17. Subject to the provisions of paragraph 16, conditions for access to and use of public telecommunications transport networks and services may include those relating to:	
5.7.1 specification of technical interfaces for inter-connection with such networks;	(a) the re-sale or shared use of such services;	This is already covered in subparagraph 5.6.3.
5.7.2 inter-operability of such services, where necessary;	(b) specification of technical interfaces with such networks;	
5.7.3 type-approval of terminal equipment to be attached to such networks;	(c) inter-operability of such services, where necessary;	
5.7.4 inter-connection of private leased or owned circuits with such networks or services or with circuits leased by another service pro-vider; or	(d) attachment of terminal equipment to such networks;	
5.7.5 notification, registration and licensing, if any.	(e) the interconnection of private leased or owned circuits with such networks or ser-vices or with circuits leased by another ser-vice provider; and	
	(f) notification, registration and licensing requirements, if any.	

1∤‑11

0178

REVISED TEXT	BRUSSELS TEXT	REMARKS
[5.8 Notwithstanding the preceding paragraphs of this Article, a developing country Party may, consistent with its level of development, place reasonable conditions on access to and use of public telecommunications transport networks and services necessary to strengthen its domestic telecommunications infrastructure and service capacity and to increase its participation in international trade in telecommunications services. Such conditions shall be specified in the Party's schedule.]	[18. Notwithstanding the previous paragraph, a developing country Party may, consistent with its level of development, place reasonable conditions on access to and use of public telecommunications transport networks and services necessary to strengthen its domestic telecommunications infrastructure and service capacity and to increase its participation in international trade in telecommunications services. Such conditions shall be specified in the Party's schedule.]	

REVISED TEXT	BRUSSELS TEXT	REMARKS
Article 6 - Technical Co-operation	Technical Co-operation	
6.1 Parties recognize that an efficient, advanced telecommunications infrastructure in countries, particularly developing countries, is essential to the expansion of their trade in services. To this end, Parties endorse and encourage the participation, to the fullest extent practicable, of developed and developing countries and their public telecommunications service suppliers and other entities in the development programmes of international and regional organizations, including the ITU, UNDP and the World Bank.	19. Parties recognize that an efficient, advanced telecommunications infrastructure in countries, particularly developing countries, is essential to the expansion of their trade in services. To this end, Parties endorse and encourage the participation, to the fullest extent practicable, of developed and developing countries and their public telecommunications service providers and other entities in the development programmes of international and regional organizations, including the ITU, UNDP and the World Bank.	
6.2 Parties shall encourage and support telecommunications co-operation among developing countries at the international, regional and sub-regional levels.	20. Parties shall encourage and support telecommunications co-operation among developing countries at the international, regional and sub-regional levels.	
6.3 In co-operation with relevant international organizations, Parties shall make available, where practicable, to developing countries information with respect to international telecommunications services and developments in telecommunications and information technology to assist in strengthening their domestic telecommunications services sector.	21. In co-operation with relevant international organizations, Parties shall make available, where practicable, to developing countries information with respect to international telecommunications services and developments in telecommunications and information technology to assist in strengthening their domestic telecommunications services sector.	

REVISED TEXT	BRUSSELS TEXT	REMARKS
6.4 Parties shall give special consideration to opportunities for the least developed countries to encourage foreign suppliers of telecommunications services to assist in the transfer of technology, training and other activities that support the development of their telecommunications infrastructure and expansion of their telecommunications services exports.	22. Parties shall give special consideration to opportunities for the least developed countries to encourage foreign providers of telecommunications services to assist in the transfer of technology, training and other activities that support the development of their telecommunications infrastructure and expansion of their telecommunications services exports.	
Article 7 - Relation to International Organizations and Agreements	Relation to International Organizations and Agreements5 5 Paragraphs 23 and 24 may need to be reviewed in light of the final text of the provisions of the Agreement on harmonization and recognition agreements and in relation to other international agreements and organizations.	
7.1 Parties recognize the importance of international standards for global compatibility and interoperability of telecommunication networks and services and undertake to promote such standards through the work of relevant international bodies, including the International Telecommunication Union and the International Organization for Standardization.	23. Parties recognize the importance of international standards for global compatibility and interoperability of telecommunication networks and services and undertake to promote such standards through the work of relevant international bodies, including the International Telecommunication Union and the International Organization for Standardization.	
7.2 Parties recognize the role played by intergovernmental and non-governmental organizations and agreements in ensuring the efficient operation of domestic and global telecommunications services, in particular the International Telecommunication Union. Parties shall make appropriate arrangements, where relevant, for consultation with such organizations on matters arising from the implementation of this Annex.	24. Parties recognize the role played by intergovernmental and non-governmental organizations and agreements in ensuring the efficient operation of domestic and global telecommunications services, in particular the International Telecommunication Union. Parties shall make appropriate arrangements, where relevant, for consultation with such organizations on matters arising from the implementation of this Annex.]	

0180

14-14

외 무 부

종   별 :

번   호 : GVW-2057   일   시 : 91 1018 2000

수   신 : 장관(수신처 참조)

발   신 : 주 제네바 대사

제   목 : UR/GNS비공식 협의

　　　　10.17(목)-10.18(금) 간 개최된 표제 20개 주요국비공식 협의 내용을 하기 보고함.

　　　1. SCHEDULING (HAWES 대사주재, 10.17 오전 및 10.18오전)

　　　가. 제 6조(국내규제)

　　　- 북구등이 제기한 하기 2개 사항에 대하여 참가국간 이견이 계속 되었음.

　　　O NATIONAL SCHEDULE 에 등재 여부를 불문하고 모든서비스 분야에 대한 정부 조치를 합리적이고,객관적이며, 공평하게 운영하도록 의무를 부과할것인지 여부

　　　O 인가기준, 기술적 표준, 자격기준 등의 국내규제에 대하여 시장접근 약속을 침해하지 않도록의무규정을 명문화할 것인지 여부(이를 명문화 할경우 NON-VIOLATION CASE 가 VIOLATION CASE 로변화되는 효과가 있음)

　　　O 한편, 북구등은 인가기준 등의 국내 규제가 NOT MORE BURDEN SOME THAN NECESSARY 등 3개 기준에기초하여야 한다는 조항은 철회하였음.

　　　나. 제 16조(시장접근)

　　　- 칠레가 자국 OFFER 에 제시한 바와 같은 관세부과를 16조 3항 상의 제한조치목록에 추가할 것을 제기하였으나

　　　O 대부분의 나라가 16조 3항의 목록이 확대되는데 반대하였으며, 동 문제는 내국민 대우 조항으로 규율될수 있다고 함.

　　　다. 제 17조(내국민 대우)

　　　- 별첨 (FAX 송부) 문안과 같이 합의 하였음.

　　　2. 분쟁해결 (JARAMILLO 의장 주재, 10.17 오후)

　　　- NON-VIOLATION CASE 에 대한 GATT 관행과관련 가스 법률국장과 기술적 사항에대한 질의응답이 있었으며, 동 문제는 제 6조 2항에서북구.호주 등이 주장하고

통상국	법무부	보사부	문화부	교통부	체신부	경기원	재무부	농수부
상공부	건설부	노동부	과기처	해항청	공보처			

PAGE 1   91.10.19   07:41 BX

외신 1과 통제관 0181

있는국내 규제로 인한 시장접근 약속 침해 금지 의무 부과 문제와 밀접한 관련이
있으므로 두가지를 함께 묶어 추후 토의키로 함.

O 한편, 호주,캐나다 등은 서비스 분야는 그 특성상 NON-VIOLATION CASE 의
구제조치도 당해 정부조치자체를 철회토록 해야 할 경우가 많다고 하여 NON-VIOLATION
CASE 를 VIOLATION CASE 화 하려는 의도를 들어냄.

3. MFN(JARAMILLO 의장 주제, 10.18 오후)

- 갓트 사무국에서 제시한 MFN 일탈 방법에관한 5개 대안(FAX 송부)과
멕시코가제시한대안 (FAX 송부)에 대하여 토의하였으나, 구체적 진전 방안은 마련하지
못하였 으며, 다음주에 재협의키로 함. 각국이 지적한 사항은 다음과같음.

O MFN 일탈에 대한 댓가 지불(PAYMENT)은 현실적으로 이행하기가 매우 어려운
문제임.

O MFN 일탈의 REVIEW 와 관련 REVIEW만으로는 불충분하며, 다자화 시행을 위한
장치가마련되어야 함.

O 사무국 대안중 4항과 관련 예외조항이 MFN일탈 수단으로 악용되는 것은
발마직하지 않음.

O 국가별 개별적 일탈도 다자간에 합의되어야 함.

첨부: 1. 내국민 대우 조항 1부

2. MFN 일탈관련 사무국 작성 대안 1부

3. MFN 일탈 관련 멕시코 제안 1부. 끝

(GVW(F)-427)

(대사 박수길-국장)

수신처:(봉기, 경기원, 재무부, 법무부, 농림수산부, 문화부, 상공부, 건설부, 보사부, 노동부
,교통부, 체신부, 과기처, 공보처, 항만청)

DRAFT

18.10.91

GVW(?)-427

11018 2000

GVW-2057 (?)

Article XVII

NATIONAL TREATMENT

1.   In the sectors or sub-sectors inscribed in its Schedule of Commitments, and subject to any conditions and qualifications set out therein, each Party shall accord to services and service providers of any other Party, in respect of all measures affecting the supply of services, treatment no less favourable than that it accords to its own like services and service providers.

2.   The requirement of paragraph 1 may be met by according either formally identical treatment or formally different treatment to the services or service providers of the Party and those of another Party.

3.   Formally identical treatment shall be considered to be less favourable if it modifies the conditions of competition [significantly] in favour of services or service providers of the Party compared to those of another Party.

Interpretative Notes

   [The assessment of whether the requirements of Article XVII are met shall not be based on economic performance in the relevant market, including market share achieved.]

   [Panels may consider statistics and other relevant factual data submitted by a Party in the application of this Article.]

   Commitments assumed under this Article shall not be construed to require any Party to compensate for any inherent competitive disadvantages which result from the foreign character or origin of the relevant services or service providers.

0183

U2-HAW

18.10.91   GATT 사무총

FIRST OPTION

Those m.f.n. inconsistent measures which participants are prepared to phase out if the appropriate amount of time is permitted to enact the phase out. The following steps would appear as candidates for action to be taken to achieve the phase out:

(a)   identification and notification of the non-conforming measures;

(b)   a commitment to phase out the non-conforming measures within the specified period of time;

(c)   a review process of xx years after the entry into force of the Agreement to ascertain whether the phasing out is indeed taking place;

(d)   in the event of an inability to phase out the measure within the specified period then resort to the waiver possibilities contained in the Article on Joint Action (Article XXIV) of the Agreement. A time bound waiver would be granted after certain conditions were met; two-thirds majority vote and proof of exceptional circumstances, etc.

SECOND OPTION

An exemption may be sought for non-conforming measures by all participants with respect to an activity within a particular sector. This exemption would be reviewed at a later date (e.g. bilaterally negotiated landing rights in civil aviation to be reviewed xx years hence but with no

0184

17 -2

- 2 -

decision necessarily being taken to bring such measures into
conformity with the m.f.n. provision).

THIRD OPTION

An exemption justified through the application of other
provisions in the Agreement (e.g. a non-conforming measure
maintained under   Article XIV - Exceptions).

FOURTH OPTION

The identification of a non-conforming measure for which
an exemption is requested but no commitment to bring the
non-conforming measure into conformity with the m.f.n.
obligation. There may be agreement to review, but without an
obligation to subject the measures to the waiver conditions.

FIFTH OPTION —→ horizontal agreements

Those measures which by their very nature are not
candidates for an extension of the m.f.n. obligation and
therefore are candidates for a permanent derogation
(e.g. double taxation agreements).

17-3

0185

INITIAL APPROACH TO THE
MFN DEROGATIONS

Type I: General derogations

The general exemptions from the MFN clause are those considered to be required by (virtually) every country in the negotiations, so that a legal instrument (an annex, a footnote to article II, additional paragraphs in article II) is needed in order to reflect the commitment in this regard. Such a multilateral instrument would contain the commitment of the PARTIES to review the situation of this derogations at the end of a period of x years or before the initiation of a new Round with the aim to decide on the future of these derogations. This type of exemption, while being necessary for all countries, would not require any kind of payment. However, the possibility of a standstill commitment so as to cover only the existing measures should be discussed. The typical example is found in the air transport agreements by which countries grant "hard rigths" on a reciprocal basis.

Type II: Time-bound general phase-out

The second kind of exemptions are those required by a number of countries and limited to certain existing measures. Examples can be found in different reciprocity provisions in bilateral agreements (i.e. co-production agreements). The legal multilateral instrument to cover these derogations should include a discipline by which Parties would commit themselves to bring into conformity with the MFN clause the measures inscribed in these exemptions, in principle at the end of a period of x years. Payment at this stage would not be necessary since the idea is to identify all the existing measures. Nevertheless, countries that do not inscribe measures in this exemption could ask for credit in the negotiations. The discipline referred to would include other elements such as the following: standstill, degressivity, surveillance and periodic review. At the end of the period, a multilateral decision would be taken either to finish the transition and apply MFN or to give an additional period under the same discipline. At this moment, and if the derogation persists, a possible payment should be considered.

Type III: Specific derogations

The last category of derogation is the one required by countries on an individual basis in order to exclude existing measures from the MFN treatment. In this case, the idea of a "negotiated exclusion" is useful. The payment should be multilaterally decided and should correspond to the size of the derogation in terms of actual or potential trade. This exclusion

0186

2

would be of a temporary nature and would be reviewed at the end of a period of x years so as to decide on its future on the basis of provisions in art. XXIV of the Framework. At this stage, the possibility of tranferring it to the type II exemption should be open. On the other hand, the renewal of the exclusion will imply a new payment. For this category of derogations, a very strong discipline is needed in order to limit them to the absolute minimum in terms of number and scope.

A summary of the proposed options at the end of the initial derogation period in each case is:

Type I

Entry into   End of
force   period
├─────────────────────────────

                             Multilateral review:
                             a)   renewal
                             b)   transfer to type II
                             c)   application of MFN

Type II

Entry into   End of
force   period
├────────────────────────────┤

                             Multilateral review:
                             a)   renewal for x years
                                  - payment?
                             b)   application of MFN

Type III

Entry into   End of
force   period
├────────────────────────────┤

"payment"   Multilateral review:
                             a)   renewal with payment
                             b)   transfer to type II
                             c)   application of MFN

0187

17~5

<u>DRAFT</u>   18 Oct 91 9:32 MFNTECH.9

18 October 1991

<u>LEGAL TECHNIQUES TO IMPLEMENT MFN EXCEPTIONS</u>

This informal note is circulated at the request of the GNS. It is intended to provide a starting point for further discussion by the GNS of points raised in a previous informal Secretariat note of 17 July on "Exceptions from the Most-Favoured-Nation (MFN) Clause of the General Agreement on Trade in Services (GATS)".

Legal techniques required to implement derogations from the MFN obligation rest on two levels: the choice of <u>limitations</u> on the MFN obligation, and the choice of legal <u>forms</u> by which such limitations are made effective. The legal form chosen can be thought of as containing the various types of MFN limitations. For this reason, the characteristics of the legal form can have important consequences on the possibility or effectiveness of certain limitations. Waivers, for example, contain widely varying limitations related to the subject matter of a measure, but can only contain certain types of time-related limitations. This note will consider both levels of legal technique: the types of MFN limitations, and the legal forms which such limitations can take.

1.   <u>What types of MFN limitation can be used?</u>

The primary legal concern in selecting MFN limitations is that they correspond as closely as possible to the intention of the negotiators. Three basic means of limiting the scope of the MFN obligation can be envisaged: limitations on the parties, on the subject matter, and on the time or duration of the derogation.

a)   <u>Limitations on parties</u>

A derogation from an MFN obligation can be limited by reference to the parties who may apply the derogation, or to those against whom a derogation can apply. The GATT contains illustrations of this: in

17-6   0188

Article $I:2$, specific countries and territories according and receiving preferences are exempted from the MFN principle, based on their dependency status or existing neighbouring-country preferential arrangements. Likewise, the 1979 Enabling Clause permits preferential treatment to be accorded one category of GATT signatories. As well, under the GATT, waivers are usually granted to single parties. However, limitations on the number of parties applying derogations, or against whom derogations can be applied, could increase the difficulty in negotiating balanced commitments.

b)   Limitations on subject matter

A derogation from an MFN obligation can also be limited by reference to the subject matter of the measure for which a derogation is sought. In this respect, the subject matter can either refer to the service sector, or to some other category, or to a combination of both. There is no essential legal difference between limitations operating on the subject matter of measures defined sectorally or non-sectorally.

c)   Limitations on time

A derogation from an MFN obligation can, as well, be limited through time conditions. These are often related to the duration of the derogation, which can be either fixed, conditional, or indefinite. A derogation of fixed duration terminates after a definite period, such as two years. A derogation of conditional duration is generally contingent on a review procedure although, as in GATS waiver provisions, it may be contingent on other factors as well. A review procedure offers several possibilities: the derogation can terminate at a definite time unless prolonged, or it may continue in force unless terminated by the review. Waivers under the GATT also generally contain such termination and review procedures.

A derogation can also be related to the date on which a measure takes effect. Thus an MFN derogation can be framed to include within its scope all measures of continuing effect which entered into force prior to the signature of the Agreement ('grandfathering'). Likewise, it could be framed to exclude all measures taking effect after the date of signature of

0189

$17-7$

the Agreement. Grandfathering is a common treaty technique and has been used in the GATT. Article I:2 effectively grandfathers preferential arrangements already existing between certain territories and contracting parties.

2. What legal forms can MFN limitations take?

The type of MFN limitations described above can only be made effective through their inclusion in certain legal forms. The choice of legal form is important because it can affect the _possibility_ of using certain types of MFN limitation, the type of _consent_ necessary for inclusion in that legal form, and the ability to _modify_ the contents of the chosen legal form.

The MFN limitations could be contained in any of the following legal forms:

- the GATS text

- a treaty reservation attached to the GATS

- a waiver decision taken under GATS Article XXIV:5

- an accession protocol of a government newly acceding to the GATS under Article XXVIII:2

a) The GATS text

Since this option makes MFN limitations an integral part of the GATS, it leaves the negotiators flexibility to choose any combination of types of MFN limitation. It is not important legally whether the derogation appear in a footnote, an annex or in the main text of the GATS. Consent for derogations within the text is clearly by consensus of the negotiators. Removal or modification of the limitations themselves can only be made, however, in accordance with the amendment provisions of Article XXXII, which require a two-thirds majority and which results in an amendment which

is only effective against those parties specifically accepting it. The
GATT in Article I:2 contains MFN limitations in this legal form.

b)   Treaty reservations

The Vienna Convention on the Law of Treaties (Articles 20-23) allows
signatories to international agreements to make reservations on obligations
contained in such agreements, unless reservations are prohibited or limited
in the agreement, or are "incompatible with the object and purpose of the
treaty". The draft GATS does not expressly prohibit or limit reservations,
but it could be argued that they are indeed incompatible with the object
and purpose of the agreement. Leaving aside that possibility, consent of
other parties is not required in order to make a reservation, but a
reservation is only effective against other parties that have accepted it.
As well, a reservation can only be made at the time of signature of,
accession to, or ratification of the GATS, and cannot subsequently be
modified, only withdrawn.

c)   Waiver decisions

A waiver decision under Article XXIV:5 of the GATS may contain
limitations on MFN. However, parties granted MFN derogations in a waiver
are subject to strict time limitations. A termination date must be
specified and the waiver, if granted for longer than one year, is
reviewable annually and may be prematurely terminated. Parties are also
limited by the requirement that the "exceptional circumstances" surrounding
the granting of the waiver still be present at the time of the review. The
consent required to obtain a waiver is a two-thirds majority comprising
more than half of the parties. Modification of the waiver can occur either
through the same procedure as for the obtention of the waiver or through
the review process.

d)   Accession Protocol

Parties acceding to the GATS after it comes into force will do so by
an accession protocol under Article XXVIII:2. This instrument could
contain conditions on derogations from MFN on a negotiated basis. This
possibility would only apply of course to a limited number of cases.

0191

3. <u>What approaches to drafting MFN derogations do the legal techniques suggest</u>?

The choice of legal technique for drafting MFN derogations should correspond to the nature of the limitations being sought. With this in mind, the following comments could be made:

a) Limitations as to <u>parties</u> able to invoke certain exceptions, while legally possible, might to raise problems in balancing commitments

b) Limitations as to <u>subject matter</u> can be partially achieved by a narrow, measure-based listing of derogations by description of the <u>right</u> to which ~~the derogation applies~~ MFN ~~is not to apply~~ (and not a description based on the name of the legislation or on an entire sector or subsector). Measures which are not sector specific can be treated in the same way as those which are sector specific.

c) Limitations as to <u>time</u> would appear to be a fruitful legal technique to develop. Thus one could envisage:

    i) measures which would be time limited and for which a ~~termination date~~ could be <u>fixed</u>

        - technique: text of the GATS or waiver decision

    ii) measures which would be time limited but for which a termination date could <u>not at present be fixed</u>

        - technique: text of GATS

    iii) measures which would <u>not be time limited</u>

        - technique: text of GATS

In each of the above cases, consideration would have to be given as to whether these limitations covered only <u>existing</u> measures, or also measures which could be taken after the entry into force of the Agreement.

17-10

In evaluating these approaches, it should also be kept in mind that certain categories of measures, while they may appear to require MFN derogations, do not for the following reasons:

a) the measure is not a measure as defined under the GATS (eg. it is non-mandatory legislation or a treaty commitment with no domestic force of law)

b) the measure is covered by the exceptions provision in Article XIV of the GATS

27.9.91

EXEMPTIONS FROM THE M.F.N. CLAUSE
Points Raised in Discussions

1. <u>Governmental actions for which an exemption from the m.f.n. clause may be sought</u>

The m.f.n. clause of Article II of the GATS applies to measures affecting the supply of services through the modes of delivery specified in Article I of the GATS. It should therefore follow that an exemption from the m.f.n. clause must be formulated as a permission to take a specified measure on specified conditions notwithstanding that clause. Practical problems with limiting such exemptions to specific measures have been identified and include the following:

- the number of specific measures relevant in the non-application of the m.f.n. clause may be very large, making the lists of exemptions unmanageable;

- the identification of specific measures places a heavy burden on countries to examine their entire regulatory systems at the most detailed level;

- it is not clear whether identifying specific measures does indeed provide an effective means of reducing the scope of exemptions from the m.f.n. clause.

It should be noted that in identifying m.f.n. exemptions, references to specific domestic legislation should in any case be avoided since this legislation is subject to interpretations by domestic courts. As pointed out in the informal note of 17 July 1991, the scope of a measure to be exempted from the m.f.n. clause should therefore be described by the participants in terms of a concrete governmental measure, and not as the

0194

I-MFN

- 2 -

exercise of particular domestic legislation or of a specified provision
thereof.

Similarly, since international agreements <u>as such</u> are not measures,
when a participant describes the scope of a measure to be exempted from the
m.f.n. clause, in general the description should refer not to an
international agreement <u>as such</u>, but to domestic measures taken to
implement it; the international agreement itself should only be referred to
if it is self-executing without further domestic implementing action under
that participant's constitutional system.

It has been suggested that an alternative to the identification of
specific measures would be the statement of the general policy pursued by
countries which would be in violation of the m.f.n. clause. A decision is
therefore necessary as to:

  - what level of specificity participants would need to have in
    their requests for exemptions, so as to limit the degree of
    detail in their lists while still retaining the precision
    necessary for assessing the value of exemptions requested and the
    overall balance at the end of negotiations.

2. <u>Factors determining whether an exemption from the m.f.n. clause is
    needed</u>

Regardless of how specific the lists of exemptions must be, the issue
arises of which factors should determine whether a particular measure or
policy may require an exemption from the m.f.n. clause. The following are
the main questions raised in discussions:

  - should requirements or policies which are applied to all trading
    partners on the basis of the same conditions be considered to be   POL
    in conformity with the m.f.n. clause if these conditions require
    actions considered m.f.n.-inconsistent (e.g. reciprocity

0195

I-MFN

- 3 -

requirements, bilateral agreements which call for
market-sharing)?

- if a measure implements a bilateral or plurilateral agreement,
should it necessarily require an exemption irrespective of the POL
nature of the agreement? Should the nature of the agreement
determine whether the exemption is needed? Should the conditions
required as a prerequisite to entering into such an agreement
determine whether the exemption is needed; if so, what sort of
conditions should be considered to be consistent with m.f.n. and
which should require an exemption for measures taken under the
resulting agreement?

- assuming that a discretionary policy or discretionary
legislation, which permits executive authorities to take   POL
m.f.n.-inconsistent action but does not require them to do so, is
not a measure (and would therefore not conflict with the m.f.n.
clause): should a discretionary policy or discretionary
legislation as such be listed as an exemption?

- if not, then would exemptions be limited to government measures
which implement discretionary policies or laws, as well as ·
mandatory policies or legislation which require an
m.f.n.-inconsistent measure to be taken?

- should an exemption permit future measures inconsistent with
m.f.n.? In other words, should an exemption for an existing   POL
measure or policy imply that a party may act inconsistently with
the m.f.n. clause in the future (e.g. renew or modify existing or
conclude new restrictive bilateral agreements)?

0196

17-14   I-MFN

- 4 -

3. Constraints limiting the scope of exemptions

There is agreement that constraints may need to be imposed on
exemptions in order to better define their extent, and to make it easier
for participants to assess the overall balance at the end of negotiations.
Exemptions may be limited in <u>duration</u> or in <u>breadth</u>, and the exemption
process may require the negotiation of <u>payment</u> for exemptions taken.

One means to limit the scope of exemptions is through the
establishment of time-limits for their <u>duration</u>. It has been suggested,
however, that in some cases it might not be feasible for participants to do
so. The following questions may be relevant to resolving the issue of
temporariness of exemptions:

-    in general, should the provisions concerning m.f.n. exemptions
     permit an exemption to continue until a party agrees to eliminate
     it, or should these provisions compel a party at some point in
     time to sunset a measure or obtain a waiver?

-    should the duration of exemptions be limited to a single
     time-limit for all parties?   Should the duration of an exemption
     be tied to other factors, and if so, then what factors?

-    what kind of flexibility could be envisaged for inconsistent
     measures when a party found it difficult to predict the time
     period necessary to bring them into conformity with the m.f.n.
     clause? Would an open-ended exemption accompanied by a review
     process be sufficient?

-    what constraints should be placed on open-ended exemptions (e.g.
     periodic review, require waiver procedures initially, require
     waiver procedures after a specific time)?

-    should all exemptions be subjected to a review procedure? If so,
     how should this procedure take place (e.g. periodically, in the
     context of a new GATS round, in conjunction with a
     report/assessment of the party taking the exemption?

0197

- 5 -

- should participants be permitted to request an exemption from the m.f.n. obligation after the entry into force of the agreement? If so, under what procedures? (e.g. Art. XXIV of the framework)

The breadth of m.f.n. exemptions has also been an issue for negotiators.

- should participants be able to take an m.f.n. exemption for an entire sector or sub-sector, or must the exemption be limited to specific measures?

Another means to deter participants from seeking exemptions is to require some form of payment for exemptions taken. It has been suggested that the "price" a participant should pay for having sought an exemption should be closely related to the effect of the exemption on the overall outcome at the conclusion of the services negotiations. There is therefore a clear linkage between the process of submitting requests for m.f.n. exemptions and the process of negotiating initial commitments. In that regard, the following questions are relevant:

- how should participants arrive at a better knowledge among themselves of requests for exemptions (e.g. dark room process, Secretariat involvement)?

- should general guidelines be adopted that could assist participants in assessing the payment they would need to make for exemptions taken?

- should each participant assess the payment "owed" by another participant based on its judgment of the overall outcome of the negotiations?

- instead of controlling the scope of exemptions through "payment" via the request/offer process, should the negotiators instead choose to provide m.f.n. exemptions only through the normal

0198

I-MFN

- 6 -

waiver procedure? To what extent would the normal waiver
procedure be a better means of controlling the scope of
exemptions than the request/offer process?

0199
I-MFN

is only effective against those parties specifically accepting it. The
GATT in Article I:2 contains MFN limitations in this legal form.

b) Treaty reservations

The Vienna Convention on the Law of Treaties (Articles 20-23) allows
signatories to international agreements to make reservations on obligations
contained in such agreements, unless reservations are prohibited or limited
in the agreement, or are "incompatible with the object and purpose of the
treaty". The draft GATS does not expressly prohibit or limit reservations,
but it could be argued that they are indeed incompatible with the object
and purpose of the agreement. Leaving aside that possibility, consent of
other parties is not required in order to make a reservation, but a
reservation is only effective against other parties that have accepted it.
As well, a reservation can only be made at the time of signature of,
accession to, or ratification of the GATS, and cannot subsequently be
modified, only withdrawn.

c) Waiver decisions

A waiver decision under Article XXIV:5 of the GATS may contain
limitations on MFN. However, parties granted MFN derogations in a waiver
are subject to strict time limitations. A termination date must be
specified and the waiver, if granted for longer than one year, is
reviewable annually and may be prematurely terminated. Parties are also
limited by the requirement that the "exceptional circumstances" surrounding
the granting of the waiver still be present at the time of the review. The
consent required to obtain a waiver is a two-thirds majority comprising
more than half of the parties. Modification of the waiver can occur either
through the same procedure as for the obtention of the waiver or through
the review process.

d) Accession Protocol

Parties acceding to the GATS after it comes into force will do so by
an accession protocol under Article XXVIII:2. This instrument could
contain conditions on derogations from MFN on a negotiated basis. This
possibility would only apply of course to a limited number of cases.

0200

[AUDIOVISUAL [, BROADCASTING, SOUND RECORDING AND PUBLISHING] SERVICES*
Annex

1.   This Annex applies to any activity related to the [production],
[publication], distribution, broadcasting or other transmission of
[audiovisual works] [films, radio and television programming, sound
recordings, [books, periodicals and newspapers]] whatever the means used.

M.f.n.

2.   The provisions of paragraph 1 of Article II of the Agreement do not
apply to measures relating to any activities described in paragraph 1
above, that are taken by a Party in pursuance of cultural policy objectives
in connection with [existing] bilateral or plurilateral agreements,
arrangements or actions of international bodies.

Other Provisions

[3.   It is recognized that in the activities referred to in paragraph 1
above, Parties may pursue cultural policy objectives;   negotiations on
specific commitments, for these activities, under Parts III and IV of the
Agreement, shall respect their cultural specificities.]

[4.   Nothing in the Agreement shall affect the status, as defined by each
Party, of the entities providing audiovisual services in its territory.]

Review

5.   Parties shall review the provisions of this annex within ... years of
the entry into force of the Agreement and periodically thereafter, pursuant
to Article XIX:I of the Agreement.]

_____

     *An alternative to an Annex could be an exception for "cultural
values" under Article XIV, relating to the list of activities in
paragraph 1 of this text.

발 신 전 보

	분류번호	보존기간

번   호 : WGV-1443   911021 1803 FN   종별 : _____

수   신 : 주   제네바   대사. 총영사

발   신 : 장 관 (통 기)

제   목 : UR/GNS(해운분야) 회의

　

대 : GVW-1794 (91.9.20)

　

10.22(화) 개최되는 표제회의 대책자료(대호 북구의 Common approach에 대한 아국 입장 포함)를 별첨 송부하니 이를 참고하여 귀관 관계관이 동 회의에 참석토록 조치하고 결과 보고바람.

　

(fax)

첨 부 : UR/해운분야 대책 자료.　　　　　　끝.　　　　(통상국장　김 용 규)

WGVF-262

보 안 통 제	

앙고재	91년 10월 21일 통기과	기안자성명 조천	과장	심의관	국장 전결		차관	장관

외신과통제

0202

UR / 해운분야 회의 대책자료

1. 기본입장

○ 해운산업은 국제적 특성으로 국제간 협력 및 .... 피할 수 없는 불가피한 분야 이므로 UR 협상에 능동적으로 대응

○ 특히, 우리나라는 미국, EC 등 선진국과의 쌍무협의를 통해 상당히 개방되어 있어 UR 협정시행에 따른 영향이 적은 분야임

○ 따라서 금번 회의에 참여하여 우리나라의 입장을 반영함과 동시에 **협상내용 및** 추이와 각국의 동향을 파악하여 향후 UR 대책에 활용

※ 단, 각국간의 입장 대립시 미국과의 쌍무해운관계와 우리나라 해운의 국제적 지위 등을 감안 적극적인 입장 자제

2. 세부입장

가. 해운분야 부속서에 대한 입장

○ 부속서 주요내용 (최혜국 대우 문제)

- 적용배제 또는 쌍무협정 및 협약에 의한 화물유보 조치는 조건부 적용 제외 (제2조)

○ 아측입장

- UN-Liner Code 와 관계없이 맺어진 쌍무협정·협약등에 의한 화물배분 **및** 유보조치는 MFN 적용 제외

- 기존 쌍무협정에 대한 MFN 일탈시한은 5년이상으로 반영

- 연안해운분야에 대하여는 기본적으로 MFN 적용 제외 입장이나 대부분의 국가가 연안해운의 MFN 일탈 입장임을 감안하여 아국으로서는 적극적인 의사표현 자제

니. 복구의 Common Approach 에 대한 입장

복 구 제 의 내 용	아 국 입 장
o 국제해운분야 - 국제해운서비스 공급에 대한 제한적 조치나 무역 왜곡 효과를 초래하는 신규조치 금지 - 협정 발효후 3년이내에 기존의 제한 조치나 무역 왜곡 효과를 초래하는 조치 철폐	o 우리나라의 국제해운분야 규제사항은 화물유보제도 뿐이며 o '95. 1 까지 화물유보제도 폐지를 Offer 했다는 점을 감안할때 특별한 문제점은 없으나 o 규제사항의 일괄철폐기간을 최대한 유보함이 바람직 (5년이상)
o 연안해운분야 - 신규 규제조치 금지 - 기존 규제사항의 완화·철폐 가능	o 연안분야에 대한 특별한 의무사항이 없으므로 복구안 지지 * 우리나라는 연안해운의 개방에는 반대
o 해운보조서비스 - 신규 규제조치 금지 - 기존 규제사항의 완화 또는 철폐를 위한 협상 가능 - 해운보조서비스의 접근 및 사용에 있어 공평한 조건 보장	o 체약국에 대한 특별한 의무규정이 없으며 o 우리나라도 항만시설 및 서비스의 이용에 있어 차별사항이 없으므로 복구안 지지하되 o 혼란방지를 위해 해운보조서비스의 개념 구체화 필요

나. 기타사항

    o 우리나라 해운실정을 고려하여 국익이 되는 방향에서 적절히 대응

0204

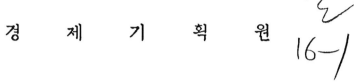

경 제 기 획 원

봉조삼 10502-<del>1738</del>   503~9149   1991. 10. 21

수 신 수신처 참조

제 목 UR/서비스협상 관계부처 회의결과 통보

　　　10.17일 개최한 MFN일탈 및 Request List에 대한 주요관계부처 회의
결과를 별첨과 같이 통보하니 협상대책추진에 만전을 기해 주시기 바라며
특히 각 분야별 Request List는 10.23일까지 기일 엄수하여 제출하여 주시기
바랍니다.

　　　첨부 : MFN일탈 및 Request List에 대한 주요관계부처 회의결과 1부.　　끝.

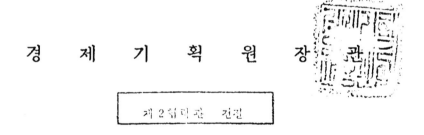

경 제 기 획 원 장 관

수신처 : <u>외무부장관</u>, 재무부장관, 문화부장관, 상공부장관, 건설부장관,
　　　　　교통부장관, 노동부장관, 체신부장관, 과학기술처장관, 공보처장관,
　　　　　해운항만청장

35134   0205

MFN逸脫 및 Request List에 대한
主要關係部處 會議結果

Ⅰ. 會議槪要

- 日　　時 : '91.10.17, 16:00〜18:20

- 場　　所 : 經濟企劃院 小會議室

- 參 席 者 : 經濟企劃院 第2協力官, 通商調整3課長, 外務部, 財務部,
　　　　　　商工部, 建設部, 交通部, 遞信部, 科技處의 擔當課長
　　　　　　또는 事務官, 海運産業研究院의 研究責任者등 참석

- 會議議題 : MFN逸脫事項 Request List 對策

Ⅱ. 會議結果

1. 水平的協定에 대한 MFN逸脫 事項

- FCN, 投資保障協定, 通商 및 貿易協定, 二重課稅防止 協定, 비자免除
協定등 수평적 협정의 MFN逸脫問題는 앞으로의 協商動向을 지켜보면서
關係部處 및 제네바 代表部의 추가 검토후 結論을 내리도록 함.

- 특히 投資保障協定, 通商 및 貿易協定은 MFN逸脫問題를 거론하지 않는
방향으로 검토

2. 分野別 MFN逸脫事項

① 視聽覺 서비스분야는 附屬書에서 "文化的 價値"가 논의되고 있는 점을
감안 일단 旣存協定에 의해서 제정한 映畵製作 및 配給業體의 설립에
대한 外國人投資 認可指針의 MFN逸脫이 필요함을 제기

0206

② 航空分野는 雙務協定에 규정되어 있는 運輸權에 대한 사항이 MFN逸脫
事項이나 協商大勢가 운수권의 MFN原則을 逸脫시키자는 상황일 경우
별도 제기 불필요

　　＊ 항공 CRS의 MFN逸脫은 상대방에 대한 설득논리가 미약하고 個別的
　　　인 自由化 措置에 대하여 MFN을 적용하는 國際貿易趨勢에 비추어
　　　MFN逸脫對象에서 제외하되 交通部와 遞信部가 필요시 추가 협의

③ 海運分野는 沿岸海運과 UN Liner Code와 관련없이 맺어진 기존 兩者
協定下의 화물분할 및 유보조치에 대한 사항(5년이상의 多者化時限
설정)

　　＊ 一般貿易業, 保險業등 韓·美 協商結果의 차별적 적용문제는
　　　MFN逸脫이 아니고 다른 차원에서 解決方法 모색

3. Request List에 대한 事項

- 各部處가 상대국에게 제시할 수 있는 형태로 核心事項을 선별·
　再作成하여 10.23일까지 經濟企劃院에 통보

- UR對策 實務委員會에서 최종 확정하여 GATT에 10월하순경에 제출

- 讓許協商過程에서 추가적인 Request List 事項을 계속 발굴

4. 其他

- 실질적인 讓許協商過程에는 各主務部處가 현지 협상에 직접 참여하여
　所管業種에 대하여 책임있게 대처

0207

경 제 기 획 원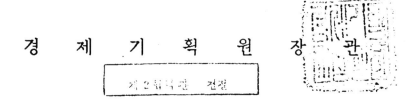

통조삼 10502-241   503~9149   1991. 10. 22

수 신 수신처 참조   통상기구~

제 목 UR/서비스 인력이동분야대책 회의결과 통보

　　　10월 19일 개최된 인력이동분야에 대한 주요관계부처 회의결과를
별첨과 같이 통보하니 UR/서비스협상대책 추진에 만전을 기해 주시기
바라며 특히 10월 28일 주간에 있게될 주요국들과의 양허협상에 귀부의
실무책임자가 반드시 참석할 수 있도록 협조해 주시기 바랍니다.

　　　첨부 : 회의결과 1부.　　끝.

경 제 기 획 원 장 관

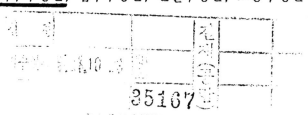

수신처 : 외무부장관, 법무부장관, 건설부장관, 노동부장관

35167   0208

人力移動分野 關係部處 會議結果

I. 會議槪要

- 日　時 : '91. 10.19(土), 10:00~11:00

- 場　所 : 經濟企劃院 第2協力官室

- 議　題 : 人力移動分野의 主要爭點에 대한 協商對策

- 參席者 : 經濟企劃院　第2協力官(會議主宰), 通商調整3課長 및
　　　　　　　　　　　　擔當事務官
　　　　　　法　務　部　出入國 企劃課長 및 擔當事務官
　　　　　　勞　動　部　海外雇傭課長 및 擔當事務官
　　　　　　建　設　部　海外協力課 방재형 事務官

II. 會議結果

① 지난 91.8월 UR/對策 實務委員會에서 결정한 基本立場을 중심으로
　대응토록 함.

　　○ 基本人力은 多者間 約束에 의해서 자유화하고 기타범주의 인력은
　　　讓許協商에 의해서 業種別로 讓許範圍를 결정

② 各分野別 전문가의 범위에 대하여는 協商의 大勢를 受容토록 함.

　　○ 전문가의 범위는 人力移動 附屬書上에 例示目錄(illustrative
　　　list)을 만드는 작업과 마찬가지로 各國마다 立場이 다르므로
　　　그 範圍를 각국 Offer에 기재하는 方式이 채택되지는 않을 것
　　　으로 예상됨.

　　○ 따라서 전문가의 범위는 결국 각국이 UR協商結果를 이행하기
　　　위하여 出入國 關係法을 운용하는 과정에서 정해질 것이며
　　　우리의 경우도 出入國 管理法 運用過程에서 각분야의 전문가
　　　범위에 대한 經濟企劃院, 法務部, 關係部處間의 基準設定過程을
　　　거쳐 case-by-case로 결정될 것임.

0209

③ 建設部가 건설서비스의 수출에 필요한 고도로 熟練된 人力(highly skilled labour)의 이동을 우리의 Offer에 포함된 개념으로 수용할 경우 이를 美國, 日本등 상대국에 대하여 專門家의 範圍에 포함시킬 수 있는지를 타진토록 함.

  ○ 다만 同 熟練人力은 배관공등의 직종별 기능공이 아니라 同一한 建設業體에 상당기간 근무한 경력을 갖고 있으며 當該企業에서 차지하는 직위에 비추어 商業的 駐在에 필수적인 인력임이 입증될 수 있어야 함.

④ 多者間 約束의 범위는 협상대세를 수용하여 讓許表에 기재한 업종 뿐만 아니라 여타개방업종에 대하여도 多者間 約束義務를 부담하는 것으로 입장을 정리토록 함.

⑤ 現地協商에 적극적으로 참석

  ○ 11월 1일 美國과의 兩者協商日程이 확정되는 등 人力移動에 대한 自由化 約束을 구체적으로 해야 하는 협상의 최종단계에 도달한 만큼 法務部, 建設部, 勞動部등 主務部處의 실무책임자가 가능한 한 직접 現地協商에 참여토록 함.

0210

조(邱호)

경 제 기 획 원

봉조삼 10502-<del>737</del>　　　　503~9149　　　　1991. 10. 21

수　신　수신처 참조

제　목　UR대책 실무위원회 개최

　　　　UR/서비스협상과 관련하여 10.28일 주간에 진행될 예정으로 있는
주요국과의 양허협상대책을 논의하기 위한 UR대책 서비스 실무위원회를
다음과 같이 개최하니 반드시 참석해 주시기 바랍니다.

다　　　　　음

가. 일　　시 : '91.10.25(금), 15:00~18:00

나. 장　　소 : 경제기획원 소회의실(과천청사 1동 721호)

다. 의　　제 : UR/서비스 양허협상대책

라. 참석범위 : (별첨1 참조)

첨부 : 참석범위 1부.

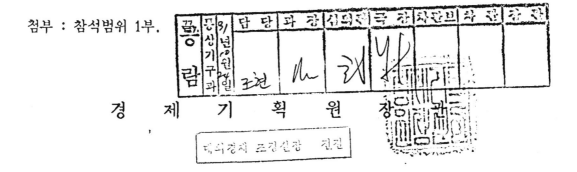

경 제 기 획 원

수신처 : <u>외무부장관</u>, 재무부장관, 법무부장관, 문화부장관, 농림수산부장관,
　　　　상공부장관, 보건사회부장관, 건설부장관, 교통부장관, 노동부장관,
　　　　체신부장관, 과학기술처장관, 공보처장관, 해운항만청장,
　　　　대외경제정책연구원장

0211　　　　　　　35135

〈 別添1 〉

參 席 範 圍

所屬 機關	參 席 對 象
經濟企劃院	對外經濟調整室長(會議主宰), 第2協力官
外 務 部	通商局長
財 務 部	關稅局長, 國際金融局長
法 務 部	涉外法務審議官, 出入國 管理局長
文 化 部	藝術振興局長
農林水産部	農業通商協力官
商 工 部	國際協力官, 産業政策局長
保健社會部	企劃管理室長
建 設 部	建設經濟局長
交 通 部	輸送政策局長
勞 動 部	職業安定局長
遞 信 部	通信政策局長
科學技術處	技術協力官
公 報 處	廣告振興局長
海運港灣廳	海運局長
KIEP	박태호博士

0212

UR 금융서비스 협정(안) 검토

'91.   10

국 제 금 융 국

0213

UR 금융서비스 협정(안) 검토

1. 금융서비스협정(안) 작성 경위

   - 금융부속서 논의를 위하여 GNS 의장과 금융부속서 협상그룹의장이 Informal Note로 제시

     o 동 제안은 기존의 선진 4개국 공동안 보다는 SEACEN 공동안을 대폭 수용한 것으로 득히 자유화 추진방식에 있어서 Two Track Approach를 명시하여 선·개도국간의 주요쟁점을 해결하였으며 우리가 수용할 수 있는 범위내에서 작성

2. 금융부속서 주요 내용

   - Annex on Financial Service
     o 정의 및 개념, 공개주의, 분쟁해결절차 등 제도적인 사항들을 명시

   - Part Ⅲ
     o 자유화 추진방식으로서 Two Track Approach 명시

   - Attachment
     o 자유화 추진방식을 Negative 방식을 채택하는 경우의 시장접근, 내국민대우에 대한 의무범위를 명시한 것으로
     o Positive 방식을 채택하는 경우는 적용대상이 아님.

0214

3. 종합 평가

- 그간의 금융부속서 협상에서 가장 쟁점이 되었던 자유화 추진방식
  논의에 있어서 각국의 여건에 따라서 자유화 추진방식을 선택할 수
  있도록 보장하는 Two Track Approach가 명시되었는 바,

  o 이로서 아국의 경우도 Positive 방식에 의한 자유화 추진방식이
    가능하며 최근에 취한 금융자율화 및 개방조치를 고려해 볼 때
    큰 문제는 없을 것임.

- 그러나, 미국은 아국에게 Attachment를 수락하는 Negative 방식의
  자유화 방식을 취하도록 요구하고 있으나,

  o 현재 우리의 여건상 모든 금융업을 개방하기에는 곤란하며 서비스
    협상이 3~5년마다 주기적으로 협상이 계속되도록 되어 있음을 감안
    하여 일단 협상 발효시에는 Positive 방식 채택이 바람직

- 따라서, 향후 협상과제는 참가국간의 양허협상이 남아있으며,
  이에 대비한 대응준비작업 준비가 중요

  o 미국, 일본, 카나다, 호주, 스웨덴 등 5개국이 아국에게 Request를
    하였으며,

  o 우리도 미국, 일본, EC, 카나다, 호주, 스위스 등 선진국에게
    Request List를 제출할 예정임.

0215

1. 금융서비스 협정(안) 작성경위

   - 브라셀 각료회의시 제출된 선진 4개국 공동안과 SEACEN 공동안을
     '91. 4 이후 토의한 결과를

     o GNS 의장과 금융부속서 협상그룹의장의 공동 Informal Note로
       제시 ('91.10)

   - 최근 11월초까지 제출키로 되어있는 UR협상 각그룹의 의장보고서
     (Chairman's Report) 작성을 위한 최종 토의 자료로서 10월 23일
     예정된 금융부속서 회의시 논의 예정

     o 기존의 선진 4개국 공동안 보다는 SEACEN 공동안을 대폭 수용한
       것으로 선.개도국간의 주요쟁점을 해결하여 우리가 수용할 수
       있는 범위내에서 작성.

2. 금융부속서 구성

   - Annex on Financial Service

     o 정의및 범위, 공개주의, 국내규제, 조화및 인정, 예외
       금융서비스기구, 분쟁해결절차.

   - Part Ⅲ

     o 자유화 추진방식으로서 Two Track Approach 명시

   - Attachment

     o 자유화 추진 방식을 Negative Approach 를 채택하는 경우의
       시장접근, 내국민대우에 대한 의무내용.

0216

3. 금융부속서 주요 내용

(1) 정의및 범위 (제1조)

- 금융서비스 공급에 영향을 주는 조치에 적용하나 다음사항 제외

    o 통화정책, 외환정책을 위한 통화당국의 활동

    o 정부보증, 공공기관의 자기 계정을 위한 활동

    o 사회보장, 공공연금제 등의 법적·제도적인 활동

< 검토의견 >

- 의견없음.

(2) 공개주의 (제2조)

- 공개주의의 적용대상은 laws, regulations, administrative
  guidelines of general application에 한정

< 검토의견 > : 의견 없음

- Framework의 공개주의 대상을 축소 (SEACEN안 반영)

    o decisions, rulings, measures of general application을 제외

(3) 국내규제 (제3조)

- 제 1 안

    o 금융제도 안정을 위한 prudential regulation 의 포괄적인 인정

0217

- 제 2 안

    o purdential regulation 의 남용방지를 위하여 협정상의 의무와
      약속을 침해하지 않는 범위로 한정.

    o 각국이 개방약속한 분야에 대한 인가시 국내법이 정한
      시한내 통보의무(Framework 제6조3항) 이외에 인가결정에
      필요한 정보제공 의무를 첨가

〈 검토의견 〉

  - 제2안이 당초 SEACEN안이었으나 Prudential regulation 남용방지
    를 위하여 제2안을 타협안으로 제시한 것으로 수용가능.

(4) 조화및 인정 (제4조)

  - 금융서비스 공급과 관련한 상호 recognition and harmonization
    협정, cooperative arrangement 체결 가능.

    o 단, 협정 체결이 모든 국가에게 개방되며, 회원국을 차별하는
      자의적이며 부당한 방법이 되어서는 안됨.

    o 협정의 합리적이고 객관적인 운영과 계약체결 내용의 통보

〈 검토의견 〉

  - 의견없음.

0218

(5) 예외 (제5조)

- 어떠한 경우라도 고객 구좌등 재산상태나 비밀사항에 관한 공개금지

〈 검토의견 〉

- 의견없음

(6) 제도조항 (제7조)

- 금융전문가로 구성된 금융서비스 기구(Financial Service Body)설립

    o 주요업무

        . 금융부속서 관련사항및 금융서비스 공급과 관련한 Framework내용
        . 서비스협정하의 금융서비스 자유화의 운영과 이행상황 점검및
          향후 계획 평가

    o FSB 구성

        . 금융서비스를 offer 한 국가로 구성.

〈 검토의견 〉

- 의견없음.

0219

(7) 분쟁 해결절차 (제8조)

- 분쟁해결 결과에 따른 보상및 보복은 원칙적으로 당해분야로 한정

  o FSB가 금융분야의 분쟁해결 절차 담당하며 서비스이사회와 같이
    관련분야에 대한 절차 제정.

- 금융서비스에 관한 분쟁을 담당하는 panel 에는 최소한 1인의
  금융전문가가 참여하며,

  o prudential regulation 에 관한 Panel의 경우 과반수를 금융
    전문가로 구성

  o 개별적인 Prudential decision 이 협정상의 의무와 약속을
    위반한 경우에만 Framework의 분쟁해결 절차에 의할 수 있음.

< 검토의견 >

- 의견없음.

  o 개별적인 prudential decision의 Framework 분쟁 해결절차 의뢰는
    국내규제의 제2안과 연결한 것임.

  o 단, 서비스분야간 보복의 경우 원칙적으로 금지하되 분야내 보복이
    불가능한 경우에만 서비스분야간 보복을 허용하는 것으로 SEACEN과
    선진국이 합의할 것으로 예상

0220

- 각국은 Attachment에 규정된 방식 또는 Framework 에 의한 방식 허용

  o 자유화 추진 방식 선택이 특정 자유화수준을 전제하지 아니하며

  o 서비스협정상의 각국의 권리, 의무및 이익에 영향을 미치지 않음.

〈 검토의견 〉

- Two Track Approach를 명시한 것으로 의견없음.

  o Lower track을 선택하더라도 불이익 없음을 명문화

Attachment

* Negative 방식을 선택할 경우 적용되는 자유화 추진방식

(1) 독점

- 각국의 독점권을 갖고 있는 금융기관 명시하고 이를 축소토록 노력

(2) 정부구매

- 정부기관의 금융서비스 구입시 MFN및 내국민대우 부여

0221

(3) Cross-Broder Trade

- 외국의 금융서비스 공급자의 다음과 같은 서비스 제공을 허용

    (a) 보험 서비스

        o 해운, 항공운송 보험(상품, 배, 항공기 및 관련 자산)

        o 적하보험

        o 재보험, 재재보험, 보험부수업(보험계리, 위험평가,
           분쟁해결 등)

    (b) 금융서비스

        o 금융정보, 자료제공및 처리업, 자문업, 신용평가업등
           금융부수업.

- 국내거주자의 해외에서의 금융서비스 구입 허용

    (a) 보험서비스

        o 해운, 항공운송보험

        o 적하보험

    (b) 금융서비스

        o 여신, 수신등 모든 금융서비스

    * 기존의 선진국 공동안에는 관련 자본거래가 자유화된 범위내로
       한정되었으나 이번 제안에는 제한 범위가 삭제되었음.

0222

(4) 상업적 주재

    - 각국은 상업적 주재기관의 설립 및 확장을 허용하되

        o 상업적 주재 인가시 서비스협정상의 의무를 위배하지 않는 범위내에서 제한 및 조건부과 가능

(5) 신상품

    - 각국은 신상품의 공급을 허용

(6) 정보의 이전및 가공처리

    - 각국은 일상적인 업무처리에 필요한 금융정보의 이전및 가공 처리를 보장하여야 하며 이를 위한 전산장치의 수입을 허용

        o 단 개인 정보및 구좌의 비밀을 보장.

(7) 인력의 이동

    - 다음의 인력이동은 허용

        o senior managerial personnel

        o specialist

    - 다음의 인력은 자국내의 인력수급상황에 따라 허용

        o 컴퓨터, 통신 및 회계전문가

        o 보험계리인, 법률전문가.

0223

(8) 무차별 조치

- 다음과 같은 무차별조치를 철폐토록 노력(shall endeavour)
  o 특정금융서비스 공급을 제한하는 무차별조치
  o 전국적인 금융서비스 공급확대를 제한하는 무차별조치
  o 겸업주의 국가에 진출한 전업주의 금융기관에 대한 조치
  o 외국 금융서비스 공급자의 경쟁능력을 제한하는 무차별 조치

(9) 내국민 대우

- 유사한 여건에서 외국서비스 공급자에게 동등한 경쟁기회
  (Equal Competitive Opportunity) 보장

  o ECO는 외국서비스 공급자의 경쟁능력을 보장해주는 것으로
     각국 조치의 영향(effect of measures)으로 평가

- 상업적 주재기관 인가 절차 조건이 내국인보다 불리하지
  않아야 함.

- 각국은 공공기관이 운영하는 payment and clearing system
  offical refinancing facility의 이용을 보장하나 lender of
  last resort의 보장은 제외

- 자율규제 단체에의 가입보장
  o 특히 동 단체가입이 서비스 공급에 필요하거나 각국이 금융
     서비스공급시 특혜나 이익을 동단체에 부여하는 경우
     내국민 대우를 부여

0224

4. 종합 평가

- 그간의 금융부속서 협상에서 가장 쟁점이 되었던 자유화 추진방식 논의에 있어서 각국의 여건에 따라서 자유화 추진방식을 선택할 수 있도록 보장하는 Two Track Approach가 명시되었는 바,

  o 이로서 아국의 경우도 Positive 방식에 의한 자유화 추진방식이 가능하며 최근에 취한 금융자율화 및 개방조치를 고려해 볼 때 큰 문제는 없을 것임.

- 그러나, 미국은 아국에게 Attachment를 수락하는 Negative 방식의 자유화 방식을 취하도록 요구하고 있으나,

  o 현재 우리의 여건상 모든 금융업을 개방하기에는 곤란하며 서비스 협상이 3~5년마다 주기적으로 협상이 계속되도록 되어 있음을 감안 하여 일단 협상 발효시에는 Positive 방식 채택이 바람직

- 따라서, 향후 협상과제는 참가국간의 양허협상이 남아있으며, 이에 대비한 대응준비작업 준비가 중요

  o 미국, 일본, 카나다, 호주, 스웨덴 등 5개국이 아국에게 Request를 하였으며,

  o 우리도 미국, 일본, EC, 카나다, 호주, 스위스 등 선진국에게 Request List를 제출할 예정임.

0225

1. 작성경위

　　브라셀 각료회의시 제출된 선진 4개국 공동안과 SEACEN 공동안을
　　'91. 4 이후 토의한 결과를

　　o GNS 의장과 금융부속서 협상그룹의장의 공동 Informal Note로
　　　 제시 ('91. 10)

―　최근 11월초까지 제출키로 되어있는 UR협상 각그룹의 의장보고서
　　(Chairman's Report) 작성을 위한 최종 토의 자료로서 10월 23일
　　예정된 금융부속서 회의시 논의 예정

　　o 기존의 선진 4개국 공동안 보다는 SEACEN 공동안을 대폭 수용한
　　　 것으로 선. 개도국간의 주요쟁점을 해결하여 우리가 수용할 수
　　　 있는 범위내에서 작성.

2. 금융부속서 구성

　　Annex on Financial Service
　　o 정의및 범위, 공개주의, 국내규제, 조화및 인정, 예외
　　　 금융서비스기구, 분쟁해결절차.

―　Part Ⅲ
　　o 자유화 추진방식으로서 Two Track Approach 명시

―　Attachment
　　o 자유화 추진 방식을 Nagative Approach 를 채택하는 경우의
　　　 시장접근, 내국민대우에 대한 의무내용.

0227

3. Informal Note 주요 내용 검토

가. Annex on Financial Service

(1) 정의및 범위 (제1조)

- 금융서비스 공급에 영향을 주는 조치에 적용하나 다음사항 제외
    o 통화정책, 외환정책을 위한 통화당국의 활동
    o 정부보증, 공공기관의 자기 계정을 위한 활동
    o 사회보장, 공공연금제 등의 법적·제도적인 활동

검토의견
- 의견없음.

(2) 공개주의 (제2조)

공개주의의 적용대상은 laws, regulations, administrative guidelines of general application에 한정

검토의견
- Framework의 공개주의 대상을 축소 (SEACEN안 반영)
    o decisions, rulings, measures of general application을 제외

(3) 국내규제 (제3조)

제 1 안
    o 금융제도 안정을 위한 prudential regulation 의 포괄적인 인정

제 2 안

o prudential regulation 의 남용방지를 위하여 협정상의 의무와

   약속을 침해하지 않는 범위로 한정.

o 각국이 개방약속한 분야에 대한 인가시 국내법이 정한

   시한내 통보의무(Framework 제6조3항) 이외에 인가결정에

   필요한 정보제공 의무를 첨가

검토의견

- 제2안이 당초 SEACEN안이었으나 Prudential regulation 남용방지

   를 위하여 제2안을 타협안으로 제시한 것으로 수용가능.

(4) 조화및 인정 (제4조)

- 금융서비스 공급과 관련한 상호 recognition and harmonization

   협정, cooperative arrangement 체결 가능.

   o 단, 협정 체결이 모든 국가에게 개방되며, 회원국을 차별하는

      자의적이며 부당한 방법이 되어서는 안됨.

   o 협정의 합리적이고 객관적인 운영과 계약체결 내용의 통보

검토의견

   의견없음.

(5) 예외 (제5조)

- 어떠한 경우라도 고객 구좌등 재산상태나 비밀사항에 관한 공개금지

< 검토의견 >

   의견없음

(6) 제도조항 <제7조>

   금융전문가로 구성된 금융서비스 기구(Financial Service Body)설립

   o 주요업무
      . 금융부속서 관련사항및 금융서비스 공급과 관련한 Framework내용
      . 서비스협정하의 금융서비스 자유화의 운영과 이행상황 점검및
        향후 계획 평가

   o FSB 구성
      . 금융서비스를 offer 한 국가로 구성.

   검토의견

   - 의견없음.

(7) 분쟁 해결절차 (제8조)

- 분쟁해결 결과에 따른 보상및 보복은 원칙적으로 당해분야로 한정

  o FSB가 금융분야의 분쟁해결 절차 담당하며 서비스이사회와 같이
    관련분야에 대한 절차 제정.

- 금융서비스에 관한 분쟁을 담당하는 panel 에는 최소한 1인의
  금융전문가가 참여하며,

  o prudential regulation 에 관한 Panel의 경우 과반수를 금융
    전문가로 구성

  o 개별적인 Prudential decision 이 협정상의 의무와 약속을
    위반한 경우에만 Framework의 분쟁해결 절차에 의할 수 있음.

  검토의견

  의견없음.

  o 개별적인 prudential decision의 Framework 분쟁 해결절차 의뢰는
    국내규제의 제2안과 연결한 것임.

  o 단. 서비스분야간 보복의 경우 원칙적으로 금지하되 분야내 보복이
    불가능한 경우에만 서비스분야간 보복을 허용하는 것으로 SEACEN과
    선진국이 합의 예정.

나. 자유화추진방식 (제6조)

　　각국은 Attachment에 규정된 방식 또는 Framework 에 의한 방식 허용

　　o 자유화 추진 방식 선택이 특정 자유화수준을 전제하지 아니하며

　　o 서비스협정상의 각국의 권리. 의무및 이익에 영향율 미치지 않음.

　　< 검토의견 >

　　- Two Track Approach를 명시한 것으로 의견없음.

다. Attachment

　　- 각국이 Attachment의 의무사항을 이행하겠다고 약속한 경우만 적용

(1) 독점

　　- 각국의 독점권을 갖고 있는 금융기관 명시하고 이를 축소토록 노력

(2) 정부구매

　　정부기관의 금융서비스 구입시 MFN및 내국민대우 부여

(3) Cross-Broder Trade

외국의 금융서비스 공급자의 다음과 같은 서비스 제공울 허용

(a) 보험 서비스

    o 해운, 항공운송 보험(상품, 배, 항공기 및 관련 자산)

    o 적하보험

    o 재보험, 재재보험, 보험부수업(보험계리, 위험평가,
       본쟁해겹 등)

(b) 금융서비스

    o 금융정보, 자료제공및 처리업, 자문업, 신능평가업틈
       금옹부수업.

- 국내거주자의 해외에서의 금융서비스 구입 허용

(a) 보험서비스

    o 해운, 항공운송보험

    o 적하보험

(b) 금융서비스

    o 여신, 수신틈 모든 금융서비스

* 기존의 선진국 공동안에는 관련 자본거래가 자유화된 멈위내로
한정되었으나 이번 제안에는 제한 범위가 삭제되었음.

(4) 상업적 주재

　　　각국은 상업적 주재기관의 설립 및 확장을 허용하되

　　o 상업적 주재 인가시 서비스협정상의 의무를 위배하지 않는
　　　범위내에서 제한 및 조건부과 가능

(5) 신상품

　　　각국은 신상품의 공급을 허용

(6) 정보의 이전및 가공처리

　　　각국은 일상적인 업무처리에 필요한 금융정보의 이전및 가공
　　　처리를 보장하여야 하며 이를 위한 전산장치의 수입을 허용

　　o 단 개인 정보및 구좌의 비밀을 보장.

(7) 인력의 이동

　　- 다음의 인력이동은 허용

　　　o senior managerial personnel

　　　o specialist

　　- 다음의 인력은 자국내의 인력수급상황에 따라 허용

　　　o 컴퓨터, 통신 및 회계전문가

　　　o 보험계리인, 법률전문가.

(8) 무차별 조치

- 다음과 같은 무차별조치를 철폐토록 노력(shall endeavour)

  o 특정금융서비스 공급을 제한하는 우차별조치

  o 전국적인 금융서비스 공급확대를 제한하는 무차별조치

  o 겸업주의 국가에 진출한 전업주의 금융기관에 대한 조치

  o 외국 금융서비스 공급자의 경쟁능력을 제한하는 무차별 조지

(9) 내국민 대우

  유사한 여건에서 외국서비스 공급자에게 동등한 경쟁기회
  (Equal Competitive Opportunity) 보장

  o ECO는 외국서비스의 경쟁능력을 보장해주는 것으로 각국
    조치의 영향(effect of measures)으로 평가

- 상업적 주재기관 인가 절차 조건이 내국민보다 불리하지
  않아야 함.

- 각국은 공공기관이 운영하는 payment and clearing system
  offical refinancing facility의 이용을 보장하나 lender of
  last resort의 보장은 제외

- 자율규제 단체에의 가입보장

  o 특히 동 단체가입이 서비스 공급에 필요하거나 각국이 금융
    서비스공급시 특혜나 이익을 동단체에 부여하는 경우
    내국민 대우를 부여

외 무 부

종 별 :

번 호 : GVW-2080   일 시 : 91 1021 2000

수 신 : 장관(수신처 참조)

발 신 : 주 제네바 대사

제 목 : UR/GNS 협상

　　　10.21(월) 당관에 전달된 스웨덴의 대아국 서비스 분야 REQUEST LIST 를 별첨 송부함.

　　　첨부: 스웨덴의 REQUEST-LIST 1 부(GVW(F)-0435).

　　　수신처:통기, 경기원, 재무부, 법무부, 농림수산부, 문화부, 상공부, 건설부, 보사부, 노동부, 교통부, 과기처, 공보처, 항만청

　　　끝

　　　(대사 박수길-국장)

　　　예고:91.12.31. 까지

일반문서로 재분류(1991. 12. 31.)

통상국	장관	차관	1차보	2차보	경제국	외정실	분석관	청와대
안기부	법무부	보사부	문화부	교통부	경기원	재무부	농수부	상공부
건설부	노동부							

SWEDISH DELEGATION

Gv W (21) - 0 —5 1102/ 2000 재무

Geneva, 21 October 1991

H.E. Ambassador
Soo Gil Park
Permanent Mission of
the Republic of Korea
Route du Pré-Bois 20

1216 Cointrin

Dear Sir,

Enclosed, please find a list of requests for
initial commitments in the services negotiations
from Sweden addressed to your country.

Our services negotiators would appreciate an
opportunity to meet with representatives from your
country, at an appropriate time, to discuss the
items on our list as well as any requests from your
country addressed to Sweden. Sweden reserves the
right to modify or make additions to the request
list for your country.

Yours sincerely,

Mikael Lindström
Minister
Acting Permanent Representative

Encl.

Postal Address	Street Address	Telephone	Telefax	Telex
Délégation Permanente de Suède	9-11, Rue de Varembé	022/734 36 00	022/733 12 09	414189
Case Postale 190				
CH - 1211 GENÈVE 20				

16-1   0237

October 21st, 1991

SWEDEN'S REQUESTS IN THE SERVICES NEGOTIATIONS

Below follows an explanation of Sweden's approach to requests.

1. GENERAL REQUESTS

The "General Requests" as well as the "General Sectors Requests" (below) are addressed to all participants in the services negotiations in order to achieve a minimum-level of binding/liberalization of certain horizontal and sector-specific regulations.

A.   We start with a request to bind a "standstill" for certain horizontal regulation under "APPLICABLE TO ALL SECTORS". This "standstill" shall apply to both national and sub-national levels.

B.   In addition, we request that all sector-specific commitments shall apply to both national and sub-national levels.

2. GENERAL SECTORS REQUESTS

After our "all-sectors-requests", we turn to the sector-specific requests, which address any sector-specific restriction that might exist in addition to any horizontal regulation mentionned under "APPLICABLE TO ALL SECTORS" (above). These requests are mainly of two types;

A.   Those where we ask for elimination of "all sector-specific restrictions on commercial presence, cross-border supply and consumption abroad" as well as "full national treatment".

        This means that any sector-specific restriction should be removed.

(Examples; Legal services, Accounting, Architectural services, etc.)

B.   Those where we ask for "a binding commitment on the present level of Market Access and National Treatment in this sector concerning commercial presence, cross-border supply and consumption abroad" (a "standstill").

        This means that any sector-specific restriction should be bound.

(Examples; Research and Development Services, Rental/Leasing Services without Operators, Distribution Services, etc.)

0238

/6~2

3. COUNTRY-SPECIFIC REQUESTS

Furthermore, we make country-specific requests addressing certain barriers to trade. These may include both sector-specific and horizontal regulations.

16-7

0239

SWEDEN'S REQUESTS IN THE SERVICES NEGOTIATIONS

GENERAL REQUESTS

SECTOR	REQUEST
APPLICABLE TO ALL SECTORS	A. Make a binding commitment, on national as well as sub-national levels, on your present level of Market Access and National Treatment concerning the following horizontal legislation: * foreign investment in commercial presence * foreign investment in real estate * foreign exchange control (including profit remittances) B. Bind also your sector-specific commitments on national as well as sub-national levels.

Furthermore, we are making the following additional sector-specific requests:

GENERAL SECTORS REQUESTS

1. BUSINESS SERVICES

A. Professional services

| a. Legal Services | Concerning advice on home country law and international law, for foreign law offices/ lawyers, provided the legal adviser fulfills the home country's professional qualification conditions:
 * eliminate all sector-specific restrictions on commercial presence, cross-border supply and consumption abroad
 * provide full national treatment |

Concerning advice on national law, for foreign law offices/lawyers, provided the legal adviser fulfills the host country's professional qualification conditions:
* eliminate all sector-specific restrictions on commercial presence, cross-border supply and consumption abroad
* provide full national treatment (including removal of nationality requirements)

b. Accounting, auditing and book-keeping services

Concerning accounting, auditing and bookkeeping services for foreign accounting firms/accountants, provided the accountant fulfills the host country's professional qualification conditions:
* eliminate all sector-specific restrictions on commercial presence, cross-border supply and consumption abroad
* provide full national treatment (including removal of nationality requirements)

d. Architectural services
g. Urban planning and landscape

* eliminate all sector-specific restrictions on commercial presence, cross-border supply and consumption abroad
* provide full national treatment (including removal of nationality requirements)

e. Engineering consulting services
f.. Integrated engineering services

* eliminate all sector-specific restrictions on commercial presence, cross-border supply and consumption abroad
* provide full national treatment (including removal of nationality requirements)

0241

B. Computer and Related Services

* eliminate all sector-specific restrictions on commercial presence, cross-border supply and consumption abroad
* provide full national treatment (including removal of nationality requirements)

C. Research and Development Services

Make a binding commitment on the present level of Market Access and National Treatment in this sector concerning:
* commercial presence,
* cross-border supply and
* consumption abroad.

E. Rental/Leasing Services without Operators

a. Relating to ships Make a binding commitment on the present level of Market Access and National Treatment in this sector concerning:
* commercial presence,
* cross-border supply and
* consumption abroad.

----

b. Relating to aircraft Make a binding commitment on the present level of Market Access and National Treatment in this sector concerning:
* commercial presence,
* cross-border supply and
* consumption abroad.

F. Other Business Services

a. Advertising services

* eliminate all sector-specific restrictions on commercial presence, cross-border supply and consumption abroad
* provide full national treatment (including removal of nationality requirements)

b. Market research and public opinion polling services

* eliminate all sector-specific restrictions on commercial presence, cross-border supply and consumption abroad
* provide full national treatment (including removal of nationality requirements)

c. Management consulting
d. Services rel. to man. consulting

* eliminate all sector-specific restrictions on commercial presence, cross-border supply and consumption abroad
* provide full national treatment (including removal of nationality requirements)

f. Consulting services incidental to agriculture, hunting and forestry

* eliminate all sector-specific restrictions on commercial presence, cross-border supply and consumption abroad
* provide full national treatment (including removal of nationality requirements)

g. Services incidental to fishing

* eliminate all sector-specific restrictions on commercial presence, cross-border supply and consumption abroad
* provide full national treatment (including removal of nationality requirements)

h. Consulting
services incidental
to mining

* eliminate all sector-specific restrictions on commercial
  presence, cross-border supply and consumption abroad
* provide full national treatment (including removal of
  nationality requirements)

i. and j. Consulting
services incidental
to manufacturing
and energy distrib.

* eliminate all sector-specific restrictions on commercial
  presence, cross-border supply and consumption abroad
* provide full national treatment (including removal of
  nationality requirements)

l. Investigation and
security

Make a binding commitment on the present level of
Market Access and National Treatment in this sector
concerning:
* commercial presence,
* cross-border supply and
* consumption abroad.

TELECOMMUNICATIONS

Make a binding commitment on the present level of
Market Access and National Treatment in this sector
concerning:
* commercial presence,
* cross-border supply and
* consumption abroad.

16-8

3. CONSTRUCTION AND RELATED ENGINEERING SERVICES

* eliminate all sector-specific restrictions on commercial
  presence, cross-border supply and consumption abroad
* provide full national treatment (including removal of
  nationality requirements :
  especially concerning

  - requirements of association with a
    domestic ompany and of local participation
  - discrimanatory duties and charges,
    including taxes

4. DISTRIBUTION SERVICES

Make a binding commitmen on the present level of
Market Access and National Treatment in this sector
concerning:
* commercial presence,
* cross-border supply and
* consumption abroad.

6. ENVIRONMENTAL CONSULTING SERVICES

Make a binding commitment on the present level of
Market Access and National Treatment in this sector
concerning:
* commercial presence,
* cross-border supply and
* consumption abroad.

16-P

7. FINANCIAL SERVICES

Make a binding commitment on the present level of Market Access and National Treatment in this sector

* commercial presence,
* cross-border supply and
* consumption abroad.

----

9. TOURISM AND TRAVEL RELATED SERVICES

REQUESTS:

* Eliminate any discriminatory duties or charges, including taxes, on all passenger departures from your country to destinations abroad, unless corresponding duties or charges also apply to departures for domestic destinations on a non-discriminatory basis.

* Eliminate any incentives available to suppliers of conferences, seminars or courses related to events located in your country, whether in the form of
a) duties or charges, including taxes, on services related to conference events located abroad or
b) exemptions from such duties or charges, including taxes, on services related to conference events located in your country.

* Eliminate any incentives available to consumers of conferences, seminars or courses related to events located in your country, whether in the form of
a) duties or charges, including taxes, on the use of services related to conference events located abroad or
b) exemptions from duties or charges, including taxes, on the use of services related to conference events located in your country.

c. Tourist guides   * Remove nationality requirements
services

11. TRANSPORT SERVICES

A. Maritime Transport Services

International
shipping services

Bind all measures that affect
a) the crossborder supply of international shipping services,
b) the purchase abroad by national consumers of international
   shipping services and
c) the commercial presence of providers of international
   shipping services
at the existing level of market access and national treatment.

Make a binding commitment to eliminate all measures that
restrict market access or condition national treatment for
a) the crossborder supply of international shipping services
   and
b) the purchase abroad by national consumers of international
   shipping services
within three years after the entry into force of the Agreement.

Maritime transport
auxiliary services

Bind all measures that affect
a) the crossborder supply of maritime transport auxiliary
   services,
b) the purchase abroad by national consumers of maritime
   transport auxiliary services and
c) the commercial presence of providers of maritime transport
   auxiliary services
at the existing level of market access and national treatment.

16-11

0247

Deinition of terms, used above:

International shipping services:

transportation of passengers or goods between ports
located in different states, including passenger cruise
traffic outside a Party's territorial waters.

Maritime transport auxiliary services:

all maritime transport related services within the confines
of the port or sea environment, limited to those which
provide an immediate, interactive, supporting role to the
primary function of the maritime transport industry, which
is the transportation of goods and/or passengers between
ports.

B. Internal Waterways Transport

Make a binding commitment on the present level of
Market Access and National Treatment in this sector
concerning:

*commercial presence
*cross-border supply and
*consumption abroad.

C. Air Transport Service

Make a binding commitment on the present level of
Market Access and National Treatment in this sector
concerning:

*commercial presence
*cross-border supply and
*consumption abroad.

16-12

E. Rail Transport Services

Make a binding commitment on the present level of Market Access and National Treatment in this sector concerning:

* commercial presence
* cross-border supply and
* consumption abroad.

F. Road Transport Services

Make a binding commitment on the present level of Market Access and National Treatment in this sector concerning:

* commercial presence
* cross-border supply and
* consumption abroad.

16-13

SPECIFIC REQUEST: Korea

Sector No.	Sector Description	Request
All	All	* Remove restrictions on remittance of profit to the service providers' home countries. * Lift credit control policies. * Liberalize the Korean foreign exchange market. * Permit all banks - domestic and foreign - to issue medium and long term debt instruments. * Remove limits on equity investments and permit greater freedom in the use of offshore loans.
1.F.a	Advertising services	* Remove restrictions on foreign produced advertising materials.
2.C	Telecommunication services	* Remove limitations on - foreign ownership, - voice and data in closed user groups, - VANS and - two-way satellite services.
3:A,B,C,D,E	Construction and related engineering services	* Remove excessive capital requirements for subsidiaries of foreign consultancy and engineering companies. * Remove preferences and subsidies given to domestic construction and consulting companies. * Remove discriminatory taxes for foreign consultancy and engineering companies. * Provide recognition of foreign engineering exams and allow foreign consultants to make contracts directly with final customer.
4:A,B,C,D,E	Distribution services	* Provide market access and liberalize restrictions concerning store size, number of stores and traded items.

0251

Financial services

* Make a binding commitment on the present level of Market Access and National Treatment.

* Concerning established companies and branches;
- make commitments in accordance with the obligations in Part III: Specific Commitments in MTN.TNC/W/50, as follows:
a) III. Financial services purchased by public entities,
b) IV. Market access
   i) B. Commercial presence, paragraph 5,
   ii) C. Transfers of information and processing of information,
   iii) D. Temporary entry of personnel, and
   iv) E. Non-discriminatory measures, and
c) V. National Treatment.

* Concerning cross-border supply;
- make commitments in accordance with the obligations in Part III: Specific Commitments in MTN.TNC/W/50; IV. Market Access, A. Cross-border trade, except for provision of credit reference.

* Concerning new establishments;
- eliminate all restrictions on the establishment of a wholly-owned subsidiary and/or branch, including the acquisition of a domestic financial Service Provider.

11.A   Maritime transport

* Remove discriminatory port duties and charges for
  foreign-flag vessels.
* Allow foreign-flag carriers to own container
  terminals and support equipment.
* Allow foreign carriers to manage port operations.
* Remove restrictions on international shipping.

11.F   Road transport services

* Eliminate restrictions on foreign establishment and
  provision of multimodal transports.

0252

(6-16
TOTAL P.01

문 화 부

영 진 35100-*14085*   720-4967   1991. 10. 21

수 신 외무부장관

제 목 UR/GNS 시청각 서비스 협상 지침 통보

1. GVW-1863('91.9.27)의 관련입니다.

1. '91.10.24 개최되는 AUDIO-VISUAL분야 협상과 관련

우리부의 지침을 별첨과 같이 통보하오니 (주)제네바대사로 하여금

동 협상에 대응토록 협조하여 주시기 바랍니다.

첨 부 : UR/GNS 시청각 서비스협상 지침 1 부. 끝.

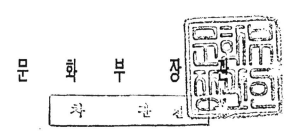

문 화 부 장

34863   0253

기 안 용 지

분류번호 문서번호	영진 35100- *140P5*	(전화 : 720-3821)	시 행 상 특별취급	
보존기간	영구 ,준영구 10, 5, 3, 1	차	관	

수 신 처 보존기간	
시행일자	'91.10

일,

보조기관	실 장		협조기관	어문출판국장	검 열 통 제 1991. 10. 21 통제관
	국 장			영상음반과장	
	과 장			심사무관	발 승 인
기안책임자	곽 영 진				

경 유		발신명의		발↑송 1991. 10 24 문화부
수 신	각 안 참 조		장 관	
참 조				
제 목	UR/GNS 시청각 서비스 협상 지침 통보			

【 제 1 안 】

수 신 : 외무부장관

제 목 : 동 건

    1. GVW-1863('91.9.27)의 관련입니다.

    1. '91.10.24 개최되는 AUDIO-VISUAL분야 협상과 관련

우리부의 지침을 별첨과 같이 통보하오니 (주)제네바대사로 하여금

동 협상에 대응토록 협조하여 주시기 바랍니다.

첨 부 : UR/GNS 시청각 서비스협상 지침 1 부. 끝.

0254

UR/GNS 시청각서비스 협상 지침

1. 입장종합

○ 우리나라는 '85. '88년 2차에 걸친 한.미영화협상 및 '89.5 한.미무역
   협상합의결과, 영화법, 음반및비디오물에관한법률의 개정으로 영화.
   비디오.음반업계의 외국인 참여 허용, 수입가격 및 편수제한 해제등
   규제사항을 폐지 또는 완화하여 그 수준에서 다른 국가에도 대등하게
   적용하고 있으며 추가개방은 없음.

○ 영화.비디오등 시청각 상품은 우리나라의 전통과 문화가 내포된 문화
   상품으로서 일반상품과 다른 차원의 교류가 불가피하므로 일반협정(안)
   제14조(예외)에 '문화적가치' 보호를 위한 조항을 반영, 각국이 이를
   위한 적절한 조치를 취할 수 있도록 하여야 함.

2. 부속서조문별 세부입장

○ 제   목 : 시청각 서비스로 규정
○ 제1조 (적용범위, 활동)
   - MFN 일탈업종은 필름.음반업으로 하고 출판.방송업은 제외
   - 활동은 배급만 포함하고 생산.출판.방송은 제외
○ 제2조(MFN) : MFN일탈대상은 현존 협정에 국한
○ 제3조, 4조, 5조 (기타 사항) : 초안 입장 지지
○ 주   석 : FRAMEWORK 제14조에 반영

3. 기타 사항은 현지의 현행 협상 입장 유지

0255

발 신 전 보

분류번호	보존기간

번   호 :　WGV-1455　911022 2013　DQ 종별 : _____

수   신 : 주 　제네바　 대사. 총영사

발   신 : 장 관 (통 기)

제   목 : UR/GNS 회의

　　　　　　　　대 : GVW-2034

1.　대호 금융부속서 초안을 검토한바 기존의 선진 4개국 공동안 보다는 SEACEN
　　공동안을 대폭 수용하여 아국으로서도 이를 기초로 협상문서 작성을 협의하는데에
　　이의가 없는 것으로 판단되니, 이를 참고하여 귀관 관계관이 10.23(수) 개최되는
　　GNS 금융부속서 회의에 참가토록 조치바람.

2.　10.24(목) 개최되는 GNS 시청각 분야 협상에는 10.15 관계부처 회의에서 결정된
　　아국 입장을 별첨 송부하니 이를 참고하여 귀관 관계관이 동 회의에 참가토록
　　조치바람.

　첨　부(fax) : GNS 시청각 서비스 협상 지침.　　　　　　　　끝.
　　　　　　(WGVF-0266)

　　　　　　　　　　　　　　　　　　　(통상국장　김 용 규)

	보 안 통 제	⋀

앙 고 재	91 년 10 월 22 일	통 기 과	기안자 성명 조현		과 장 ⋀	심의관 ⋀	국 장 전결		차 관	장 관 ⋀	외신과통제

0256

외 무 부

종 별 :

번 호 : GVW-2082   일 시 : 91 1022 1200

수 신 : 장관(수신처참조)

발 신 : 주 제네바 대사

제 목 : UR/GNS 회의(1)

10.21(월) 개최된 표제 GNS 공식회의 및 20개 주요국 비공식 협의 내용을 하기 보고함.

1. GNS 공식 회의

- 공식회의는 다음 두가지 사항만 처리한후 곧바로 주요국 비공식 협의로 전환 하였음.

0 HAWES 호주대사로 부터 SCHEDULING 에 관한 비공식 협의 경과에 대한 설명 및 JARAMILLO의장으로부터 분쟁해결 및 MFN 에 관한 비공식 협의 경과에 대한 설명

0 OFFER 를 제출한 모로코(GNS/W/141),엘살바도르, 니카라과, 과테말라, 혼두라스(4개국공동 OFFER: GNS/W/142)의 제안 설명

2. 주요국 비공식 협의

가. 협정 부적용(JARAMILLO 의장 주재 10.21 오전)

- 동 조항(제 30조) 관련 다음 쟁점에 대하여 선.개도국간 입장이 반복 되었으며, 의장은 사무국과 협의하여 새로운 초안을 제시하겠다고함.

0 분야별 협정 부적용의 반영 여부(동 개념에 대한 반대 의견이 대세를 이룸)

0 양 허협상을 하지 않은 국가에 대하여만 협정 부적용 조항 원용을 인정할 것인지, 양허협상을 하였으나 상대국의 양허 수준에 만족하지 않는 경우에도 협정 부적용 조항 원용이 가능하도록 할 것인지(개도국들은 갓트 35조와 같이 양허 협상을 하지않은 경우에 한정할 것을 주장)

0 협정 부적용 국가에 대한 다자간 REVIEW 제도 도입 여부

0 UR 에 참여한 국가에 대해서는 협정 부적용 조항을 원용하지 못하도록 할것인지 여부(이에대한 반대의견이 대세를 이룸)

나. SCHEDULING (HAWES 대사 주재 10.21. 오후)

통상국	2차보	법무부	보사부	문화부	교통부	체신부	경기원	재무부
농수부	상공부	건설부	노동부	과기처	해항청	공보처		

PAGE 1

- 사무국에서 지난주 협의 결과를 반여하여 새로운 초안을 작성 배부하였으며 제6조(국내규제) 및16조(시장접근)에 대하여 토의하였음.

1) 제 6조

- NATIONAL SCHEDULE 에 반영여부를 막론하고 모든 분야에 대하여 관련 조치를 합리적이고,객관적이며 공평한 방법으로 운영하도록 일반적 의무를 부과하는 문제에 대하여 미국, 아국, 인도,이집트, 유고, 일본등은 다음과 같은 이유로 유보입장을 표명하였음.

0 조치자체와 조치의 운영을 구분하기 곤란함.

0 분쟁발생시 PANEL 에서 동 의무를 해석하는데 명확한 기준이 없어 법적으로 불안정하게됨.

2) 제 16조

- 양적 제한 조치 목록(16조 3항)의 성격

0 대부분의 나라가 동 조치 유형이 한정적 열거목록(EXHAUSTIVE LIST)이라고 하였으나, 캐나다는 원칙적으로 이에 동의하나 동 목록에서 누락된 경우에는 SCHEDULING하지 않은채 계속 무역제한 행위를 할수 있게되는 위험이 있다는 이유로 SPECIFIC LIST 임을 강조함.

- 상업적 주재 형태 제한(16조 3항 C)의 포함여부

0 일본은 이를 질적인 규제 조치라고 주장하였으나 대부분의 국가가 시장진입에대한 제한이라고 함

- 영업시간, 영업장 면적 제한 (16조 3항 D 의주석)의 SCHEDULING 여부

0 일본을 제외한 모든 나라가 동 제한 조치의SCHEDULING 입장을 견지함. 끝

(대사   박수길-국장)수신처:
(봉기, 경기원, 재무부, 법무부,농림수산부,문화부, 상공부, 건설부,보사부,노동부 교통부, 체신부,과기처,공보처,항만청)

외 무 부

종 별 :

번 호 : GVW-2084   일 시 : 91 1022 1600

수 신 : 장관(수신처 참조)

발 신 : 주제네바대사

제 목 : UR/분야별 협상 대책(서비스)

연: GVW-2083

연호 서비스분야 협상 현황 및 전망 아국의 대책방향등을 보고함.

1. 협상현황

가. FRAMEWORK

- '91.2 협상재개이후 양허 협상의 필수전제조건인 SCHEDULING 관련 조문(시장접근, 내국민 대우, 국내규제)에 협상 집중,

0 일부 미결사항이 있으나 거의 마루리 단계에 있으며 사실상 법적 문안 정리 단계에 진입

- 미결상태에 있는 다음 조문들중 4조, 5조, 23조, 30조, 34조에 대한 토의가 있었으나 아직 최종합의에는 이르지 못하였으며 양허 협상의 실질적 기준도 미합의 상태

0 서비스 무역의 정의(1조), 개도국 무역증대(4조), 경제통합(5조), 세이프가드(10조), 지급 및 이전(11조), BOP(12조), 예외(14), 분쟁해결(23조), 협정부적용(30조), 용어의 정의(34조)

나. 분야별 부속서

- 분야별 MFN 일탈(해운, 육운, 내수로 운송, 항공, 기본통신, AUDIO VISUAL, 노동력 이동등 7개분야)문제에 대해서는 MFN 일탈의 법적기술에 관한 토의에 한정

0 구체적인 MFN 일탈 대상 정부 조치를 비밀 유지조건하에 사무국에 제출키로 하여 일부 국가가 제출하였으나 아직 협상 진전의 MODALITY 는 찾지 못한 상태

- 통신 부속서는 브랏셀 TEXT 에 대한 토의를 거쳐 통신분야 공동 의장이 수정 초안을 배부(10.14)

- 금융 부속서는 브랏셀 회의시 TEXT 가 없었으나 최근(10.14) 금융 분야

통상국	2차보	법무부	보사부	문화부	교통부	체신부	경기원	재무부
농수부	상공부	건설부	노동부	과기처	해항청	공보처		

PAGE 1

91.10.23 05:55 DQ

외신 1과 통제관

0259

공동의장이 부속서 초안을 작성 배부

- 노동력 이동 부속서는 브랏셀 TEXT 로 부터 일부진전이 있었으며 인력의 종류에 관한 ILLUSTRATIVE LIST 제정 여부가 주요 쟁점

　다. INITIAL COMMITMENT

- 각국의 자유화 계획 작성의 기초가 되는 OFFER는 현재까지 43개국이 제출

0 OFFER 제출 의사만 표명한 태국, 필리핀, 일부분야에 대한 동결 약속만 제시한루마니아, 체코등을 제외하면 사실상 39개국

- 국가간 양허협상 개시를 위한 REQUEST-LIST 는 일본,호주,캐나다, 미국, 스웨덴 만이 개별적으로 배부한 상태

　2. 전망

　가. FRAMEWORK

- 미결 조문이 많기 때문에 물리적 작업량은 많으나 상대적으로 이해 대립의 정도가 약하기 때문에 11월초까지 CLEAN TEXT 또는 이에 가까운 TEXT 가 작성될 수 있을것으로 전망

　나. 분야별 부속서

- 분야별 MFN 일탈 문제는 실질적 이해관계가 큰 주요 정치적 쟁점 일뿐만 아니라 국가간 양허협상과도 연계되기 때문에 11월초까지 합의안 도출 가능성은 불투명

- 금융 부속서는 주요쟁점인 TWO TRACK APPROACH 와PRUDENTIOL REGULATION 에 대하여 선진국과 SEACEN이 의견 접근을 보이고 있어 단일안을 작성 할수 있을 것으로전망

- 봉신 부속서와 노동력 이동 부속서 역시 합의에 도달할 수 있을 것으로 전망

　다. INITIAL COMMITMENT

- 10.28 주부터 양자협상이 개시되나 서비스 분야의특성, MFN 일탈과의 연계등의이유때문에 '92년 초까지 협상이 계속 될것으로 예상

③. 아국 입장 및 대책

- FRAMEWORK 및 분야별 부속서는 각 잇슈별로 아국이 다수쪽에 속해 있기 때문에 별다른 문제가 없는 상태

- 그러나, 실질 자유화 약속을 위한 양허협상에서는 미국, EC등의 강한 압력이 예상되는바 동양허협상에 대한 철저한 준비 및 국내 홍보대책 강구 필요

　0 아국의 REQUEST-LIST 준비

PAGE 2

0260

0 주요국과의 서비스 무역 통계 작성등

(대사 박수길-국장)

수신처:통기, 경기원, 재무부, 법무부, 농림수산부, 문화부, 상공부, 건설부, 보사부, 노동부
,교통부, 체신부, 과기처, 공보처, 항만청

외 무 부

종 별 :

번 호 : GVW-2108
일 시 : 91 1023 1600

수 신 : 장 관(수신처참조)

발 신 : 주 제네바대사

제 목 : UR/GNS 회의(2)

　　　10.22(화) 개최된 해운 분야 GNS 회의와 FRAMEWORK에 관한 20개 주요국 비공식 협의내용을 하기 보고함.

　　1. 해운 분야 회의(10.22 오전, JARAMILLO 의장주재)

　　가. GNS 공식 회의

　　- 노르웨이는 지난 9.19 회의시 제시된 북구제안중 해운 보조 서비스에 대한 비공식 문서(FAX송부)를 배부하는 한편 동 제안 5항과 6항의 관계를 다음과 같이 설명함.

　　0 5항은 해운 보조 서비스 제공 사업의 개방에 관한 사항이며, 6항은 보조 서비스에의 접근 보장의무(서비스의 사용측면)를 부과하기 위한 것임.

　　- 말련, 인니를 포함 많은 아프리카 국가들은 5항의 보조 서비스 개방 상태 동결 및 6항의 보조 서비스접근 보장 의무는 자국의 해운 산업 발전 상태 및 항구시설을고려할때 수락하기 어렵다고 하였으며, 미국 역시 그간 국제해운 산업이 쌍무적 접근 방식에 의해 발전되어 왔음을 들어 다자간 접근방식을 취하는데 반대 의사를 표명함

　　- 한편 EC 는 5항과 A 와 같은 현존 개방상태의 동결만으로는 불충분하여 국제 해운에 대한 제한 조치의 공통철폐(3항 B)와 같이 일정기간내에 해운 보조 서비스도 자유화 되어야 한다고 함.

　　나. 비공식 협의

　　- 브랏셀 TEXT 와 달리 북구 제안 부속서 6항과 같이 해운 보조 서비스 접근 보장 의무를 규정하는경우 동 의무에 위배되는 조치의 SCHEDULING 가능여부에 대하여 EC, 카나다등은 동 부속서 규정에 기초하여 SCHEDULING 할수 있다고 한 반면

　　0 대부분의 개도국은 부속서에 의해 의무를 규정하는데 반대 의사를 표명함.

　　- 한편 미국은 일반 협정에 의하면 해운 관련 각종 제한이 무조건 동결 대상이 아

통상국	2차보	문화부	교통부	체신부	경기원	재무부	농수부	상공부
건설부	과기처	해항청	공보처					

91.10.24　08:46 WH

외신 1과　통제관

0262

니며 또한 몇개국이 이러한 접근 방식에 의해 COMMITMENT 할수 있는지 의문을 제기함.

- 이에 대해 EC 는 일부국가(주로 아프리카)가 보조서비스 관련기존 조치의 동결과 이에 대한 접근보장에 어려움이 있음을 인정하나 EC는 서비스 특히 해운 분야에있어서 동결(STANDSTILL)이 아주 중요하며, 회원국들의 이해가 지대하다고 강조함.

0 특히 EC는 서비스 협정에 UNIVERSAL COUERAGE와 UNCONDITIONAL MFN 원칙이 적용되어야 하며,해운 분야 협상 결과가 극히 중요하다고 함. 다만 UN LINER CODE 를협정 당사국(주로 아프리카)의 이해를 고려하여 MFN 원칙과 어떻게 적절히 조화시키느냐 는 검토가 필요하다고 함.

2. RRAMEWORK 에 관한 주요국 비공식 협의 (10.22오후 JARAMILLO 의장 주재)

가. 제 5조 (경제 통합)

- 일본이 지난 9월 회의시 제시한 TEXT 를 수정배부하였는 바, 브랏셀 TEXT 제 1안에 상당히 가깝게 된 것으로서 타협안의 기초문서가 될수 있는 것으로 평가를 받았으며, 일본이 각국 논평(대체로 9월 회의시 논평과 동일)을 반영하여 새로운 초안을작성 제시키로 함.

나. 제 8조(독점)

- 각항별로 EC 가 일부 자귀 수정을 제의하였으며, 주요 쟁점인 제 6항(독점이 아 닌복점등 소수 지배적 사업자에 의무 부과 여부)에 대하여는 토의하지 않았음.

다. 제 9조(사기업자의 행위)

- 제 1항 관련 1안을 지지하는 EC와 2안을 지지하는 인도의 입장 표명외에 별다른 진전이 없었음.

라. 제 10조(세이프 가드)

- 협정 발효후 2년내에 세이프가드 조항에 대한 협상을 완료토록 하는 ALTERNATIVE TEXT를 채택하기로 합의 하였으며, 다만 동 조항 마련이전에 세이프가드 발동이 필요한 사례등에 대처하기 위한 점등을 보완하기로 하였음.

첨부: 해운 보조 서비스 정의에 관한 북구의 비공식문서 1부. 끝

(GVW(F)-439)

(대사 박수길-국장)

수신처:(통기,경기원,재무부,농림수산부,문화부,상공부,건설부,보사부,노동부, 교통부 ,체신부,과기처,공보처,항만청)

22.10.91

Gvw(h) - 43p //023/800
Gvw - 2158 첨부

<u>Group of Negotiations on Services</u>

<u>INFORMAL NOTE BY THE NORDIC COUNTRIES</u>

The following informal note is circulated at the request of the permanent delegation of Sweden on behalf of the Nordic countries.

———————————————

The following definition relates to Maritime Transport Auxiliary Services referred to in paragraph 6 of MTN.GNS/W/135:

Maritime Transport Auxiliary Services are all maritime transport related services, within the confines of the port or sea environment, limited to those which provide an immediate, interactive, supporting role to the primary function of the maritime transport industry which is the transportation of goods and/or passengers between ports. For the purpose of the Agreement, these services are understood to include:

- Towing and tug assistance, including for and by sea-going vessels;
- Pilotage, anchorage and berths, and berthing services;
- Lightering and water taxi services;
- Provisioning, fuelling and watering;
- Garbage collection and ballast waste disposal;
- Stevedoring and terminal services, including warehousing and storage;
- Port captains' services attached to specific foreign vessels;
- Navigation aid services;
- Freight transport agency services;
- Cargo handling services (container and other cargo);
- Shore based operational services essential to ship operations including communications and electronic data interchange networks and water and electrical services;
- Marine surveys and classification societies for the purpose of providing accurate documentation and certification of cargo and vessels;
- Multi-modal transportation services limited to those aspects which involve the movement of goods within the port environment; and
- Customs clearance

/-7

13-TRAN 0264

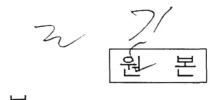

관리번호	91-705

외　무　부

종　별 :

번　호 : GVW-2118　　　　　　　　　일　시 : 91 1023 2030

수　신 : 장 관(수신처 참조)

발　신 : 주 제네바 대사

제　목 : UR/GNS 협상

　　10.23(수) 당관에 전달된 핀란드의 대 아국 서비스 분야 REQUEST LIST 를 별첨 송부함.

　　수신처:(봉기, 경기원, 재무부, 법무부, 농림수산부, 문화부, 상공부, 건설부, 보사부, 노동부, 교봉부, 체신부, 과기처, 공보처, 항만청)

　　첨부: 필랜드의 REQUEST LIST 1 부.(GVW(F)-442) 끝

　　(대사 박수길-국장)

　　예고 91.12.31. 까지

일반문서로 재분류(1991.12.31.)

통상국	장관	차관	1차보	2차보	경제국	외정실	분석관	정와대
안기부	법무부	보사부	문화부	교통부	체신부	경기원	재무부	농수부
상공부	건설부	과기처	노동부	공보처	해항청			

PAGE 1

91.10.24　09:37

외신 2과　통제관 BS

0265

PERMANENT MISSION OF FINLAND
      IN GENEVA

No. 2446   Geneva, 22 October 1991

Dear Ambassador Park,

I have the honour to attach Finland's general requests
for all participants of the services negotiations and
detailed requests on your country with respect to
initial commitments to be entered into as a part of the
Services Agreement in the Uruguay Round.

The aim of the general requests is to obtain a minimum
level of binding and liberalisation in the negotiations.

I am looking forward in having an opportunity to discuss
of these requests bilaterally between our services
negotiators.

                          Yours sincerely,

                          Antti Hynninen
                          Ambassador
                          Permanent Representative

His Excellency
Mr. Soo Gil Park
Ambassador
Permanent Representative
Permanent Mission of the Republic of Korea
GENEVA

                                                    0266

FINLAND'S GENERAL REQUESTS

SECTOR

REQUEST

APPLICABLE TO ALL SECTORS

Make a binding <u>commitment</u>, on national as well as sub-national levels, on your present level of Market Access and National Treatment concerning:

* foreign investment in commercial presence
* foreign investment in real estate
* foreign exchange control (including profit remittances)

Bind your commitments on national as well as sub-national levels.

Furthermore, we are making the following additional sector-specific requests:

1. BUSINESS SERVICES

A. Professional services

a. Legal Services CPC 861

Concerning advice on <u>home country law and international law</u>, for foreign law offices/lawyers, provided the legal adviser fulfills the <u>home</u> country's professional qualification conditions:

* eliminate all sector-specific restrictions on commercial presence, cross-border supply and consumption abroad
* provide full national treatment

b. Accounting, auditing and book-keeping services CPC 862

Concerning <u>accounting, auditing and book-keeping</u> <u>services</u> for foreign accounting firms/accountants, provided the accountant fulfills the <u>host</u> country's professional qualification conditions:

* eliminate all sector-specific restrictions on commercial presence, cross-border supply and consumption abroad

d. Architectural services, CPC 8671
g. Urban planning and landscape, CPC 8674

* eliminate all sector-specific restrictions on commercial presence, cross-border supply and consumption abroad
* provide full national treatment (including removal of nationality requirements)

e. Engineering consulting services CPC 8672
f. Integrated engineering services CPC 8673

* eliminate all sector-specific restrictions on commercial presence, cross-border supply and consumption abroad
* provide full national treatment (including removal of nationality requirements)

B. Computer and Related Services (including categories a,b,c,d,e,)

CPC 841-845, 849

* eliminate all sector-specific restrictions on commercial presence, cross-border supply and consumption abroad
* provide full national treatment (including removal of nationality requirements)

C. Research and Development Services (including categories a,b,c,)

CPC 851-853

Make a binding commitment on the present level of Market Access and National Treatment in this sector concerning:
* commercial presence,
* cross-border supply and
* consumption abroad.

E. Rental/Leasing Services without Operators

a. Relating to ships
CPC 83103

Make a binding commitment on the present level of Market Access and National Treatment in this sector concerning:
* commercial presence,
* cross-border supply and
* consumption abroad.

b. Relating to aircraft
CPC 83104

Make a binding commitment on the present level of Market Access and National Treatment in this sector concerning:
* commercial presence,
* cross-border supply and
* consumption abroad.

F. Other Business Services

a. Advertising services, CPC 871

* eliminate all sector-specific restrictions on commercial presence, cross-border supply and consumption abroad
* provide full national treatment (including removal of nationality requirements)

b. Market research and public opinion polling services CPC 864

* eliminate all sector-specific restrictions on commercial presence, cross-border supply and consumption abroad
* provide full national treatment (including removal of nationality requirements)

c. Management consulting, CPC 865
d. Services rel. to man. consulting CPC 866

* eliminate all sector-specific restrictions on commercial presence, cross-border supply and consumption abroad
* provide full national treatment (including removal of nationality requirements)

10-8

f. Consulting services incidental to agriculture, hunting and forestry CPC 881

* eliminate all sector-specific restrictions on commercial presence, cross-border supply and consumption abroad
* provide full national treatment (including removal of nationality requirements)

g. Services incidental to fishing CPC 882

* eliminate all sector-specific restrictions on commercial presence, cross-border supply and consumption abroad
* provide full national treatment (including removal of nationality requirements)

h. Consulting services incidental to mining CPC 883 + 5115

* eliminate all sector-specific restrictions on commercial presence, cross-border supply and consumption abroad
* provide full national treatment (including removal of nationality requirements)

i. and j. Consulting services incidental to manufacturing and energy distrib. CPC 884, 885 (except for 88442) and CPC 887

* eliminate all sector-specific restrictions on commercial presence, cross-border supply and consumption abroad.
* provide full national treatment (including removal of nationality requirements)

l. Investigation and security, CPC 873

* eliminate all sector-specific restrictions on commercial presence, cross-border supply and consumption abroad
* provide full national treatment (including removal of nationality requirements)

2. COMMUNICATION SERVICES

C. Telecommunication Services

Make a binding commitment on the present level of Market Access and National Treatment in this sector.

---

3. CONSTRUCTION AND RELATED ENGINEERING SERVICES
(including a,b,c,t,e,)

CPC 511-518

* eliminate all sector-specific restrictions on commercial presence, cross-border supply and consumption abroad
* provide full national treatment (including removal of nationality requirements); especially concerning
  - requirements of association with a domestic company or of local participation
  - discriminatory duties and charges, including taxes

---

4. DISTRIBUTION SERVICES
(including A,B,C,l,E,)
CPC 621, 622, 631
632, 6111, 6113,
6121, 8929

Make a binding commitment on the present level of Market Access and National Treatment in this sector concerning:

* commercial presence,
* cross-border supply and
* consumption abroad.

---

6. ENVIRONMENTAL SERVICES
(including A,B,C,L)
CPC 9401-9403)

* eliminate all sector-specific restrictions on commercial presence, cross-border supply and consumption abroad
* provide full national treatment (including removal of nationality requirements)

7. FINANCIAL SERVICES

Make a binding commitment on the present level of Market Access and National Treatment in this sector.

9. TOURISM AND TRAVEL RELATED SERVICES
(including C)

Tourist guides services CPC 7472

* Remove nationality requirements

11. TRANSPORT SERVICES

A. Maritime Transport Services

International shipping services

Bind all measures that affect
a) the crossborder supply of international shipping services,
b) the purchase abroad by national consumers of international shipping services and
c) the commercial presence of providers of international shipping services
at the existing level of market access and national treatment.

Make a binding commitment to eliminate all measures that restrict market access or condition national treatment for
a) the crossborder supply of international shipping services and
b) the purchase abroad by national consumers of international shipping services
within three years after the entry into force of the Agreement.

Maritime transport auxiliary services

Bind all measures that affect
a) the crossborder supply of maritime transport auxiliary services,
b) the purchase abroad by national consumers of maritime transport auxiliary services and

0273

c) the commercial presence of providers of maritime transport auxiliary services at the existing level of market access and national treatment.

Definition of terms, used above:

International shipping services:
transportation of passengers or goods between ports located in different states, including passenger cruise traffic outside a Party's territorial waters.

Maritime transport auxiliary services:
all maritime transport related services within the confines of the port or sea environment, limited to those which provide an immediate, interactive, supporting role to the primary function of the maritime transport industry, which is the transportation of goods and/or passengers between ports.

B. Internal Waterways Transport

Make a binding commitment on the present level of Market Access and National Treatment in this sector concerning:
* commercial presence
* cross-border supply and
* consumption abroad.

C. Air Transport Services

Make a binding commitment on the present level of Market Access and National Treatment in this sector concerning:
* commercial presence
* cross-border supply and
* consumption abroad.

0274

E. Rail Transport Services

Make a binding commitment on the present level of
Market Access and National Treatment in this sector
concerning:
* commercial presence
* cross-border supply and
* consumption abroad.

F. Road Transport Services

Make a binding commitment on the present level of
Market Access and National Treatment in this sector
concerning:
* commercial presence
* cross-border supply and
* consumption abroad.

FINLAND'S SPECIFIC REQUEST: Korea

Sector No.	Sector Description	Request
All	All	* Remove restrictions on remittance of profit to the service providers' home countries. * Lift credit control policies. * Liberalize the Korean foreign exchange market. * Permit all banks – domestic and foreign – to issue medium and long term debt instruments. * Remove limits on equity investments and permit greater freedom in the use of offshore loans.
1.F.a	Advertising services	* Remove restrictions on foreign produced advertising materials.
2.C	Telecommunication services	* Remove limitations on VANS.
3:A,B,C,D,E	Construction and related engineering services	* Remove excessive capital requirements for subsidiaries of foreign consultancy and engineering companies. * Remove preferences given to domestic construction and consulting companies. * Remove discriminatory taxes for foreign consultancy and engineering companies. * Provide recognition of foreign engineering exams and allow foreign consultants to make contracts directly with final customer.
4:A,B,C,D,E	Distribution services	* Provide market access and liberalize restrictions concerning store size, number of stores and traded items.
7	Financial services	* Make a binding commitment in accordance with the obligations in MTN.TNC/W/50.

TOTAL P.10

기 안 용 지

분류기호 서번호	통기 20644-	(전화: 720 - 2188)	시 행 상 특별취급
보존기간	영구 . 준영구 10. 5. 3. 1.	장　　　　　　　관	
수 신 처 보존기간			
시행일자	1991.10.23.		

보 조 기 관	국 장	전 결	협 조 기 관		문 서 통 제
	심의관				
	과 장				
기안책임자		조 현			발 송 인

경 유 수 신 참 조	건 의	발 신 명 의	

제 목	UR/서비스 협상 정부대표단 임명

　91.10.23-25간 제네바에서 개최되는 UR/GNS 통신분야 부속서

제정을 위한 공식 및 비공식 회의에 참가할 정부대표단을 "정부대표 및

특별사절의 임명과 권한에 관한 법률"에 의거 아래와 같이 임명할 것을

건의하오니 재가하여 주시기 바랍니다.

- 아　　　　　　　래 -

- 1 -

0276

1. 회 의 명 : UR/GNS 통신분야 부속서 회의

2. 개최일시 :

   o 공식회의 : 10.25(금)

   o 비공식 회의 : 10.23(수)-24(목)

3. 정부대표단

   o 주 제네바 대표부 관계관

   o 체신부 행정사무관   노영규

   o 통신개발연구원 연구위원   최병일 (자문)

4. 출장기간 : 91.10.23(수)-27(일) (4박5일)

5. 소요경비 : 체신부 소관예산

6. 훈   령 :

   o 아래 기본입장을 견지하며 통신서비스 이용 보장 문제가

   UR/GNS 협상에서 타결될 수 있도록 협의에 적극적으로 대처

- 2 -   0277

- 통신부속서상의 의무 부과시 경쟁상태에 있는 민간

공중 통신 사업자에게 부속서 의무를 적용시키는

문제와 관련, 부속서 의무를 모든 공중 통신

사업자에게 적용하여 각국 사업자간 균형을 유지해야

할 것임.

- 기업내 통신의 허용은 각국의 공중 통신 사업자에게

미칠 영향을 충분히 고려하여 업무상 긴밀한 사항에

한정, 허용해야 할 것임.

- 공중 통신 사업자의 서비스 공공제공 의무 수행을 위해

공중 통신 서비스의 접근 및 이용에 대한 제한을

허용하는 문제는 우선 서비스 공공 제공 의무의

개념을 구체화 하여야 할 것임.

- 공중 통신 서비스의 요금은 기본적으로 원가를

지향하여야 함.   끝.

- 3 -   0278

분류기호 문서번호	통기 20644- 13ㅏ	(2170, 2391)	결	담 당	담당관	심의관
시행일자	1991.10.23.		재	조현	대결	
수　신	영사교민국장	발　신	통상국장			
재　목	정부대표 출국 협조					

91.10.25(금) 개최되는 UR/GNS 통신부속서 협상에 참가할

정부대표단을 아래와 같이 임명 하였으니, 동 대표단의 출국에 필요한

조치를 취하여 주시기 바랍니다.

- 아　　　　　래 -

1. 회 의 명 : UR/GNS 통신분야 부속서 회의

2. 개최일시 :

　ㅇ 공식회의 : 10.25(금)

　ㅇ 비공식 회의 : 10.23(수)-24(목)

3. 정부대표단 :

　ㅇ 체신부 행정사무관　　　　　노영규

　ㅇ 통신개발연구원 연구위원　　　최병일 (자문)

0279

- 1 -

4. 출장기간 : 91.10.23(수)-27(일) (4박5일)

5. 소요경비 : 체신부 소관예산

첨　부 : 원칙결재 사본 1부.　　　　　　　끝.

0280

- 2 -

"피땀흘려 이룬 경제 사치,낭비로 무너진다"

체   신   부

110-777 서울 종로구 세종로 100번지   /(02)750-2341/(02)750-2915

문서번호 통협 34470-7631

시행일자 1991· 10· 21·

수   신 외무부장관

제   목 UR/GNS통신분야 전문가회의 참가

　　　　　1· UR/GNS 통신분야 부속서 제정을 위한 공식 및 비공식회의가 '91·
10· 23(수)-10·25(금)스위스 제네바에서 개최될 예정인 바. 동 회의에 우리부
대표단을 아래와 같이 참석케 하고자 하오니 적극 협조하여 주시기 바랍니다·

　　　　　가· 참가자 및 출장기간

소 속	직 위	성 명	출 장 기 간	비 고
체 신 부	행정사무관	노영규	91·10·23-10·27 (5일간)	UR/GNS통신 부속서 제정을 위한 공식· 비공식회의 참가
통신개발 연구원	연구위원	최병일	91·10·22-10·27 (6일간)	

붙임 : 훈령(안) 1부· 끝·

체   신   부   장

차   관   전   결

'91.10 23

35136

0281

훈 령 (안)

1. 기본훈령

o 금번 UR/GNS 통신분야 전문가회의는 지난 90.12월에 확정이
  보류된 통신부속서를 협의하는 중요한 회의이므로

  - 통신서비스 이용보장문제가 UR서비스 다자간협상을 통하여
    해결될 수 있도록 적극적으로 협의에 임할 것

2. 세부훈령

o 통신부속서상의 의무를 부과함에 있어 경쟁상태에 있는 민간
  공중통신사업자에게 부속서의 의무를 적용시키는 문제에
  대해서는

  - 부속서의 의무를 모든 공중통신사업에게 적용하여 각국
    사업자간 균형을 유지해야 한다는 입장을 견지할 것

o 기업내통신의 허용에 대해서는 기업내통신의 허용이 각국의
  공중통신사업자에게 미칠 영향을 충분히 고려하여 업무상긴밀
  관계자로 한정하여 허용해야한다는 입장을 견지할 것

o 공중통신사업자의 서비스 공공제공의무 수행을 위해 공중통신
  서비스의 접근 및 이용에 대한 제한을 허용하는 문제는

  - '서비스 공공제공의무'의 개념을 구체화할 필요는 있으나
    by-pass 방지등을 위한 규제는 필요하다는 입장을 표명할 것

o 원가를 지향한 요금제도에 대해서는 요금결정시 각국의 국내
  정책이 고려될 수 있어야 하지만 기본적으로 공중통신서비스의
  요금은 원가를 지향해야 한다는 입장을 견지할 것

0282

51907

분류기호 서번호	통기 20644-	(전화 : 720 - 2188)		시 행 상 특별취급	
보존기간	영구. 준영구 10. 5. 3. 1.	장		관	
수 신 처 보존기간					
시행일자	1991.10.23.				

보 조 기 관	국 장	전 결	협 조 기 관		문 서 통 제	검열 1991
	심의관					
	과 장	대결			발 송 인	
기안책임자		조 현				

경유 수신 참조	체신부장관	발신명의	

제 목   UR/서비스 협상 정부대표단 임명 통보

1. 91.10.23-25간 제네바에서 개최되는 UR/GNS 통신분야 부속서

제정을 위한 공식 및 비공식 회의에 참가할 정부대표단이 "정부대표

및 특별사절의 임명과 권한에 관한 법률"에 의거 아래와 같이 임명

되었음을 통보합니다.

- 아   래 -

- 1 -   0283

가. 회 의 명 : UR/GNS 통신분야 부속서 회의

나. 개최일시 :

　　ㅇ 공식회의 : 10.25(금)

　　ㅇ 비공식 회의 : 10.23(수)-24(목)

다. 정부대표단

　　ㅇ 주 제네바 대표부 관계관

　　ㅇ 체신부 행정사무관　　　　노영규

　　ㅇ 통신개발연구원 연구위원　　최병일 (자문)

라. 출장기간 : 91.10.23(수)-27(일) (4박5일)

마. 소요경비 : 체신부 소관예산

2. 출장 결과 보고서는 대표단 귀국후 2주일이내 당부로

송부하여 주시길 바랍니다.　　　　　　　끝.

- 2 -

0284

발 신 전 보

			분류번호	보존기간

번　　호 : WGV-1460　　911023 1524　FN 종별 : 암호통신

수　　신 : 주 제네바　　대사. 총영사

발　　신 : 장 관 (통 기)

제　　목 : UR/GNS(통신 부속서) 협상

　　　　10.25(금) 개최되는 UR/GNS 동신부속서 협상에 본부대표가 아래 임명 되었으니 귀관 관계관과 함께 참석토록 조치바람.

1. 본부대표

　　ㅇ 체신부 행정사무관　　　　　　　　노영규

　　ㅇ 동신개발연구원 연구위원　　　　　최병일(자문)

2. 출장기간 : 91.10.23-27 (4박5일)

3. 훈　　령 :

　　ㅇ 아래 기본입장을 견지하여 동신서비스 이용 보장 문제가 UR/GNS 협상에서

　　　타결될 수 있도록 협의에 적극적으로 대처바람.

　　- 부속서의 의무는 모든 민간 공중 동신 사업자에게 적용하여 각국 사업자간

　　　균형을 유지해야 할 것임.

　　- 기업내 동신의 허용은 각국의 공중 동신 사업자에게 미칠 영향을 충분히

　　　고려하여 업무상 긴밀한 사항에 한정, 허용해야 할 것임.

　　- 공중 동신 사업자의 서비스 공공 제공 의무 수행을 위해 공중 동신 서비스의

　　　접근 및 이용에 대한 제한을 허용하는 문제와 관련, 우선 서비스 공공 제공

　　　의무의 개념을 구체화 하여야 할 것임.

　　- 공중 동신 서비스의 요금은 기본적으로 원가를 지향하여야 함.　　끝.

　　　　　　　　　　　　　　　　　　　　　　　(통상국장보 김안용 규)

앙고재	91년 10월 22일 통기과	기안자 성명 조현	과 장	심의관	국 장	차 관	장 관	외신과통제
				전결				

0285

외 무 부

종 별 :

번 호 : GVW-2131

일 시 : 91 1024 1930

수 신 : 장 관(수신처참조)

발 신 : 주 제네바대사

제 목 : UR/GNS 협상

　　10.28 주간에 개최 예정인 서비스 분야 양자 협의관련 현재까지 잠정 합의된 국별 일정을 하기보고함.

　　1. 국별 일정

　- 10.31(목) 16:30 : 캐나다(대상분야: 모든 서비스 분야)

　- 11.1(금) 11:30 : 호주(모든 서비스 분야)

　　14:30 : 미국(금융, 증권을 제외한 전분야, 보험포함)

　　2. 양자 협상 성격

　- UR/GNS 허버상 진행상황 및 국별 양자 협의시간이 약 두시간여에 불과한 점을고려할때 본격적인 양허 협상 진입은 어려울 것으로 판단되며, REQUEST LIST 에 대한 설명 및 상대국의 개괄적 반응 탐지등에 한정될 것으로 전망됨.

　- 참고로 지금까지의 아국에 전달된 REQUEST LIST는 미국, 일본, EC, 캐나다, 호주, 스웨덴, 핀랜드 등 7개국임. 끝

　　(대사 박수길-국장)

　　수신처:(봉기, 경기원, 재무부, 법무부, 농림수산부, 문화부, 상공부, 건설부, 보사부, 노동부, 교통부, 체신부, 과기처, 공보처, 항만청)

통상국 농수부	2차보 상공부	법무부 건설부	보사부 노동부	문화부 과기처	교통부 해항청	체신부 공보처	경기원	재무부

91.10.25　08:16 WH

외신 1과　통제관

0286

외 무 부

원 / 본

종 별 :

번 호 : GVW-2132

일 시 : 91 1024 1930

수 신 : 장관(수신처 참조)

발 신 : 주 제네바 대사

제 목 : UR/GNS 협상

10.24(목) 당관에 전달된 일본의 서비스 분야 추가 REQUEST-LIST 및 EC 의 금융분야 REQUEST-LIST(기타분야는 추후 전달예정)를 별첨 송부함.

첨부: 1. 일본의 추가 REQUEST-LIST 1 부

2. EC 음 금융분야 REQUEST-LIST 1 부.

(GVW(F)-0444)

수신처: 통기, 경기원, 재무부, 법무부, 농림수산부, 문화부, 상공부, 건설부, 보사부, 노동부, 교통부, 체신부, 과기처, 공보처, 항만청

(대사 박수길-국장)

예고:91.12.31. 까지

일반문서로 재분류(1991. 12. 31.)

통상국	장관	차관	2차보	청와대	안기부	법무부	보사부	문화부
교통부	체신부	경기원	재무부	농수부	상공부	건설부	노동부	과기처
해항청	공보처							

PAGE 1

91.10.25   06:58

외신 2과   통제관 CE

0287

UR(우루과이라운드).GNS(서비스협상그룹) 회의, 1991. 전5권(V.4 9-10월) (2)   181

Grw(h)-444 11024 1800
권방 '

1.   In accordance with the Procedural Guidelines for
Negotiations on Initial Commitments agreed at the Group
of Negotiaions on Services of 28 June 1991, Japan presents
to the Republic of Korea initial requests for liberalization
of restrictions to trade in services in the sectors/sub-
sectors and activities as described in the attached list.

        This list is of initial and provisional nature in
the light of the ongoing negotiations on the General
Agreement on Trade in Services and Japan reserves its rights
to modify or to make technical changes to this list as
necessary and appropriate in the course of the process
of initial commitment negotiations.

        Japan intends to make additional requests for
liberalization in other sectors such as the financial
services sector, the maritime transport services sector
and the tourism and travel related services sector in the
near future.

2.   "Sector/Sub-sector/Activities" column in the request
list is described on the basis of Service Sectoral
Classification List prepared by the Secretariat as
MTN.GNS/w/120.

3.   Trade restrictive measures of horizontal nature
are described as "Horizontal Measure(s)" in the Sector/Sub-
sector/Activities column.

4.   The terms used in the category column mean as
follows:

   (1) MA: Trade restrictive measures considered to fall
             under the category of the market access
             provision (Article XVI) of the General Agreement
             which is being developed in negotiations in
             the GNS.

   (2) NT: Trade restrictive measures considered to fall
             under the category of the national treatement
             provision (Article XVII) of the General
             Agreement which is being developed in
             negotiations in the GNS.

0288

(Country) The Republic of Korea

Sector/Sub-sector/Activities	Description	Category
TRANSPORT SERVICES		
Maritime Transport	(requests)	
	1. Under the Shipping Industry Promotion Law, only ship operators of a country which is not a party to a multilateral convention acceded by the Republic of Korea or which does not have a bilateral agreement with the Republic of Korea are required to obtain waiver in order to be engaged in liner trade with the Republic of Korea.	MA, NT
	2. Designated cargoes including cement and steel for export, crude oil, raw material of steel, raw material fertilizer, government purchased cargo are only reserved for Korean flag carriers. The government of the Republic of Korea may add other cargoes as designated cargo.	MA, NT
	3. Foreign investment in oceangoing shipping is restricted to a minority share.	MA, NT

(continued)

0289

(Country) The Republic of Korea

Sector/Sub-sector/ Activities	Description	Category
	4. A shipping agent shareholded by foreign ship operators may undertake business only for the shareholding ship operators.	MA, NT
	5. The Republic of Korea keeps discriminatory charge on harbour dues for vessels under foreign flags.	MA, NT
	Japan requests the rollback of such measures and restrictions.	

*Advanced copy. Other requests will
follow.   24/10/9*

EUROPEAN COMMUNITY REQUEST LIST ON SERVICES

PART II - PARTICULAR REQUESTS FOR FINANCIAL SERVICES

- Individual request to KOREA -

1. General request

In addition to the general request made by the Community to all participants for all sectors indicated in Part I of the Community request and in
particular to the commitment not to introduce any new restrictions as of
[....... 1991], as regards the financial services sector the Community
seeks from Korea participants to the services negotiations that the
following undertakings are entered in their schedules:

1. To bind all the financial services sector, without excluding any
   particular financial sector, subsector or transaction.

2. Unless otherwise indicated in the schedule for existing measures, with
   due respect to the principle of progressive liberalization and without
   prejudice to the application of measures justified on prudential grounds
   as defined in the financial services annex (as ultimately agreed by
   participants), to undertake:

   a) to eliminate any restrictions not justified on prudential grounds on
      the establishment, including - without prejudice of the application
      of anti-trust laws - through acquisition of existing enterprises, of
      a commercial presence, in particular in the form of branches or
      wholly-owned subsidiaries, and on the expansion of the activities of
      financial service providers;

   b) to eliminate any measures which disadvantage foreign financial
      service providers in their ability to compete effectively on equal
      terms with domestic financial service providers, including as regards
      participation in payments and clearing systems operated by public
      institutions and access to official funding and refinancing
      facilities;

   c) to allow foreign financial service providers to compete effectively
      on equal terms, in each segment or geographical part of the market,
      with domestic financial service providers which operate in that
      segment or geographical part of the market, regardless of the
      affiliation or ownership links of the foreign financial service
      provider with other financial or non-financial enterprises;

0291

d) to liberalize the cross-border provision of reinsurance, transport
insurance, banking auxiliary services as defined in the annex, either
at the initiative of the consumer or of the financial service
provider, and to liberalize the purchase by its residents abroad of
all banking and other financial services other than insurance;

e) to allow the introduction of new financial services and products
insofar as host regulatory authorities are satisfied as to the
soundness of these new services and products;

f) to allow cross-border transfers of information and equipment
necessary for the conduct of ordinary business of financial service
providers;

g) to list in the schedule existing monopoly rights and to commit to
endeavour to eliminate them or reduce their scope as soon as
circumstances permit;

h) to grant most favoured nation and national treatment as regards the
purchase of financial services by public institutions.

These commitments should be applied at all levels of regulation - central,
sub-national or local government. These commitments should also apply to
the activities of non-governmental bodies or of other self-regulatory
organizations enjoying regulatory powers or other privileges or benefits
granted by the Government.

2. Specific request

In addition to the commitment not to introduce any new restrictions on
market access and national treatment and to the undertaking to apply the
general principles indicated in No II.1 of the Community request concerning
financial services unless otherwise specified in the schedules, the
European Community seeks from Korea the concessions listed below, which
refer to specific restrictions. The Community is ready to negotiate with
Korea on the modalities and possible time limits for the progressive
implementation of these concessions.

The Community reserves its right to amend or complement this request in
light of the evolution of the negotiations and of the requests made by
other participants.

a) Banking

- To allow the establishment of subsidiaries of foreign banks, including
through the acquisition by foreigners of majority shareholdings in
Korean banks, and to allow them to operate under conditions of national
treatment, in particular as regards access by companies established in
Korea to foreign banks ("prime banking system").
- Liberalization of the conditions for establishment of branches of
foreign banks in Korea on the basis of national treatment, including
requirements concerning separate capitalization; improvement of the
conditions for the availability of adequate funding in domestic
currency, in particular through the removal of restrictions on new money
market instruments and the development of an efficient interbank market.

0292

- 31 -

- Liberalization of the restrictions on the creation of additional branches.
- Liberalization of the restrictions on the granting of "trust licences".
- Liberalization of conditions for access to Korea's ATM networks and electronic clearning house networks, and of conditions for expansion of ATM networks.
- To ease the restrictions concerning ownership of real estate.

b) <u>Insurance</u>

- To allow foreign insurance companies to establish subsidiaries and branches in Korea and to allow them to operate under conditions of national treatment, in particular by easing licensing conditions.
- To authorize foreign state owned insurance companies to establish operations in Korea
- To permit MAT insurance abroad
- To relax the conditions on compulsory reinsurance
- To liberalize restrictions on insurance broking
- Introduction of more flexibility in the system for checking policy conditions to ensure a quick approval of new policy contracts after a short period of time and as regards regulations on premium rates and other policy conditions.

c) <u>Securities Trading</u>

- To allow any suitably qualified foreign securities firm to establish branches and subsidiaries in Korea, including through acquisition of majority shareholdings in domestic securities firms, and to allow them to operate under conditions of national treatment.
- To relax conditions on branch licences, in particular as regards minimum capital.
- Liberalization of access to and membership of the stock exchange
- Liberalization of access by foreign companies to the unit trust market.
- To continue to liberalize access by foreign investors to the stock market.

0293

외 무 부

종 별 :

번 호 : GVW-2126

일 시 : 91 1024 1700

수 신 : 장 관(봉기, 경기원, 재무부, 상공부, 한국은행)

발 신 : 주 제네바대사

제 목 : UR/GNS회의(3)

10.23(수) 개최된 금융분야 GNS 회의 내용을하기 보고함.

1. GNS 전체 비공식 (10.23 오전 JARAMILLO 의장 및 FRANK SWEDLOVE 의장 공동 주재)

- FRANKS SWEDLOVE 공동 의장이 작성, 배부한 비공식 금융 부속서 초안(10.14 자)에 대하여 알젠틴, 브라질, 이집트, 베네쥴엘라, 유고, 인도, 칠레, 모로코, 멕시코등 개도국들은 분야별 부속서는 FRAMEWORK 규정을 명료화 하는데 한정하여야 하지 이를 수정하는 역할을 해서는 안되며, 단일 서비스 협정이 되어야 한다는 전제하에 다음 사항들을 지적함.

0 제 1조(SECOPE/DEFINITION) 2항: FRAMEWORK 1조3항B를 제외토록 하는 것은 FRAMEWORK 제 1조 각항이 서로 연결되어 있는 점을 고려할때 서비스협정 전체의 적용을배제할 우려가 있음.

0 제 3조 (PRUDENTIAL CARVE-OUT): 구체적 문안에 대하여 협상할 용의가 있음. 인가 신청 관련당국의 정보 제공의무는 FRAMEWORK 6조 4항에 규정된대로 당해사안의처리 상태에 한정하여야 하며, 인가 결정에 필요한 사항은 동 대상에 포함할수 없음. 0 제 4조(조화 및 인정): FRAMEWORK 제 7조 갈이 조화 및 인정 협정의 협상에관심이 있는 국가가 모두 참여할수 있는 기회가 보장되어야 함.

0 제 5조(예외): FRAMEWORK에서 다루어야 할 사항임.

0 제 7조(기구): 너무 자세할 뿐만 아니라 금융 분야에 대하여 별도 독립 기구를상정하고 있는바 이는 서비스 협정을 분할 하는 결과가 됨. 또한 동조3항의 금융 서비스 기구에 대한 MANDATE (추가자유화 범위 평가)는 FRAMEWORK 에서 결정되어야 할사항이므로 수용할수 없음.

금융 서비스 기구에 참여 자격을 금융분야에 자유화 약속을 한 나라에

통상국   2차보   경기원   재무부   상공부

PAGE 1

91.10.25   07:59 WH

외신 1과 통제관

0294

한정하고있으나, 이는 부당하며, 서비스 협정 가입국은 모두 참가자격이 부여되어야 함.

0 제 8조 (분쟁해결): FRAMEWORK 에서 다루어야 하문제임.

금융분야만 별도로 취급하는 것은 상품 분야까지 포함하여 통합된 분쟁해결 시스템을 구성코자하는 선진국 입장과 모순됨., 개별결정의 분쟁해결 의뢰 여부도 FRAMEWORK에서 결정되어야 할 사항이며, 부속서에 규정할 필요없음.

0 제 3부(SPECIFIC COMMITMENT): FRAMEWORK 의SCHEDULING 에 대한 합의가 형성되고 있는바 금융 부속서에 규정하고자 하는 것과 유사하므로 별도로 다시 규정할 필요가 없음.

- 이에 대하여 미국 및 EC 는 금융 및 통신분야는 FRAMEWORK과 일체를 이루는 가운데 구체적 규정이 필요하다는 가정하에 작업이 진전되어 왔으며, 의장 초안이 별도 협정을 의미하는 것이 아니라 금융 서비스의 특성에 따른 것이라고 전제하고 다음과 같이 논평함.

0 FRAMEWORK 16조, 17조와 일부 중복되는 부분이 있으나 보완 가능함.

0 금융 서비스의 특성상 시장접근과 내국민 대우관련 구속력 있는 규정이 필요하며, 이를 의무로 규정하더라도 유보가 허용되므로 융통성이 있기 때문에 2 TRACK 이불필요하며, 부속서에 따른 ONE TRACK 이 되어야 한다는 것이 자국입장임.(종전에는EC만이 부속서상의ONE TRACK 채택 입장을 표명하였으나 미국도 이에 가세 보다 경화된 입장을 견지)

0 금융 서비스 기구 및 분쟁해결 은 전체적 분쟁해결 메카니즘과는 별개 문제이며, 금융서비스의 특성에 따른 것임.

- 한편 GATT 법률국은 의장 초안 관련의문사항에 대하여 다음과 같이 답변함

0 제 1조 2항의 효력은 FRAMEWORK 제 1조 전체가 아니라 제 1조 3항(B)만 제외하는 것임.

0 제 8조 4항은 FRAMEWORK 에 따를 경우 모든 INDIVISUAL CASE 에 대한 분쟁해결의뢰가 가능하나 이중 NON-VIOLATION CASE 는 제외하는 효과가 있음.

0 제 2조는 FRAMEWORK 제 3조중 일반적 적용효력을 가지는 RULINGS 와 DECISIONS를 공표대상에서 제외하는 효과가 있음.

2. 주요국 비공식 협의(10.23 오후 HAWES 대사 및 FRANK SWEDLOVE 공동주재, 약 25개국 참석)

PAGE 2

0295

가. 제 1조 (SCOPE/DEFINITION)

- 미국, 스웨덴, SWEDLOVE 의장등은 FRAMEWORK에 따를 경우 정부 기능에 따른 ACTIVITY 는 모두 제외되는 바, 공공기관이 종종 외국인 서비스공급자를 차별하므로 상기 ACTIVITY 를 모두 제외하기 보다는 외국 서비스 공급자에게 똑같은 시장접근 기회를 부여하기 위한 것이라고 하였으며

0 특히 EC 는 제 1조가 의장 초안과 같이 규정되지 않을 경우 독점관련 조항이 무의미하게 된다고 함.

- 싱가폴은 공공기관의 서비스 공급자에 대한 업무지정은 차별의 문제가 아니라 신용등급에 따른 재량의 문제라고 반박함.

나. 제 3조(DOMESTIC REGULATION)

- 브라질은 일반적 의무인 제 6조에 REASONABLEMEASURE에 한한다는 조건하에 PRUDENTIAL CARVE OUT을 규정할 경우 시장접근 약속을 하지 않은 분야에 있어서도 국내규제(즉 PRUDONTIALREGULATION)가 REASONABLE 해야 하는 의무가 생기므로 이는 FRAMEWORK 과 부합하지 않느냐고 함.

3. 상기 주요국 비공식 협의는 10.24 오후 속개될 예정임. 끝

(대사 박수길-국장)

외 무 부

종 별 :

번 호 : GVW-2133   일 시 : 91 1024 1930

수 신 : 장 관(봉기, 경기원, 문화부, 상공부, 체신부, 과기처, 공보처)

발 신 : 주 제네바대사

제 목 : UR/GNS 회의(4)

10.24(목) JARAMILLO 의장 주재로 개최된 AUDIOVISUAL 서비스 분야 표제회의 내용을하기 보고함.

1. EC, 호주, 북구, 스위스, 말련등은 AUDIO VISUAL서비스 분야의 문화적 특성을강조하고 부속서 제정이 동 특성을 반영하는데 제일 적당한 방법이며, FRAMEWORK 제14조에 CULTURAL EXCEPTION은 너무 광범위하여 남용 가능성이 많다고 함. (예: 특정국가의 은행 설립을 문화적 이유로 거부하는 경우)

0 동 국가들은 부속서에 포함할 요소로서 MFN일탈만으로는 부족하며, 문화 정책목표에 대한 인정이 반영되어야 한다고 하는 한편 MFN일탈의 경우 영화 공동 생산 협 정등에 한하여 MFN 일탈을 하고자 하는 것이므로 무역에 미치는 영향이 작으며, 그일탈 범위도 점차 축소될 것이라고 함.

2. 아국, 캐나다, 인도등은 MFN 일탈은 CULTURALIDENTITY 보존에 적당한 방법이되지 못하며, FRAMEWORK 상의 예외조항으로 반영하여야 한다고 전제하고 예외 조항으로 반영하더라도 14조 조문에 의하여 문화 정책상 필요한 경우에 한정될 것이므로 남용 가능성이 없다고 지적함.

3. 미국, 일본은 문화적 이유로는 것은 매우 주관적이며, 사실상 경제적 보호를위한 도피수단으로 악용되기 용이한 것이라고 전제하고 FRAMEWORK 상의 예외 조항뿐만 아니라 부속서를 제정하여 MFN 일탈을 허용하는 것은 판도라상자를 여는 것이라고 하는 한편 STRONG MFN을 주장하는 EC 가 분야별로 일관성을 잃고 있다고 지적함.

4. 의장은 각국간 합의가 도출되지 않고 있다고 지적하고 각국과 비공식 협의를거쳐 추후 재토의할 것을 제의하고 회의를 종결하였음. 끝

(대사 박수길-국장)

통상국   2차보   문화부   체신부   경기원   상공부   과기처   공보처

PAGE 1   91.10.25   08:21 WH

외신 1과 통제관

0297

원 본

외 무 부

종 별 :

번 호 : GVW-2151

일 시 : 91 1025 1920

수 신 : 장 관(수신처 참조)

발 신 : 주 제네바대사

제 목 : UR/GNS 회의(5)

10.25(금) 오후 개최된 20개 주요국 비공식 협의와 동일 17:00 GNS 전체 비공식회의 내용을 하기보고함.

1. 주요국 비공식협의(JARAMILLO 의장주재)

0 다음과 같이 다음주 협의 진행계획을 정하였으며 동 협의는 20개 주요국 비공식 협의로 진행될 예정임.

- 10.28(월) 오전 : FRAMEWORK 제 7조, 14조(HAWES호주대사 주재, 금융전문가 참석가능)

0 오후: 금융서비스(HAWES 대사 및 FRANK SWEDLOVE공동주재)

0 저녁: AUDIO VISUAL 서비스(JARAMILLO 의장주재)

- 10.29(화) 오전: FRAMEWORK 제 13조, 15조,34조(JARAMILLO 의장주재)

0 오후: FRAMEWORK 제 5조, 8조, 9조,10조,30조(JARAMILLO의장주재)

0 저녁: 해운서비스(JARAMILLO 의장주재)- 10.30(수) 오전: 인력이동부속서, FRAMEWORK 제 1조,2조, 23ㅈ A(JARAMILLO 의장주재)

0 오후: SCHEDULING(HAWES 대사주재)

0 저녁: 해운, AUDIOVISUAL, 항공서비스(JARAMILLO의장주재)

- 10.31(목) 오전: FRAMEWORK 제 11조, 12조(JARAMILLO의장주재)

- 10.31(목) 오후- 11.1(금): 상기 과제중 미결사항 및 마무리 작업

0 제 4조(개도국 무역비중 증대) 및 양허협상의 실질적 기준 초안을 배부하였음(FAX 송부)

2. GNS 전체비공식(JARAMILLO 의장주재)

0 JARAMILLO 의장은 금추 비공식협의 경과 및 다음주 협의진행계획을 다음과 같이 보고함.

통상국 농수부	2차보 상공부	법무부 건설부	보사부 노동부	문화부 과기처	교통부 해항청	체신부 공보처	경기원	재무부

91.10.26   09:53 WH

외신 1과 통제관

0298

- 제 4조 및 양허협상의 실질적 기준: 많은 진전이 있었으며 오직 남은 문제는 최저개발국에 대한 우대문제임. 다음주총에 결론을 제시할 예정임.

- 인력이동부속서: 어느정도 진전은 있었으나 새로운 초안은 만들지 못하였음.

- MFN: MFN일탈에 관한 법적 대안에 대하여 토의하였으며 서비스협정의 근본취지가 퇴색하지 않도록 일탈을 최소화하고 이를 절감(DEGRESSIVITY)시키는 대안을 찾아야 함

- FRAMEWORK 제 5조, 8조,9조, 10조, 23조: 새로운 초안을 마련중에 있음

- AUDIOVISUAL 및 해운: 다음주에 협의를 계속할예정임.

- 금융서비스 및 FRAMEWORK 제 7조, 14조, SCHEDULING: HAWES 대사 주재로 협의를 계속할 예정

- 통신부속서: TRITT 의장이 개별적 협의를 계속할 예정

3. 협상진행 전망

0 다음주에 계속될 주요국 비공식 협의에서는 각국의 입장반복은 지양되고 타협안을 모색하되 참가국간 합의가 불가능할 경우에는 사무국에서 대안을 제시 이의 선택여부를 묻는 형태로 최종 합의안 도출을 시도할 전망

- 상기 최종 합의안 도출작업은 남은 작업량과 주어진 시간을 고려할때 늦어질 가능성도 있으며 금융부속서가 최대 난관으로 대두될 전망   ?

- 분야별 MFN 일탈은 주요정치적 쟁점으로 서양허협상과도 연계되어 있기때문에 11월초까지 결론 도출은 쉽지 않을 것으로 판단됨

- 통신부속서는 각 쟁점별로 이의가 있는 국가를 개별 접촉하여 타협안을 모색할예정인바 합의안 도출이 비교적 용인할 것으로 전망

0 동협의관련 현지 출장중인 최병일박사의 출장연장을 건의함.   ⟶ 으르리

첨부: 1. 양허협상의 실질적 기준초안 1부

2. 제 4조 초안

(GVW(F)-0452).끝

(차석대사   김삼훈-국장)수신처:

통기, 경기원, 재무부, 법무부, 농림수산부, 문화부, 상공부, 건설부, 보사부, 노동부, 교통부, 체신부, 과기처, 공보처, 항만청

본 전문의 누락부분은 재송 요청중이므로
추후 재대무 하겠습니다. 등재관: /l/

			기 안 용 지		시 행 상	
분류기호 문서번호	통기 20644-		(전화: 720 - 2188)		특별취급	
보존기간	영구. 준영구 10. 5. 3. 1.		차 관		장 관	
수 신 처 보존기간			전결			
시행일자	1991.10.26.					
보 조 기 관	국 장		협 조 기 관	제2차관보	문 서 통 제	
	심의관					
	과 장				발 송 인	
기안책임자	조 현					
경 유 수 신 참 조	건 의		발 신 명 의			
제 목	UR/서비스 협상 정부대표단 임명					

91.10.31-11.2기간중 제네바에서 개최되는 UR/GNS 주요국간

양자협의(Request/Offer 협상)에 참가할 정부대표단을 "정부대표 및

특별사절의 임명과 권한에 관한 법률"에 의거, 아래와 같이 임명할 것을

건의하오니 재가하여 주시기 바랍니다.

- 아   래 -

0300

- 1 -

1. 회 의 명 : UR/GNS 주요국간 양자협의	
2. 개최일시 :	
ㅇ 한.일본 : 10.31(목) 시간미정	
ㅇ 한.스웨덴 : 10.31(목) 시간미정	
ㅇ 한.카나다 : 10.31(목) 16:30-	
ㅇ 한.호주 : 11.1(금) 11:30-	
ㅇ 한.미국 : 11. 1(금) 15:00-	
3. 정부대표단	
ㅇ 경제기획원 제2협력관	이윤재
ㅇ 경제기획원 통상조정3과 사무관	김용준
ㅇ 경제기획원 통상조정2과 사무관	신호현
ㅇ 건설부 해외협력과 사무관	방재영
ㅇ 과학기술처 기술개발국 전기기좌	송우근
ㅇ 대외경제정책연구원 연구위원	김태준(자문)
ㅇ 김 & 장 법률사무소 변호사	신희택(자문)

- 2 -

0301

4. 출장기간 : 10.28-11. 3

    ㅇ 단, 이윤제 협력관, 김용준 사무관은 91.10.28-11.10

    (UR/GNS 여타 협상 참가)

5. 소요경비 : 해당부처 소관예산

6. 훈　령 :

    ㅇ 91.10.25 관계부처 UR/서비스 협상 대책 회의에서

    결정된 각 분야별 아국 입장을 기초로 양자협의에 적극

    대처토록 함.

    ㅇ 주요국의 대아국 요청사항 및 새로운 양허표 작성 방식에

    관한 정보를 입수, 아국의 Initial offer 수정에

    대비토록 함.　　　　　끝.

- 3 -

0302

경 제 기 획 원

봉조삼 10502-745   503~9149   1991. 10. 23

수 신 수신처 참조

제 목 UR/서비스 양허협상 참석요청

　　　1. 국내 서비스시장의 실질적 개방수준을 결정하는 양허협상이 10월 28일부터 본격적으로 진행될 예정이며 미국과는 11월 1일 스위스 제네바에서 1차 협상을 갖기로 확정되었읍니다.

　　　2. 이에따라 경제기획원 및 미국측 Request에서 제기된 업종관련 주무부처의 실무책임자와 관련연구기관의 전문가로 별첨과 같이 본부대표단을 구성하여 현지 협상에 참석코자 하니 해당되는 부처 및 기관은 협조해 주시기 바랍니다.

　　　3. 참고로 현재까지 우리에 대하여 Request List를 제시한 국가는 일본, 호주, 캐나다, 미국, 스웨덴이며 미국이외에 다른 국가들과의 협상일정은 아직 확정되지 않았음을 첨언합니다.

첨부 : UR/서비스 양허협상 대표단 구성(안) 1부.　　끝.

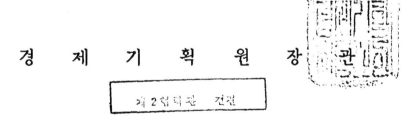

경 제 기 획 원 장

제 2협력관 건전

수신처 : <u>외무부장관</u>, 재무부장관, 법무부장관, 건설부장관, 노동부장관, 과기처장관, 대외경제정책연구원장, 한국개발연구원장, 김&장 법률사무소장

0303   35423

UR/서비스 讓許協商代表團 構成(案)

Ⅰ. 出張期間 : 10.29〜11.3(5박 6일)

Ⅱ. 代表團構成(총13명)

- 首席代表 : 經濟企劃院 第2協力官

- 代　　表

〈 政府 〉

○ 經濟企劃院 : 通商調整3課長, 김용준 事務官
　　　　　　　　 通商調整2課 신호현 事務官
○ 外　務　部 : 通商機構課 조현 書記官
○ 財　務　部 : 證券業務課長(또는 保險政策課長)
○ 法　務　部 : 涉外法務擔當檢事
○ 建　設　部 : 海外建設課長
○ 勞　動　部 : 海外雇傭課長
○ 科學技術處 : 技術用役課長

〈 專門家 〉

○ KIEP　 : 성극제博士
○ KDI　　 : 김지홍博士
○ 김&장法律事務所 : 신희택 辯護士

0304

경 제 기 획 원

통조삼 10502- 25/   503~9149   1991. 10. 26

수 신 외무부장관
참 조 통상국장
제 목 UR/서비스 양자협의 참석

      1. 스위스 제네바에서 개최되는 UR/서비스 양자협의에 아국대표단의
일원으로 다음과 같이 참석코자 하니 협조하여 주시기 바랍니다.

다   음

   가. 출장자

소 속	직 위	성 명	출 장 기 간
경제기획원 대 조 실	제2협력관	이 운 재	'91. 10.28~11.10(11.3~11.10간 은 UR/실무협상대표단 참여예정)
〃	통상조정3과 사무관	김 용 준	〃
〃	통상조정2과 사무관	신 호 현	'91. 10.28 ~ 11. 3
K I E P	연구위원	김 태 준 (자문역)	〃
김&장 법률사무소	변호사	신 희 택 (자문역)	'91. 10.30 ~ 11.3

     나. 경비부담 : 당원, KIEP

첨부 : 출장일정 각 1부.   끝.

경 제 기 획 원 장   관

0305

건 설 부

우 427-760   경기 과천 중앙 1   /   전화 (02) 503 - 7396   /   전송 503 - 7409

문서번호 해외 30600-29800

시행일자 1991. 10. 26   (1년)

선결			지	
접	일자 시간	11.10.29	시 결 재 · 공 람	
수	번호	35662		
처리과				
담당자				

수신 수신처 참조

참조

제목 UR/서비스협상 회의 참가에 따른 협조 요청

─────────────────────────────────

　　1. 경제기획원 동조삼 10502-745('91. 10. 23)의 관련임.

　　2. '91. 10. 30 ~ 11. 1간 스위스 제네바에서 있을 UR 서비스협상의 정부대표단의

일원으로 우리부 관계관을 다음과 같이 참석시키고자 하니 필요한 협조를 하여 주시기

바랍니다.

　　　　가. 협상기간 : '91. 10. 30 ~ 11. 1

　　　　나. 장 소 : 스위스 제네바

　　　　다. 참가자 소속 및 직.성명

　　　　　　　건설경제국 해외협력과 행정사무관 방 재 영

　　　　　　　　　　(영문 : JAI YOUNG BANG)

　　　　라. 출장기간 : '91. 10. 29 ~ 11. 3.　

건　설　부　장

건설경제국장 전결

수신처 : 경제기획원장관, 외무부장관.

0306

조한여기본

과 학 기 술 처

우 427-760 경기 과천 중앙 1, 정부 제2종합청사내 / (02)503-7619 / 전송

문서번호 기용16331-12042

시행일자 1991. 10.   .

선결			지시	
접수	일자시간		결재·공람	
	번호			
처 리 과				
담 당 자				

수신 수신처참조

참조

제목 UR/서비스 양허협상 참가 (정부 대표)

　　　1. 관련 : 경기원 통조삼 10502-745('91.10.23)

　　　2. UR/서비스 양허협상을 위해서 아래와 같이 우리처 대표를 파견코자 하오니
정부대표임명등 필요한 조치를 취하여 주시기 바랍니다.

　　　　　가. 피파견자 : 기술개발국 기술용역과 전기기좌 송우근

　　　　　나. 파견기간 : 1991.10.28 - 11.3.

　　　　　다. 장　　　소 : 스위스 제네바

　　　　　라. 파견경비 : 당처 예산

　　　　　　- 항공료 : US$2,108

　　　　　　- 체재비 : US$830

　　　　　　- 판공비 : US$300

　　　　　마. 예산지변과목 : ┌ 체재비 및 항공료 : 1112-213

　　　　　　　　　　　　　　└ 판　공　비 : 1112-234

첨부 국·영문 이력서 각1부. 끝.

과 학 기 술 처 장 관

수신처 경제기획원장관(참조 : 제2협력관), 외무부장관(참조 : 통상기구과장)

0307

52601

기 안 용 지

분류기호 문서번호	통기 20644-	(전화 : 720 - 2188)	시 행 상 특별취급	
보존기간	영구. 준영구 10. 5. 3. 1.	장 관		
수 신 처 보존기간				
시행일자	1991.10.28.			

보 조 기 관	국 장	전 결	협 조 기 관	문 서 통 제
	심의관			검열 1991. 10. 28 통지관
	과 장	대결		
기안책임자		조 현		발 송 인

경 유 수 신 참 조	수신처 참조	발 신 명 의	

제 목	UR/서비스 협상 정부대표단 임명 통보

　　　1.　91.10.31-11.2기간중 제네바에서 개최되는 UR/GNS 주요국간

양자협의(Request/Offer 협상)에 참가할 정부대표단이 "정부대표 및

특별사절의 임명과 권한에 관한 법률"에 의거, 아래와 같이 임명

되었음을 통보합니다.

　　　　　　　　　- 아　　　　　　　　　래 -

　　　　　　　　　　　- 1 -　　　　　　　　　　0308

가 . 회 의 명 : UR/GNS 주요국간 양자협의
나 . 개최일시 :
ㅇ 한 . 일본　 : 10.31(목) 시간미정
ㅇ 한 . 스웨덴 : 10.31(목) 시간미정
ㅇ 한 . 카나다 : 10.31(목) 16:30-
ㅇ 한 . 호주　 : 11.1(금) 11:30-
ㅇ 한 . 미국　 : 11. 1(금) 15:00-
다 . 정부대표단
ㅇ 경제기획원 제2협력관　　　　　 이윤제
ㅇ 경제기획원 통상조정3과 사무관　 김용준
ㅇ 경제기획원 통상조정2과 사무관　 신호현
ㅇ 건설부 해외협력과 사무관　　　 방재영
ㅇ 과학기술처 기술개발국 전기기좌 송우근
ㅇ 대외경제정책연구원 연구위원　　 김태준(자문)
ㅇ 김 & 장 법률사무소 변호사　　　 신희택(자문)

- 2 -

0309

라. 출장기간 : 10.28-11. 3

　　　o 단, 이윤제 협력관, 김용준 사무관은 91.10.28-11.10

　　(UR/GNS 여타 협상 참가)

마. 소요경비 : 해당부처 소관예산

2. 출장 결과 보고서는 대표단 귀국후 2주일이내 당부로

송부하여 주시기 바랍니다.　　　　　　　끝.

수신처 : 경제기획원, 건설부, 과학기술처장관

- 3 -

0310

발 신 전 보

분류번호	보존기간

번   호 : WGV-1480   911028 1644 FO 종별 :

수   신 : 주 제네바 대사. 총영사

발   신 : 장 관 (통 기)

제   목 : UR/GNS 양자협의

        10.31-11.2중 개최될 UR/GNS 양자협의에 참가할 본부대표단이 아래 임명 되었으니
귀관 관계관과 함께 참석토록 조치바람.

        ㅇ 본부대표단

            - 경제기획원 제2협력관   이윤제

            - 경제기획원 통상조정3과 사무관   김용준

            - 경제기획원 통상조정2과 사무관   신호현
            - 건설부 해외협력과 사무관 방재명
            - 과학기술처 기술개발국 전기기좌   송우근

            - 대외경제정책연구원 연구위원   김태준 (자문)

            - 김 & 장 법률사무소 변호사   신희택 (자문)

            (법무부, 노동부, ~~건설부~~, 문화부 대표도 정부대표 임명 절차 진행중)

        ㅇ 출장기간

            - 이윤재 협력관, 김용준 사무관 : 10.28-11.10

            - 여타 대표 : 10.28-11.3

보 안 통 제	〰

양 고 재	91년 10월 28일	통 기 과	기안자 성 명 조현		과 장 〰	심의관 홍장웅	국 장 전결		차 관	장 관 〰	외신과통제

0311

o 훈 령

- 91.10.25 관계부처 UR/서비스 협상 대책 회의에서 결정된 각 각야별 아국

  입장을 기초로 양자협의애 적극 대처토록 함.

- 주요국의 대아국 요청사항 및 새로운 양허표 작성 방식에 관한 정보를

  입수, 아국의 Initial offer 수정에 대비토록 함.   끝.

                                        (통상국장   김 용 규)

0312

외 무 부

종 별 :

번 호 : GVW-2158 　　　　　　　　　　　　일 시 : 91 1028 1830

수 신 : 장 관(통기,경기원,상공부,체신부)

발 신 : 주 제네바 대사

제 목 : UR/GNS 회의`(6)

　　10.25(금) TOBER TRITT 공동의장 주재로 개최된 통신부속서 수정안 에 대한 GNS전체 비공식회의 내용을 하기 보고함.

　　1. 부속서 적용 범위와 관련 공중 통신망의 사용및 접근에 영향을 미치는 정부조치를 부속서 적용대상으로 한다는데 대체적으로 합의가 형성되었으나 이와 관련 미국은 수정안 5.1 항의 통신망 사용 및 접근 보장의무 규정이 정부로 하여금 민간업자에 적극적인 조치를 취하도록 강제하는 문제가 있다고 지적함.

　　0 PTTS 의 정의에 관해서는 국가의 명시적인 요구에 의해 공중에게 일반적으로 제공되는 공중통신 서비스와 국가의 명시적인 요구가 없이 공중에게 일반적으로 제공되는 공중 통신서비스가 모두 포함되어야 한다는 수정안의 정의에 대체로 의견이 접근

　　2. 기업내 통신의 정의와 관련 아국은 시장접근이 허용된 분야의 서비스 제공업자의 자회사, 지점, 계열회사(AFFICIALTE)로 할 것을 주장한 반면, EC 등 일부 국가는` 계열회사` 의 정의가 없는 상태라고 하면서 이로 인해 발생가능한 문제에 대한 우려를 표명함.

　　3. 수정안 제 5조의 PTTN 및 PTTS 의 접근 및 이용에 관해서 미국, 스웨덴은 금번 수정안에서 이용자의 권리가 구체적으로 명시되어 이용권과 규제 권한과의 균형이이루어졌다고 환영한 반면, 개도국들은 기존의 의장 부속서와 많이 달라진 것으로 반대의사 표명

　　0 수정안 5.3 에 구체적으로 명시된 이용자의 권리와 관련 아국, EC, 일본을 포함한 다수국가가 명시된 내용들이 다소 모호한 점이 있음을 지적하면서 이를 보다 구체화 시킬것으로 주장함.

　　0 이와 함께 PTTN 및 PTTS 의 접근 및 이용에 대한 규제 권한을 행사할수 있는 경

통상국　　2차보　　청와대　　안기부　　체신부　　경기원　　상공부

PAGE 1 　　　　　　　　　　　　　　　　　　　91.10.29　　06:43 FN

　　　　　　　　　　　　　　　　　　　　　　외신 1과　통제관

　　　　　　　　　　　　　　　　　　　　　　　　　0313

우와 관련, 아국, 일본을 포함한 많은 국가가 기존안의 내용이 유지될 것을 주장하였으며, 공동사용(SHARED USE)에 대한 규제권한이 명시되어야 한다고 언급함.

4. 한편, 요금 조항, 국경간 정보이동을 위한 PTTN및 PTTS 의 접근 및 이용 보장, 개도국 특별고려 조항은 금번 회의에서 토의하지 않았으나 이견이 계속되는 상태임.

5. 금번 회의 결과 부속서 적용 범위에 있어서 상당한 의견 접근이 이루어졌으며, 기업내 통신의 정의 및 PTTN 및 PTTS 의 접근 및 이용보장(제 5조)과 관련 문제를제시한 국가들에 대하여서는 공동의장인 TRITT 가 개별 접촉하여 견해차이를 좁힌후 내주말까지는 수정된 통신부속서를 GNS 에 제출할 것으로 예상됨. 끝

(대사 박수길-국장) FN

외 무 부

종 별 :

번 호 : GVW-2159   일 시 : 91 1028 1830

수 신 : 장 관(수신처 참조)

발 신 : 주 제네바 대사

제 목 : UR/GNS 회의(7)

　　10.26(토) HAWES 대사 및 FRANKS SWEDLOVE 공동주제로 개최된 금융부속서에 대한주요국(약 30개국) 비공식 협의 내용을 하기보고함.

　　1. 협의 개요

　　- 10.25(목) 오후 협의에 이어 금융 서비스기구, 분쟁해결, SPECIFIC COMMITMENT에 대하여 논의하였는 바, 금융 서비스 기구 및 분쟁해결에 대하여는 갓트 법률국의조언에 의하여 선진국의 입장이 약화되는 경향을 보였으며, 금융 서비스기구 관련규정에 대하여 갓트 사무국이 대안을 작성 제시키로 함.

　　- SPECIFIC COMMITMENT 에 대하여는 근본적 입장대립이 계속 되었는 바, TWO TRACK APPROACH 공동제안 4개국(스위스, 스웨덴, 캐나다, 일본)은 TWO TRACK APPROACH 자체가 타협안인데도 불구하고 호주, 헝가리를 제외하고는 선.개도국 양쪽으로 부터 지지가 없음에 실망을 표시하고 자국의 최초 입장인 부속서상의 ONE TRACK 으로 입장을바꾼다고 하였으며, 이에 대해 인도는 자국의 본래 입장인 금융 부속서가 불필요하다는 입장을 견지하겠다는 등 감정 대립 양상을 보임.

　　0 한편, SEACEN 의 요청에 의하여 FRAMEWORK과 금융부속서 초안상의 자유화 추진방식이 서로 어떻게 다른지 비교표를 사무국 주도로 작성키로 함.

　　2. 토의 내용

　　가. 금융 서비스 기구(제 8조)

　　- SEACEN 을 제외한 대부분의 개도국들은 동기구의 설치 시기 및 방법(부속서에규정할 것인지, 협정 발효이후 COUNCIL의 결정에 의하여 설치할 것인지), 동기구의역할 및 구성, COUNCIL 과 관계등에 대하여 다음과 같이 논평함.(동기구의 필요성자체 는 부인하지 않음)

　　0 FRAMEWORK 상에 COUNCIL이 하부 기구를 설치할수 있으므로 부속서에 관련

통상국	2차보	법무부	보사부	교통부	체신부	경기원	재무부	농수부
상공부	건설부	노동부	과기처	해항청	공보처			

PAGE 1

91.10.29　　08:45 DQ

외신 1과 통제관

0315

사항규정 불필요. 협정 발효전부터 이를 규정코자 한다면 예산행정위원회, 양허위원회, 통신등 기타 분야별기구도 동시에 규정하여야 함.

0 금융 서비스 기구의 구성원은 각 체약국 정부가 결국 자국 금융 전문가를 선임하게 될 것이므로 별도 규정 불요

0 서비스 협정 관련 모든 조항은 해석은 일관성있게 COUNCIL 에 의하여 행해져야함.

0 7조 2항의 'ALL OTHER MATTERS AS MAY BE ASSIGNED TO IT'는 언제, 누가, 어떻게 금융 서비스 기구에 임무를 부여하는지 불명확함.

0 7조 3항의 추가 자유화 범위 평가는 중요한 정치적문제로서 금융 서비스 기구가 다룰 사항이 아님.

- 미국, EC, 스웨덴 등은 동 기구의 규정이 필요하다는 전제하에 다음 구체적 사항을 언급함.

0 금융 서비스 기구의 역할과 관련 금융 부속서 및 FRAMEWORK 중 관련 규정의 해석, 이행 및 적용, 관련 국제기구 관계 업무, 추가 자유화협상을 위한 GUIDELINE 개발, 금융 분야의 보복, 보상 관련 공동 해동등 LIST 작성이 필요함(EC 및 스웨덴)

0 금융 서비스 기구 자체의 운영에 관한 절차적 규정도 필요(미국)

나. 분쟁해결(제 8조)

- SEACEN 을 제외한 대부분의 개도국들이 금융분야에 FRAMEWORK 과는 다른 별도의 분쟁 해결체제를 유지할 필요가 없으며, 금융 서비스 기구가 체약국단의 역할을 대체해서는 안된다는 전제하에 다음 사항을 지적함.

0 패널 구성등 절차적 규정은 모두 협정 발효이후 체약국단의 결정에 의하도록 하는 것이 타당함.

0 패널에 금융 전문가의 참여를 명시적으로 규정하지 않더라도 실제 분쟁해결시당연히 각 분야별 전문가가 참여하게 될 것임.

0 8조 2항에 의할 경우 COUNCIL이 설치하는 패널과 금융 서비스 기구가 설치하는패널 두개가 존재하게 될것이므로 혼란이 발생하게 됨.

0 NON-VIOLATION CASE 도 중요한 것이 많으므로 일율적으로 분쟁해결 대상에서 배제하여서는 안되며, FRAMEWORK 에 따라야 함.

- 개도국들이 지적한 사항과 같은 맥락에서 갓트법률국은 갓트 분쟁 체제에 대하여 다음과 같이 설명함.

PAGE 2

0316

0 체약국단이 협정을 운영할 모든 권한을 갖기 때문에 자세한 절차적 규정은 법률적으로 불필요하며 협정 외곽의 문제임.

0 갓트 분쟁해결은 근본적으로 CONSENSUS체제이며 당사국이 PANELIST 선정에 합의하게되며 관련 분야 전문가가 PANEL 에 참여하게 됨

0 서비스 협정 체계상 금융 서비스 기구가 패널을 설치해도 COUNCIL 이 또한 패널을 설치할수 있으며, 부속서 초안은 금융 서비스 기구에 태타적 권한을 부여하는 규정임. 구 기구중 한기구가 우위에 있을 때에는 여러분야가 관련되는 사항에 대하여상부 기구가 권한을 갖는 것이 명백하나 두기구가 대등할 경우에는 관할권에 관한 명백한 것이 명백하나 두기구가 대등할 경우에는 관할권에 관한 명백하정이 있어야만하며, 이는 아주 중요한 문제임.

- 이에 대하여 미국, EC, 스위스등의 금융 대표는갓트 법률국의 설명에 상당 부분 수긍하면서 최대한 봉일된 분쟁해결 체제를 유지하는 것이 바람직하며, 금융 서비스기구는 COUNCIL의 하부기구가 될것이라고 함.

0 한편, 이들은 금융 분야는 특히 민감하고 복잡한 분야이므로 안정성을 유지하기 위하여 패널에 금융전문가가 꼭 참여하도록 패널 리스트 명부가 만들어져야 한다고함.

0 한편, 서비스 분야간 보복과 관련 원칙적으로 분쟁대상 당해 서비스 분야에 보복을 한정하도록 하는데 대하여는 선.개도국간 별다른 이견이 없었음.

다. SPECIFIC COMMITMENT

- SEACEN 을 포함한 대부분의 개도국들이 '90년도중반 금융부속서 초안이 처음 제시될 당시에는 FRAMEWORK의 시장접근과 내국민 대우 조항이 엄격하지 못하였으나 그후 많은 발전이 있어 지금은 금융 부속서 초안과 사실상 다를 것이 없으므로 이에 관한별도 규정이 불필요하다고 함.

0 특히 인도는 두가지의 차이점은 오직 자유화 대상분야 열거에 있어서 각각 NEGATIVE 방식과 POSITIVE 방식이라는 것이며, 최종 결과는 똑같이 되게 될것이나 부속서상의 접근 방법이 FORMULA 방식으로서 시장접근과 내국민 대우를 표준화하기 때문에반대하는 것이라고 함.

- 이에 대하여 EC 는 이부분 없이는 금융 부속서제정이 불가능하다고 간단히 논평하였고 미국은 FRAMEWORK 규정은 실제 해석이 매우 어려우며, 현존 제한의 동결등 FRAMEWORK 에는 없는 사항들이 부속서에는 많으므로서 전적으로 다르다고 함.

- 한편 갓트 법률국은 법률적 관점에서 볼때 FRAMEWORK과 부속서상의 내국민 대우

및 시장접근의 정의가 실제 서로 다를 것이 없으며, 자유화 대상 분야가 NEGATIVE냐 POSITIVE 냐 하는것도 SECTORAL COVERAGE 에 관한 LIST 가 없을 경우에는 서로 다르나 이에 관한 DEFINITE LIST 가있는 경우에는 차이가 없다고 언급함. 끝

(대사 박수길-국장)

수신처:(봉기, 경기원, 재무부, 법무부, 농림수산부, 상공부, 건설부, 보사부, 노동부, 교통부, 채신부, 과기처, 공보처, 항만청)

외 무 부

원 본

종 별 :

번 호 : GVW-2163

일 시 : 91 1028 1800

수 신 : 장관(수신처참조)

발 신 : 주 제네바 대사

제 목 : UR/GNS 협상

10.28 (월) 당관에 전달된 EC 의 대아국 서비스 분야 REQUEST LIST 를 별첨송부함.

첨부: EC 의 REQUEST LIST 1 부. 끝

(GVW(F)-456)

(대사 박수길-국장)

예고: 91.12.31 까지

수신처: (통기, 경기원, 재무부, 법무부, 농림수산부, 문화부, 상공부, 건설부, 보사부, 노동부, 교통부, 체신부, 과기처, 공보처, 항만청)

일반문서로 재분류(1991 . 12. 31 .)

통상국	장관	차관	2차보	경제국	청와대	안기부	법무부	보사부
문화부	교통부	체신부	경기원	재무부	농수부	상공부	건설부	노동부
과기처	해항청	공보처						

PAGE 1

91.10.29 08:43

외신 2과 통제관 BW

0319

ADVANCE COPY — KOREA

GVW (万)-0456   1/028 1.800   "첨부"

EUROPEAN COMMUNITY REQUEST LIST ON SERVICES

The European Community is submitting to its negotiating partners a two-part request list with a view to the negotiations on specific commitments to be undertaken in the framework of the GNS. The first part is a general request made to all participants, while the second contains specific requests regarding measures of one participant, the removal of which is sought by the Community. This request is made without prejudice to the Community's proposals regarding the text of Article XIX.3 of the draft GATS (document MTN.GNS/W/35/Rev.1).

PART I

1. The first part of the Community's request list constitutes a general request of all participants for commitments as follows :

    a) not to maintain, with respect to the sectors covered by the commitment, any measures inconsistent with Articles XVI and XVII of the draft Agreement (as set out in the document submitted to the GNS by Ambassador HAWES on 25 July 1991), other than those actually applied on 31 December 1991, whether through legislation, administrative regulation or by any other administrative method, and

    b) to undertake the commitment, in relation to the sectors covered in their respective Schedules, regarding the movement of natural persons providing services under the Agreement set out as an Annex to this request.

2. This commitment would apply from the date of entry into force of the Agreement.

3. The commitment would cover at least the following sectors (as described in the Services Sectoral Classification List MTN.GNS/W/120) :

    Professional Services, other than Legal, Medical, Dental, Veterinary, Para-medical and Other Services (Section 1.A.b-g.)
    Computer and Related Services (Section 1.B)
    Other Business Services (Section 1.F)
    Value-Added Telecommunications Services (Section 2.C.f-o.)
    Construction and Related Engineering Services (Section 3)
    Distribution Services (Section 4)
    Financial Services (Section 7)
    Tourism and Travel Related Services (Section 9)
    Maritime Transport Services (Section 11.A)
    Internal Waterways Transport (Section 11.B)
    Air Transport Services, other than Traffic Rights and directly related Activities (ex Section 11.C.c-e.)
    Road Transport Services (Section 11.F)
    Services Auxiliary to all Modes of Transport (Section 11.H)

0320

P .

- 2 -

4. Any measure forming part of the régime actually applied on 31 December 1991 which is inconsistent with the provisions of Article XVI or XVII of the Agreement shall be listed, according to the provisions of the Agreement, in the Schedule of the party concerned.

5. The Community is ready to examine positively any proposals by other participants which would achieve equivalent or more substantial commitments, by all parties to the Agreement, in these sectors or in others.

6. The Community would underline that both it and its Members States have legislation regarding reciprocity affecting a number of services sectors. Consistent with the application of unconditional MFN under the GATS, the Community is ready to renounce recourse to such measures in relation to GATS parties, providing that a satisfactory balance of commitments can be achieved through negotiation. It requests its partners to act in the same way.

PART II

1. The Community is in addition making individual specific requests to certain other participants, including those who have already submitted offers, regarding actual liberalisation going beyond the régime actually applied on 31 December 1991 which it seeks from that participant.

2. The timetable for implementation of such liberalisation would be the subject of bilateral negotiations.

3. The request lists will be submitted in confidence to the individual participant concerned. The Community reserves its right to modify and add to such requests in the course of negotiations.

The Community is ready to discuss, clarify and elaborate all elements of its request, whether under Part I or Part II.

0321

- 3 -

LIBERALISATION COMMITMENT ON THE MOVEMENT OF NATURAL PERSONS PROVIDING SERVICES UNDER THE AGREEMENT

All Parties shall permit, without requiring compliance with economic needs tests :

(I) the temporary movement, as intra-corporate transferees, of natural persons in the following categories, provided that such persons have been employed by the company concerned for at least the year immediately preceding such movement :

a) Senior employees of an organisation who primarily direct the management of the organisation, receiving general supervision or direction principally from the board of directors or stockholders of the business, including :

- directing the organisation or a department or sub-division of the organisation;

- supervising and controlling the work of other supervisory, professional or managerial employees;

- having the authority personally to hire and fire or recommend hiring, firing or other personnel actions.

b) Persons employed by an organisation who possess high or uncommon :

- qualifications referring to a type of work or trade requiring specific technical knowledge;

- knowledge essential to the organisation's service, research equipment, techniques or management.

These may include, but are not limited to, members of accredited professions.

(II) the temporary movement of natural persons in the following categories :

a) Persons not based in the territory of a Party who are representatives of a service provider and are seeking temporary entry for the purpose of negotiating for the sale of services or entering into agreements to sell services for that service provider, where those representatives will not be engaged in making direct sales to the general public or in supplying services themselves.

b) Persons meeting the criteria of category (I) a) who are responsible for the setting-up, in a Party, of a commercial presence of a service provider of a Party when:

- the representatives are not engaged in making direct sales or supplying services, and

- the service provider has no representative, branch or subsidiary in that Party

All other requirements of Parties' laws and regulations regarding such movement shall continue to apply.

0322

0323

KOREA PART II

Sector No.	Sector description	Measure	Action requested
.a	Legal Advice Activities on Home Country Law and International Law	- market access (commercial presence) - national treatment	Access for individuals and law firms without limitations and conditions
.b.c	Accounting, Auditing and Bookkeeping Services	- market access - national treatment	- Ease the foreign ownership restrictions - Remove reciprocity condition on certified tax accountant business - Remove restrictions on financial cooperation between local and international firms
	Taxation Services		- Remove limitations on the scope of practice: allow foreign accredited accountants to provide services to host country nationals and expand scope of practice beyond technical consultancy - Allow for possibility to have qualifications recognized
.a.b	Computer and Related Services	- market access - national treatment	Confirm elimination of restrictions on market access, including 50% foreign equity limitation for computer communication services
.a	Advertising	- market access	Remove restrictions on foreign television and radio advertisements including requirement that the importation and use of foreign made marketing materials requires a letter of recommendation from the Minister concerned

0324

KOREA PART II

or No.	Sector description	Measure	Action requested
	Telecommunications – "value-added services (excludes voice telephony, telegraph, telex)	– market access	– Possibility to provide real-time facsimile services
		Real-time transmission of data for the provision of facsimile services is prohibited	
	– packet- and circuit-switched data transmission services	– national treatment	– The possibility to provide international data transmission services by any company, and without equity restrictions
		Domestic and international data transmission services are only allowed to companies which are providing computer communication services and with less than 50% foreign equity (subject to legislation)	
	General construction	– market access	Allow for establishment of branch offices prior to 1996
	Retailing Services	– market access (commercial presence)	Make a commitment on provision of retail services for shops with more than 700 m² floor area
	Financial Services	See attachment	See attachment (ADVANCE COPY ALREADY SUPPLIED)
	Hotels and Restaurants	– market access (commercial presence)	Remove foreign-owned equity requirement
	Travel Agencies, Tour Operators, Tour Managers	– market access – national treatment	Liberalise current restrictions on the establishment and operation of travel agencies, tour operators and tour managers owned by foreign entities
A.	Maritime Transport	– market access – national treatment	Removal of restrictions on the establishment of agencies by foreign shipowners
A.b	Maritime Transport – Freight Transportation	– market access – national treatment	Immediate elimination of remaining cargo preferences and cargo sharing restrictions
A.c	Maritime Transport – Port Services	– market access	Allow access to port services on a non-discriminatory and economically reasonable basis

KOREA PART II

...r No.	Sector description	Measure	Action requested
f	Maritime Transport - Supporting Services	- national treatment	- Elimination of nationality requirement for local agents - Elimination of joint venture requirements for auxiliary services as well as limitation on operations of foreign owned shipping agencies to to own cargoes and vessels only
c	Air Transport - Ground Handling Services	- market access	- Advance proposed elimination of ground handling monopoly and ease restrictions on foreign participation - Allow access to ground handling services on a non-discriminatory and economically reasonable basis
	- Computer Reservation Systems	- market access	Eliminate restrictions on domestic and international services
	- Sales and Marketing	- market access - national treatment	Eliminate restrictions and discriminatory treatment
b	Road Transport - Freight Transportation	- market access - commercial presence	- Advance proposed opening of market - Eliminate restrictions on foreign-owned companies
	Auxiliary Transport Services - Freight forwarding	- market access	Removal of restrictions on establishment of commercial presence for foreign companies

Advanced copy. Other requests will follow. 24/10/91

EUROPEAN COMMUNITY REQUEST LIST ON SERVICES

PART II - PARTICULAR REQUESTS FOR FINANCIAL SERVICES

- Individual request to KOREA -

1. General request

In addition to the general request made by the Community to all participants for all sectors indicated in Part I of the Community request and in
particular to the commitment not to introduce any new restrictions as of
[....... 1991], as regards the financial services sector the Community
seeks from Korea participants to the services negotiations that the
following undertakings are entered in their schedules:

1. To bind all the financial services sector, without excluding any
   particular financial sector, subsector or transaction.

2. Unless otherwise indicated in the schedule for existing measures, with
   due respect to the principle of progressive liberalization and without
   prejudice to the application of measures justified on prudential grounds
   as defined in the financial services annex (as ultimately agreed by
   participants), to undertake:

   a) to eliminate any restrictions not justified on prudential grounds on
      the establishment, including - without prejudice of the application
      of anti-trust laws - through acquisition of existing enterprises, of
      a commercial presence, in particular in the form of branches or
      wholly-owned subsidiaries, and on the expansion of the activities of
      financial services providers;

   b) to eliminate any measures which disadvantage foreign financial
      service providers in their ability to compete effectively on equal
      terms with domestic financial service providers, including as regards
      participation in payments and clearing systems operated by public
      institutions and access to official funding and refinancing
      facilities;

   c) to allow foreign financial service providers to compete effectively
      on equal terms, in each segment or geographical part of the market,
      with domestic financial service providers which operate in that
      segment or geographical part of the market, regardless of the
      affiliation or ownership links of the foreign financial service
      provider with other financial or non-financial enterprises;

0326

P- 1

d) to liberalize the cross-border provision of reinsurance, transport insurance, banking auxiliary services as defined in the annex, either at the initiative of the consumer or of the financial service provider, and to liberalize the purchase by its residents abroad of all banking and other financial services other than insurance;

e) to allow the introduction of new financial services and products insofar as host regulatory authorities are satisfied as to the soundness of these new services and products;

f) to allow cross-border transfers of information and equipment necessary for the conduct of ordinary business of financial service providers;

g) to list in the schedule existing monopoly rights and to commit to endeavour to eliminate them or reduce their scope as soon as circumstances permit;

h) to grant most favoured nation and national treatment as regards the purchase of financial services by public institutions.

These commitments should be applied at all levels of regulation - central, sub-national or local government. These commitments should also apply to the activities of non-governmental bodies or of other self-regulatory organizations enjoying regulatory powers or other privileges or benefits granted by the Government.

2. Specific request

In addition to the commitment not to introduce any new restrictions on market access and national-treatment and to the undertaking to apply the general principles indicated in No II.1 of the Community request concerning financial services unless otherwise specified in the schedules, the European Community seeks from Korea the concessions listed below, which refer to specific restrictions. The Community is ready to negotiate with Korea on the modalities and possible time limits for the progressive implementation of these concessions.

The Community reserves its right to amend or complement this request in light of the evolution of the negotiations and of the requests made by other participants.

a) Banking

- To allow the establishment of subsidiaries of foreign banks, including through the acquisition by foreigners of majority shareholdings in Korean banks, and to allow them to operate under conditions of national treatment, in particular as regards access by companies established in Korea to foreign banks ("prime banking system").
- Liberalization of the conditions for establishment of branches of foreign banks in Korea on the basis of national treatment, including requirements concerning separate capitalization; improvement of the conditions for the availability of adequate funding in domestic currency, in particular through the removal of restrictions on new money market instruments and the development of an efficient interbank market.

0327

P - 8

- 31 -

- Liberalization of the restrictions on the creation of additional branches.
- Liberalization of the restrictions on the granting of "trust licences".
- Liberalization of conditions for access to Korea's ATM networks and electronic clearning house networks, and of conditions for expansion of ATM networks.
- To ease the restrictions concerning ownership of real estate.

b) <u>Insurance</u>

- To allow foreign insurance companies to establish subsidiaries and branches in Korea and to allow them to operate under conditions of national treatment, in particular by easing licensing conditions.
- To authorize foreign state owned insurance companies to establish operations in Korea
- To permit MAT insurance abroad
- To relax the conditions on compulsory reinsurance
- To liberalize restrictions on insurance broking
- Introduction of more flexibility in the system for checking policy conditions to ensure a quick approval of new policy contracts after a short period of time and as regards regulations on premium rates and other policy conditions.

c) <u>Securities Trading</u>

- To allow any suitably qualified foreign securities firm to establish branches and subsidiaries in Korea, including through acquisition of majority shareholdings in domestic securities firms, and to allow them to operate under conditions of national treatment.
- To relax conditions on branch licences, in particular as regards minimum capital.
- Liberalization of access to and membership of the stock exchange
- Liberalization of access by foreign companies to the unit trust market.
- To continue to liberalize access by foreign investors to the stock market.

P- P

0328

기 안 용 지

분류기호 문서번호	통기 20644-	기 안 용 지 (전화 : 720 - 2188)	시 행 상 특별취급	
보존기간	영구 . 준영구 10. 5. 3. 1.	장		관
수 신 처 보존기간				
시행일자	1991.10.29.			

보조기관	국 장	전 결	협조기관		문 서 통 제	
	심의관	출장중 1				
	과 장					
기안책임자	조 현			발 송 인	

경 유 수 신 참 조	~~수신처 참조~~ 건 의	발 신 명 의	

제 목	UR/서비스 협상 정부대표단 임명

91.10.31-11.2기간중 제네바에서 개최되는 UR/GNS 주요국간

양자협의(Request/Offer 협상)에 참가할 정부대표단을 "정부대표 및

특별사절의 임명과 권한에 관한 법률"에 의거, 아래와 같이 임명할 것을

건의하오니 재가하여 주시기 바랍니다.

- 아   래 -

- 1 -   0329

1. 회 의 명 : UR/GNS 주요국간 양자협의
2. 개최일시 :
ㅇ 한.일본   : 10.31(목) 시간미정
ㅇ 한.스웨덴 : 10.31(목) 시간미정
ㅇ 한.카나다 : 10.31(목) 16:30-
ㅇ 한.호주   : 11.1(금) 11:30-
ㅇ 한.미국   : 11. 1(금) 15:00-
3. 정부대표단
ㅇ 문화부 영상음반과장   이돈종
ㅇ 노동부 해외고용과 사무관   김규하
4. 출장기간 : 10.28-11. 3
5. 소요경비 : 해당부처 소관예산
6. 훈   령 :
ㅇ 91.10.25 관계부처 UR/서비스 협상 대책 회의에서
결정된 각 분야별 아국 입장을 기초로 양자협의에 적극
대처토록 함.

- 2 -

0330

ㅇ 주요국의 대아국 요청사항 및 새로운 양허표 작성 방식에

관한 정보를 입수, 아국의 Initial offer 수정에

대비토록 함.   끝.

0331

- 3 -

" 노 사 관 계 안 정 "

노 동 부

해고 32481-/5485   503-9751   1991. 10. 28,

수신 수신처참조

제목 UR/ 서비스 정부대표단 출장협조 요청

1. 경제기획원 통조삼 10502-741 (91.10.23)의 관련입니다.

2. UR/ 서비스 양허협상 대표단 파견계획에 의거 다음과 같이

스위스에 정부대표를 출장코저 하오니 협조하여 주시기 바랍니다.

　　　　가. 기   간 : '91.10.30 - 11.7 (8박 9일간)

　　　　나. 출장지역 : 스위스 (제네바)

　　　　다. 출 장 자 : 노동부 직업안정국 ~~사라관 신재현~~, 5급 김규하

　　　　라. 출장목적

　　　　　　O UR/ 서비스 노동력 이동분야 양허협상.   끝.

노 동 부 장

수신처 : 경제기획원장관, 외무부장관.

" 산 업 평 화 정 착 "

0332

226 우루과이라운드 서비스 협상 3

5940

기 안 용 지

분류기호 문서번호	통기 20644-	(전화 : 720 - 2188)	시 행 상 특별취급	
보존기간	영구. 준영구 10. 5. 3. 1.	장	관	
수 신 처 보존기간				
시 행 일 자	1991.10.29.			

보 조 기 관	국 장	전 결	협 조 기 관		문 서 통 제
	심의관				검열 1991. 10 ⊃ 0 통제관
	과 장	대결			
기안책임자		조 현			발 송 인

경 유 수 신 참 조	수신처 참조	발 신 명 의	

제 목	UR/서비스 협상 정부대표단 임명 통보

  1. 91.10.31-11.2기간중 제네바에서 개최되는 UR/GNS 주요국간

양자협의(Request/Offer 협상)에 참가할 정부대표단이 "정부대표 및

특별사절의 임명과 권한에 관한 법률"에 의거, 아래와 같이 임명

되었음을 통보합니다.

- 아   래 -

- 1 -

0333

가 . 회 의 명 : UR/GNS 주요국간 양자협의
나 . 개최일시 :
ㅇ 한.일본 : 10.31(목) 시간미정
ㅇ 한.스웨덴 : 10.31(목) 시간미정
ㅇ 한.카나다 : 10.31(목) 16:30-
ㅇ 한.호주 : 11.1(금) 11:30-
ㅇ 한.미국 : 11. 1(금) 15:00-
다 . 정부대표단
ㅇ 문화부 영상음반과장   이돈종
ㅇ 노동부 해외고용과 사무관   김규하
라 . 출장기간 : 10.28-11. 3
마 . 소요경비 : 해당부처 소관예산
2. 출장 결과 보고서는 대표단 귀국후 2주일이내 당부로
송부하여 주시기 바랍니다.   끝.
수신처 : 문화부장관 , 노동부장관
- 2 -   0334

발 신 전 보

분류번호 | 보존기간

번   호 : WGV-1488   911029 1537 WI종별 : _____

수   신 : 주   제네바   대사. 총영사

발   신 : 장 관 (통 기)

제   목 : UR/GNS 양자협의

연 : WGV-1480

연호 UR/GNS 양자협의 본부대표단에 아래 2명이 추가 임명 되었음

(출장기간 : 10.30-11.3)

   ㅇ 문화부 영상음반과장   이돈종

   ㅇ 노동부 해외고용과 사무관   김규하.   끝.

(통상국장   김 용 규)

앙고재	91년 10월 29일	통기 과	기안자 성명 조현	과 장	심의관 출장중	국 장 전결	차 관	장 관	보 안 통 제	외신과통제

외 무 부

종 별 :

번 호 : GVW-2179

일 시 : 91 1029 1930

수 신 : 장관(수신처참조)

발 신 : 주 제네바 대사

제 목 : UR/GNS 협상

　　　10.29(화) 당관에 전달된 스위스의 서비스 분야 대아국 REQUEST LIST 를 별첨 송부함.

　　　첨부: 스위스의 REQUEST - LIST 1 부 끝

　　　(GVW(F)-458)

　　　수신처: 통기, 경기원, 재무부, 법무부, 농림수산부, 문화부, 상공부, 건설부, 보사부, 노동부, 교통부, 체신부, 과기처, 공보처, 항만청

　　　(대사 박수길-국장)

　　　예고: 91.12.31. 까지

일반문서로 재분류(1991 . 12 . 31.)

통상국	장관	차관	1차보	2차보	경제국	분석관	청와대	안기부
법무부	보사부	문화부	교통부	체신부	경기원	재무부	농수부	상공부
건설부	노동부	과기처	공보처	해항청				

GUWG31-458 1102P 1800

Le Chef
de la Délégation Suisse
près
l'AELE et le GATT

Geneva, October 28, 1991

Dear Ambassador Park

In accordance with procedures agreed upon by the Group of Negotiations on Services, Switzerland submits a list of initial requests with respect to your country. The attached list contains the following three parts: A) requests of a general nature, B) requests addressing specific barriers to trade in non financial services and C) requests in the financial services area.

Switzerland reserves the right to modify or to amend the request list in the light of the negotiations.

Switzerland would appreciate the opportunity to discuss these requests with your government at your earliest convenience.

Yours sincerely

William Rossier
Ambassadeur

H.E. Mr. Soo Gil Park
Ambassador
Permanent Representative of Korea to GATT
Geneva

0337

/ - /

GATS: Initial Requests by Switzerland: Republic of Korea

A) Requests of general nature:

1. Please list in your national schedule all services sectors as set out in the Services Sectoral Classification List (see MTN.GNS/W/120, 10 July 1991)

2. We would appreciate if your country would at least accept a freeze in all sectors/sub-sectors and rollback the obstacles in accordance with our specific requests set out below

B) Requests which address specific barriers to trade in non financial services:

Distribution:

*   Complete liberalization of the access for foreign companies to the Korean distribution market and ensure during the liberalization phase a transparent and stable transitory regime

C) Requests in the financial services area:

The requests on services in the financial services area are listed on the following pages which are an integral part of this request list.

0338

BANKING AND OTHER FINANCIAL SERVICES

Country   REPUBLIC OF KOREA

		Market Access		Remarks
1.	Acceptance of deposits and other repayable funds from the public.	R	EB, ES	NT	
2.	Lending of all types, including, inter alia, consumer credit, mortgage credit, factoring and financing of commercial transactions.	R	EB, ES,CB	NT	Financing of commercial transactions only
3.	Financial leasing.				
4.	All payment and money transmission services.	R	EB, ES	NT	
5.	Guarantees and commitments.	R	EB,ES,CB	NT	
6.	Trading for own account or for account of customers, whether on an exchange, in an over the counter market or otherwise, the following:				
	(a) money market instruments (cheques, bills, certificates of deposits, etc).	R	EB, ES	NT	
	(b) foreign exchange.	R	EB, ES	NT	
	(c) derivative products including, but not limited to, futures and options.	R	EB, ES	NT	
	(d) exchange rate and interest rate instruments, including products such as swaps, forward rate agreements, etc.	R	EB, ES	NT	
	(e) transferable securities.				
	(f) other negotiable instruments and financial assets, including bullion.				
7.	Participation in issues of all kinds of securities, including underwriting and placement as agent (whether publicly or privately), and provision of services related to such issues.	R	ES	NT	
8.	Money broking.	R	EB, ES	NT	
9.	Asset management, such as cash or portfolio management, all forms of collective investment management, pension fund management, custodial depository and trust services.	R	ES	NT	
10.	Settlement and clearing services for financial assets, including securities, derivative products, and other negotiable instruments.				
11.	Advisory and other auxiliary financial services on all the activities listed in Article 1B of this Annex, including credit reference and analysis, investment and portfolio research and advice, advice on acquisitions and on corporate restructuring and strategy.	R	EB,ES,CB	NT	
12.	Provision and transfer of financial information, and financial data processing and related software by providers of other financial services.	R	EB,ES,CB	NT	

R : Liberalisation of transaction requested
EB: Commercial presence in form of branch
ES: Commercial presence in form of subsidiary
CB: Cross-border provision
NT: National treatment requested

0339

BANKING AND OTHER FINANCIAL SERVICES

Specific obstacles

Country: REPUBLIC OF KOREA

- Quantitative limits concerning the attribution of licences, be it rep. office or branch ones. The same applies for additional branches of already established foreign banks;

- Foreign banks are not allowed to establish banking subsidiaries;

- Financial participation of foreign banks in existing banks' equity is limited de facto to 10 %;

- Discriminatory restrictions for foreign banks wishing to establish or take financial participation in non-bank financial institutions;

- Each branch of a foreign bank has to be capitalized separately; the lending capacity of the branch of a foreign bank is determined by its local capital;

- Foreign banks do not have direct access to the clearing system;

- Regulations and administrative procedures are not transparent;

- Foreign banks have not the same access to rediscount facilities as domestic banks;

- Foreign banks have limited access to local funds; they suffer a disadvantage on the call market in terms of interest rates;

- The qualification of foreign banks for trust banking licences is subject to hard conditions and burdensome procedures;

- Funding possibilities for foreign banks are not adequate due to interest rate regulation, specific rules for the calculation of limits on CD issuance and the lack of an efficient interbank market;

- Very restrictive conditions severely limit the possibilities of foreign financial service providers to establish or acquire a commercial presence on the Korean Securities' market;

- Korean investors are not allowed to purchase foreign investment products;

- Foreign investors have only indirect access to Korean Securities through investment funds;

0340

INSURANCE SERVICES

Country :   REPUBLIC OF KOREA

		MARKET ACCESS		REMARKS
CROSS-BORDER OPERATIONS				
(1) insurance of risks relating to maritime shipping and commercial aviation covering both vehicles, goods and liability arising therefrom or either of them, and insurance of risks relating to goods in international transit;	R	CB	NT	
(2) reinsurance and retrocession and the services auxiliary to insurance as defined in paragraph 1.A.4. of the Definitions;	R	CB	NT	

		MARKET ACCESS		REMARKS
COMMERCIAL PRESENCE				
1. Direct insurance (including co-insurance) (i) life (ii) non-life	R	EB, ES	NT	
2. Reinsurance and retrocession				
3. Insurance intermediation, such as brokerage and agency	R	EB	NT	
4. Services auxiliary to insurance, such as consultancy, actuarial, risk assessment and claim settlement services	R	EB, ES	NT	

R : Liberalisation of transaction requested
EB : Commercial presence in form of branch
ES : Commercial presence in form of subsidiary
CB : Cross-border provision
NT : National treatment requested

0341

INSURANCE SERVICES

Specific obstacles

Country: REPUBLIC OF KOREA

- Quantitative limits concerning the authorisation of foreign insurers;

- Licensing conditions are severe;

- No cross-border insurance business is allowed;

- Reinsurance is not liberalized. Obligation of priority reinsurance cession to domestic insurers;

- Foreign insurance brokers are only permitted to represent an exclusive agent for domestic and foreign non-life insurance companies operating in Korea;

- In life insurance, foreign brokers access is exclusively permitted to foreign corporations operating in Korea and to foreigners;

- Foreign-invested companies are unable to allocate a portion of their investable funds for real estate;

- An insurance broker has to incorporate 100 Millions won or more and deposit 10 Million won or 10 % of the paid-in capital with a banking institution designated by the Ministry;

0342

외 무 부

종 별 :

번 호 : GVW-2209　　　　　　　　　일 시 : 91 1031 1730

수 신 : 장 관(수신처참조)

발 신 : 주 제네바대사

제 목 : UR/GNS 회의(10)

10.30(수) 개최된 주요국 비공식 협의 내용을 하기보고함.

1. 인력이동 부속서(10.30 오전, JARAMILLO 의장주재)

- 갓트사무국에서 작성, 배부한 부속서초안(10.30자)에 대하여 토의 하였는바 인력의 종류에 관한 ILLUSTRATIVE LIST 제정 첨부조항을 삭제하고 모든 범주의 인력이양허협상 대상이 된다는 점만 명시하고 MFN 일탈 문제는 FRAMEWORK 제2조(MFN) 및 14조(예외)에서 다루기로 하는등 상당한 진전을 이루었으며 오직 일부사항에 대하여만법률적 관점에서 이견을 보이고 있음.

2. FRAMEWORK 제 1조(정의 및 범위)

- 상업적 주재에 의한 서비스 무역에의 제한조건(제한된 기간, 특정목적)은 인도가 계속하여 동 조건 규정입장을 견지하였으나 1조 3항 A)II)의 비정부 기구의 정의 규정에 대하여는 합의를 도출하였음.

3. 금융부속서(10.30 오후, HAWES 대사 및 FRANKSWEDLOVE 공동주재)

- 사무국에서 작성한 부속서 초안(별도 FAX송부)에 대하여 토의하였는 바 조문별 각국 논평사항은 다음과 같음.

0 제 2조(PRUDENTIAL REGULATION): 동 초안이 엄격하지 못하기 때문에 제 3부(SPECIFIC COMMITMENT) 에강한 의무 규정이 마련되지 않으면 수용할 수 없음(EC, 스웨덴)

0 제 3조(조화 및 인정) : FRAMEWORK 제 7조의 조화및 인정 대상은 자격 기준 및기술적 표준인데비하여 금융부속서 초안에는 MEASURE 를 대상으로하고 있는바 이는너무 광범위하여 각국의 규제체계의 조화까지 시도하는 것으로서 수용할 수없음.(인도)

0 제 4조(예외) : 비밀정보의 공개금지는 FRAMEWORK제 3조(공개주의) 및 제

통상국	2차보	법무부	보사부	문화부	교통부	체신부	경기원	재무부
농수부	상공부	건설부	노동부	과기처	해항청	공보처		

PAGE 1

6조(국내규제)에 이미 반영되어 있는 사항이므로 동조문에 필요한 요소만 반영하면 되며 부속서에 예외로 규정할 사항이 아님.(인도)

0 제 6조(금융서비스 기구) 및 7조(분쟁해결): 동초안은 실체적 규정과 절차적 규정이 혼합되어 있는 바 이와같은 부속서 제정 필요성에 회의적이며 금융서비스 기구설치 문제가 참가국간 이의가 없는 사항이라면 FRAMEWORK 에 규정하는게 바람직함.(인도) 한편 동 6조 및 7조 초안은 그간 개도국들이 지적한 사항을 상당부분 수용한것인바 미국, 스위스, 스웨덴, 선진국들은 대체적으로 균형된 초안이라고 지지하면서일부자 귀에 대한 의견만 개진하였음.

첨부: 금융부속서 1부

(GVW(F)-0467).끝

(대사   박수길-국장)

수신처:통기, 경기원, 재무부, 법무부, 농림수산부, 문화부, 상공부, 건설부, 보사부, 노동부, 교통부, 체신부, 과기처, 공보처, 항만청

외 무 부

종 별 :

번 호 : GVW-2227   일 시 : 91 1101 1830

수 신 : 장 관(수신처참조)

발 신 : 주 제네바대사

제 목 : UR/GNS 회의(11)

　　10.31(목) 종료된 주요국 비공식 협의 내용을 하기보고함.

　　1. FRAMEWORK 제 11조(지급 및 이전) (10.31오전JARAMILLO 의장 주재)

　　- IMF 법률 전문가가 참석하여 다음과 같이 IMF관할 사항과 GATS 규정이 서로 상치될 가능성에 대하여 우려를 표명함

　　O IMF 에서는 인정된 규제 조치가 GATS 규정에 위배될 경우가 있음.

　　O 상품 무역의 경우 무역은 GATT, 이에 대한 지불은 IMF 로 그관할이 명백히 구분 되나 서비스는 서비스의 국경간 거래 그 자체가 경상거래인 경우가 있음.

　　O 자본 거래의 경우 어떤 제한을 하든 하지 않든 전적으로 회원국의 자유임

　　- 이에 대하여 EC, 미국은 GATS 규정중 어느것도 IMF 하의 권리, 의무에 영향을미치지 않으며 비록 GATS 체약국이 COMMITMENT 한 사항이라하더라도 IMF 하에서 인정된 제한은 할 수 있다고 반박함.

　　- 반면 인도 및 말련은 각국이 개별적으로 기업설립에 대한 자국의 COMMITMENT와관계되는 자본 이동에 대한 의무를 부담하는 것은 관계 없으나 일반적 의무로 규정하는 것은 수용할수 없다고 함.

　　- 아국은 시장접근에 관한 COMMITMENT 가침해되지 않기 위해서는 이에 관계되는자본이동도 보장되어야 마땅하다고 전제하고 다만 자본의 과다 유입에 따른 거시 경제상의 문제를 규율할 규정이 마련되어야 한다고 언급함.

　　2. SCHEDULING(10.31 오후 HAWES 대사 주재)

　　- 제 16조(시장접근) 및 제 17조(내국민 대우)에 해당하지 않는 국내규제에 대한ADDITIONALCOMMITMENT 근거 조항 설정 여부에 대하여선,개도국간 의견이 대립하여 결론을 내리지 못하고 협의를 종결하였음.

　　3. 관찰 및 평가

통상국	2차보	법무부	보사부	문화부	교통부	체신부	경기원	재무부
농수부	상공부	건설부	노동부	과기처	해항정	공보처		

PAGE 1

91.11.02　　08:19 WH

외신 1과 롱제관

0345

- 당초 GNS 협상 계획은 11.1 까지 모든 작업을 종료할 계획이었으나 남아있는 물리적 작업량이 많을 뿐만 아니라 UR 전체 협상의 부진으로 인하여 작업이 미루어지게 되었음.(11.1 GNS 전체회의를 개최하여 그동안의 비공식협의 경과를 보고하고 약 1주후에 협상을 속개할 계획을 수립할 것으로 예상)

- 10.16 부터 진행된 GNS 공식회의 및 주요국비공식 협의 성과를 요약하면 다음과 같음.

1) 상당한 진전을 이룬 분야

O FRAMEWORK: SCHEDULING 관련 조문(제 6조, 16조,17조), 제 4조(개도국 무역비중 증대), 제10조(세이프가드), 제 13조(정부조달), 제18조(양허협상), 양허협상의 실질적 기준

O 분야별 부속서: 인력이동 부속서, 통신부속서

2) 의견 대립이 심한 분야

O FRAMEWORK: 제 11조(지급 및 이전), 제 12조(BOP),제 14조(예외), 제 23조(분쟁해결), 제 30조(협정부적용)

- 기타 제 1조(정의 및 범위), 제 5조(경제통합), 제8조(독점), 제 9조(사기업의행위), 제34조(용어의정의)등도 미결 사항이 남아 있음.

O 분야별 부속서: 금융부속서, AUDIO VISUAL

- 상기와 같이 FRAMEWORK 및 분야별 부속서에 물리적 작업량이 많이 부과됨으로써 실질적자유화 약속을 위한 양자 협상도 예정보다 늦어지게 되었으며 특히 가장 중요한 정치적 쟁점인 분야별 MFN 일탈 문제는 협상진전의 MODALITY 를 찾지 못하고 암중 모색단계에 있음.끝

(대사 박수길-국장)

수신처:총기, 경기원, 재무부, 법무부, 농림수산부, 문화부, 상공부

건설부, 보사부, 노동부, 교통부, 체신부, 과기처, 공보처, 항만청

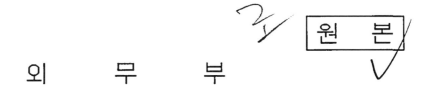

외 무 부

종 별 :

번 호 : GVW-2229

일 시 : 91 1101 1930

수 신 : 장관(수신처참조)

발 신 : 주제네바대사

제 목 : UR/GNS 회의(12)

11.1(금) 오후 개최된 표제 공식회의 내용을 하기보고함(본직 및 이경협관 참석)

1. 공식문서 제안설명

- 태국이 제출한 OFFER(GNS/W/132/ADD.1)에 대한 제안설명이 있었음.

0 쿠바는 OFFER 제출의사만 표명한제안(GNS/W/143)을 제출하였으며 EC 는 제3차OFFER 수정안(MTN.TNC/W/53/REV.3)을, 북구 및기타국가는 해운보조서비스의 접근보장의무와 관련 해운보조서비스의 정의규정(GNS/W/135/ADD.1)을 공식문서로 제출하였음(상기 모든 문서 본부대표지참)

2. 비공식 협의경과 보고

- JARAMILLO 의장은 10.16-10.31간 진행된 FRAMEWORK 각조문 및 각분야별 부속서에 대한 협의 경과를 설명하고 SCHEDULING 관련조문 및제 4조, 10조, 양허협상의 실질적기준,인력이동부속서초안등(기송부)을 배부하였음.

0 특히 동 의장은 MFN 일탈과 관련 MFN일탈 메카니즘의 개요를 가까운 시일내에제시하겠다고 하였으며 해운부속서는 북구제안 제6항(해운보조서비스 접근보장의무)을중심으로추가작업이 진행될 것이라고 함.

3. 향후 작업계획

- 의장은 다음 GNS 회의는 11.11.시작주부터시작하되 DEADLINE 은 협상대표 자신들에 의하여 정하여 질것이라고 하고 회의형태는 지금까지와같은 형태(주요국비공식협의)가 될것이라고 함

0 한편 11.11.주에는 주로 FRAMEWORK 조문들을 토의하고 11.18 주에는 각분야별부속서 또는 NOTE에 대하여 토의하되 FRAMEWORK 조문에 대한 토의도 계속하겠다고 함(각분야별 전문가가참석할 수 있도록 보다 자세한 일정은 다음주에 마련하겠다고 함) 0 또한 금주의 협의결과를 반영하여 사무국이 협정초안 전체를

통상국	장관	차관	2차보	청와대	안기부	법무부	보사부	문화부
교통부	체신부	경기원	재무부	농수부	상공부	건설부	노동부	과기처
해항청	공보처							

PAGE 1

91.11.02 08:26 BX

외신 1과 통제관

0347

새로이 작성 배부하겠다고함(TNC/W/35.REV.2 는 아님)

 - 한편 미국은 '92년 2월까지 모든 협상을 완료하기 위해서는 양자협의의 촉진이중요하다고 전제하고 12.8주에 양자협의 개최를 제의하여의장이 이를 수락함.끝

　(대사 박수길-국장)

　수신처:　　　총기,경기원,재무부,법무부,농림수산부,문화부,상공부,건설부,보사부,노동부,교통부,체신부,과기처,공보처,항만청)

외 무 부

종 별 :

번 호 : GVW-2240　　　　　　　　　　일 시 : 91 1104 1600

수 신 : 장 관(수신처참조)

발 신 : 주 제네바대사

제 목 : UR/GNS 양자협의

　　10.31(목)-11.1(금) 개최된 카나다, 호주, 미국과의 양자 협의내용을 하기 보고함.

　　1. 협의 개요

　　- 각국의 REQUEST LIST 내용을 구체적으로 명료화하고 아국의 규제도 내용을 설명하는 작업에 한정하였으며, 실질적 자유화 약속에 관한 협상은 하지 않았음.

　　2. 국가별 주요 협의 내용

　　가. 카나다의 양자 협의(10.31 오후)

　　- 카나다측은 106 개국에 대해서 COMMON REQUEST(인력이동과 사업 서비스등 일부분야)를 하였고 37개국에 대하여 구체적인 REQUEST LIST 를 제출하였으며, 금번에는16개국을 아래와 같이 세그룹 구분하여 양자 협의를 진행하고 있다고 함.

　　O OECD 국가(1군), 한국, 홍콩, 싱가폴, 브라질, 알젠틴등(2군)과 이집트, 모로코, 인도, 파키스탄 등(3군)

　　- 카나다측은 자국의 COMMON REQUEST에 대한 배경을 관심 업종별로 설명하였는바, 광산건설 엔지리어링, 사업서비스(인가 및 비인가 업종),운송, 컴퓨터 관련 서비스, 화물주선업 및 해운분야의 자유화가 그 주요 내용임.

　　- 아측은 기 제출한 아국의 INITIAL OFFER 를 바탕으로 구체적인 교역 장벽의 완화 내지 제거에 관한 REQUEST 를 요구한데 반하여 카나다측은 아국의 규제 제도 파악에 한계가 있기 때문에 자국의 관심 업종에 대하여 모든 규제 조치를 철폐하라는 COMMON REQUEST 를 제시한 것이라 설명함.

　　- 아측은 재차 아국의 OFFER LIST 를 기초로 하여 카나다가 구체적인 개선 사항을 요구할때 협상이 실질적으로 진행될수 있을 것이라는 입장을 제시하였고, 카나다측은 아측의 입장을 수용하겠다는 뜻을 밝힘.

통상국　2차보　보사부　경기원　재무부　농수부　동자부　건설부　과기처
공보처

　　　　　　　　　　　　　　　　　91.11.05　08:45 WH

외신 1과 통제관

0349

- 한편 카나다측은 CPC 분류에 따라 보완된 자국의 REQUEST 를 아측에 전달항였으며 아측은 추가 검토하겠다고 언급함.

나. 호주와의 양자 협의(11.1 오전)

- 호주는 자국의 수정 OFFER 를 아측에 전달하였으며, 아국에 대하여 건설 엔지니어링, 금융, 통신, 해운등의 업종에 주요 관심을 표명하였음.

- 아국에 대한 호주의 REQUEST 에 대하여 양국은 업종별로 협의를 진행하였는 바, 회계, 광고,항공(CRS), 건설, 엔지니어링, 금융, 보험,법무, 하운, 통신 분야에 대하여 아측은 현행제도를 설명하고 기존 입장을 견지하는 선에서 대응하였으며, 다만엔지니어링 서비스에 대하여 현재 관련 법인 기술 용역 육성법의 개정작업이 진행중임을 언급함.

다. 미국과의 양자 협의(11.1 오후)

- 미국은 그간 38개국(EC 를 1개국 간주)에 대하여 REQUEST 하였으며 금번에는 27 개국과 양자 협의를 하고 있다고 함.

- 보험통신 분야에 있어서 미측은 UR/서비스 양자협상의 결과가 <u>기존 한.미 쌍무협상 결과에 영향을 미치지 않을까 우려하</u>였는바, 아측은 기본적으로 기 약속한 사항에 대하여 일관성있는 입장을 유지해 나갈 것이라고 언급함.

- 미국이 REQUEST 한 업종별로 상세한 협의가 진행되었는바, 미측의 주요 질의,확인 요구사항은 아래와 같으며, 아측은 현재 국내 규제상황 및 추가 양허의 어려움에대한 설명을 중심으로 대응함.

0 회계: FINANCIAL LINKS의 의미는 JOINT VENTURE부자와 PARTNERSHIP 을 포괄함.자격의 상호인정과 관련하여 미국의 STATE 별 CPA협회와 협상 용의가 있는지 여부,외국 공인회계사의 작격 취득에 있어 간소화 절차를 BINDING 할 용의여부, 한국 CPA와PARTNERSHIP 관계 설정의 가능 여부

0 광고: 해외 광고물 심의 기준 및 절차의 명료화

한국 방송광고 공사의 역할과 방송광고 시간의배분 기준의 명료화

0 시청각: SCREEN QUOTA 의 제한 완화 및 영화PRINT 별 수의 철폐 계획에 대한 양허 용의

0 엔지니어링: 외국 용역 발주 승인제 및 등록제등 현 규제 제도의 개선

0 건설: 도급한도제 폐지

0 법무: 외국법 및 국제법 자문에 대한 추가 OFFER

PAGE 2

0350

0 관광: CREDIT CARD 사용 규제에 대한 우려표명 및 이의 개선

- 한편 아측은 미측의 REQUEST 하였던 부문중 보건 (HEALTH SERVICE)부문의 명확한 의미 및 포괄범위에 대한 질문과 건설 부문의 미측 규제사항에 대한 확인을 요구하는 질의서를 작성하여 미측에 전달하였으며, 미측은 이를 검토 회신할것을 약속함. 끝

(대사 박수길-국장)

정 리 보 존 문 서 목 록

기록물종류	일반공문서철	등록번호	2019080106	등록일자	2019-08-14
분류번호	764.51	국가코드		보존기간	영구
명 칭	UR(우루과이라운드) / GNS(서비스협상그룹) 회의, 1991. 전5권				
생 산 과	통상기구과	생산년도	1991~1991	담당그룹	
권 차 명	V.5 11-12월				
내용목차					

0001

관리 번호	91-84?

외 무 부

종 별 :

번 호 : GVW-2256   일 시 : 91 1106 1500

수 신 : 장관(경협)

발 신 : 주 제네바 대사

제 목 : UR/GNS 협상

　　11.6(수) 당관에 전달된 노르웨이의 대아국 서비스분야 REQUEST-LIST 를 별첨 송부함.

　　첨부: 노르웨이 REQUEST LIST 1 부

　　(GVW(F)-0483). 끝

　　(대사 박수길-국장)

　　예고:91.12.31. 까지

일반문서로 재분류 (1991 . 12 . 31 .)

경제국

DÉLÉGATION DE NORVÈGE

58, RUE DE MOILLEBEAU, CASE POSTALE 274
1211 GENÈVE 19

Geneva, 31 October 1991

GVW (ㅠ) - 0483   11/06 1500 Enclosure

"첨부"   경협

Dear Colleague,

In accordance with the procedures agreed to by the GNS, we are submitting to you an initial list of request from Norway with respect to your country.

Norway reserves the right in the course of the negotiations on specific commitments on services to modify the request list for your country, including the addition of further requests.

Norway would appreciate the opportunity to discuss at an appropriate time, the attached requests and would be pleased to provide clarification or background details.

Yours sincerely,

Erik Selmer
Ambassador

H.E. Mr. Soo Gil Park
Permanent Mission of the Republic of Korea
20, route de Pré-Bois
1216 COINTRIN GE

0003

SPECIFIC REQUEST: Korea

Sector No.	Sector Description	Request
All	All	* Remove restrictions on remittance of profit to the service providers' home countries. * Lift credit control policies. * Liberalize the Korean foreign exchange market. * Permit all banks - domestic and foreign - to issue medium and long term debt instruments. * Remove limits on equity investments and permit greater freedom in the use of offshore loans.
1.F.a	Advertising services	* Remove restrictions on foreign produced advertising materials.

2.C	Telecommunication services	* Remove limitations on
		  - foreign ownership,
		  - VANS

3:A,B,C,D,E	Construction and related engineering services	* Remove excessive capital requirements for subsidiaries of foreign consultancy and engineering companies. * Remove discriminatory taxes for foreign consultancy and engineering companies. * Provide recognition of foreign engineering exams and allow foreign consultants to make contracts directly with final customer.
4:A,B,C,D,E	Distribution services	* Provide market access and liberalize restrictions concerning store size, number of stores and traded items.
7	Financial services	* Make a binding commitment on the present level of Market Access and National Treatment.

Sector No.	Sector Description	Request

		* Concerning established companies and branches;
		 - make commitments in accordance with the obligations in Part III: Specific Commitments in MTN.TNC/W/50, as follows;
		 a) III. Financial services purchased by public enteties,
		 b) IV. Market access
		     i) B. Commercial presence, paragraph 5,
		     ii) C. Transfers of information and processing of information,
		     iii) D. Temporary entry of personnel, and
		     iv) E. Non-discriminatory measures, and
		 c) V. National Treatment.
		
		 * Concerning cross-border supply;
		 - make commitments in accordance with the obligations in Part III: Specific Commitments in MTN.TNC/W/50; IV. Market Access, A. Cross-border trade.

11.A	Maritime transport	* Concerning new establishments; - eliminate all restrictions on the establishment of a wholly-owned subsidiary. * Remove discriminatory port duties and charges for foreign-flag vessels. * Allow foreign-flag carriers to own container terminals and support equipment. * Allow foreign carriers to manage port operations. * Remove restrictions on international shipping for certain items.
11.F	Road transport services	* Eliminate restrictions on foreign establishment and provision of multimodal transports.

NORWAY'S GENERAL REQUESTS
(to be addressed to all participants in the services negotiations)

SECTOR   REQUEST

APPLICABLE TO ALL SECTORS

Make a binding commitment, on national as well as sub-national levels, on your present level of Market Access and National Treatment concerning:
* foreign investment in commercial presence
* foreign investment in real estate
* foreign exchange control (including profit remittances)

Furthermore, we are making the following additional sector-specific requests:

1. BUSINESS SERVICES

A. Professional services

a. Legal Services
CPC 861

Concerning advice on home country law and international law, for foreign law offices/ lawyers, provided the legal adviser fulfils the home country's professional qualification conditions:
* eliminate all sector-specific restrictions on commercial presence, cross-border supply and consumption abroad
* provide full national treatment

Concerning advice on national law, for foreign law offices/lawyers, provided the legal adviser fulfils the host country's professional qualification conditions:
* eliminate all sector-specific restrictions on commercial presence, cross-border supply and consumption abroad

* provide full national treatment (including removal of nationality requirements)

12-5

0007

b. Accounting, auditing and book-keeping services CPC 862

Concerning accounting, auditing and bookkeeping services for foreign accounting firms/accountants, provided the accountant fulfils the host country's professional qualification conditions:
* eliminate all sector-specific restrictions on commercial presence, cross-border supply and consumption abroad
* provide full national treatment (including removal of nationality requirements)

d. Architectural services, CPC 8671
g. Urban planning and landscape, CPC 8674

* eliminate all sector-specific restrictions on commercial presence, cross-border supply and consumption abroad
* provide full national treatment (including removal of nationality requirements)

e. Engineering consulting services CPC 8672
f. Integrated engineering services CPC 8673

* eliminate all sector-specific restrictions on commercial presence, cross-border supply and consumption abroad
* provide full national treatment (including removal of nationality requirements)

B. Computer and Related Services (including categories a,b,c,d,e,)

CPC 841-845, 849

* eliminate all sector-specific restrictions on commercial presence, cross-border supply and consumption abroad
* provide full national treatment (including removal of nationality requirements)

1991-11-06 11:00   KOREAN MISSION GENEVA   022 791 0525   P.06

UR(우루과이라운드).GNS(서비스협상그룹) 회의, 1991. 전5권(V.5 11-12월)   253

1~-6

C. Research and Development Services
(including categories a,b,c,)

CPC 851-853 — Make a binding commitment on the present level of Market Access and National Treatment in this sector concerning:
* commercial presence,
* cross-border supply and
* consumption abroad.

E. Rental/Leasing Services without Operators

a. Relating to ships
CPC 83103 — Make a binding commitment on the present level of Market Access and National Treatment in this sector concerning:
* commercial presence,
* cross-border supply and
* consumption abroad.

b. Relating to aircraft
CPC 83104 — Make a binding commitment on the present level of Market Access and National Treatment in this sector concerning:
* commercial presence,
* cross-border supply and
* consumption abroad.

F. Other Business Services

a. Advertising services, CPC 871 —
* eliminate all sector-specific restrictions on commercial presence, cross-border supply and consumption abroad
* provide full national treatment (including removal of nationality requirements)

b. **Market research and public opinion polling services** CPC 864	* eliminate all sector-specific restrictions on commercial presence, cross-border supply and consumption abroad * provide full national treatment (including removal of nationality requirements)
c. **Management consulting, CPC 865** d. Services rel. to man. consulting CPC 866	* eliminate all sector-specific restrictions on commercial presence, cross-border supply and consumption abroad * provide full national treatment (including removal of nationality requirements)
f. Consulting services incidental to agriculture, hunting and forestry CPC 881	* eliminate all sector-specific restrictions on commercial presence, cross-border supply and consumption abroad * provide full national treatment (including removal of nationality requirements)
g. Services incidental to fishing CPC 882	* eliminate all sector-specific restrictions on commercial presence, cross-border supply and consumption abroad * provide full national treatment (including removal of nationality requirements)
h. Consulting services incidental to mining CPC 883 + 5115	* eliminate all sector-specific restrictions on commercial presence, cross-border supply and consumption abroad * provide full national treatment (including removal of nationality requirements)

i. and j. Consulting services incidental to manufacturing and energy distrib. CPC 884, 885 (except for 88442) and CPC 887

* eliminate all sector-specific restrictions on commercial presence, cross-border supply and consumption abroad
* provide full national treatment (including removal of nationality requirements)

l. Investigation and security, CPC 873

* eliminate all sector-specific restrictions on commercial presence, cross-border supply and consumption abroad
* provide full national treatment (including removal of nationality requirements)

TELECOMMUNICATIONS

Make a binding commitment on the present level of Market Access and National Treatment in this sector.

3. CONSTRUCTION AND RELATED ENGINEERING SERVICES (including a,b,c,d,e,)

CPC 511-518

* eliminate all sector-specific restrictions on commercial presence, cross-border supply and consumption abroad
* provide full national treatment (including removal of nationality requirements); especially concerning
    - requirements of association with a domestic company or of local participation
    - discriminatory duties and charges, including taxes

4. DISTRIBUTION SERVICES
(including A,B,C,D,E,)
CPC 621, 622, 631
632, 6111, 6113,
6121, 8929

Make a binding commitment on the present level of
Market Access and National Treatment in this sector
concerning:
* commercial presence,
* cross-border supply and
* consumption abroad.

6. ENVIRONMENTAL SERVICES
(including A,B,C,D,)
CPC 9401-9403)

* eliminate all sector-specific restrictions on commercial
presence, cross-border supply and consumption abroad
* provide full national treatment (including removal of
nationality requirements)

7. FINANCIAL SERVICES

Make a binding commitment on the present level of
Market Access and National Treatment in this sector.

9. TOURISM AND TRAVEL RELATED SERVICES
(including A,B,C,D,)

CPC 641-643,
7471, 7472

REQUESTS:
* Remove nationality requirements.

* Eliminate any incentives available to suppliers of
conferences, seminars or courses related to events
located in your country, whether in the form of
a) duties or charges, including taxes, on services
related to conference events located abroad or
b) exemptions from such duties or charges, including
taxes, on services related to conference events
located in your country.

* Eliminate any incentives available to consumers of conferences, seminars or courses related to events located in your country, whether in the form of
a) duties or charges, including taxes, on the use of services related to conference events located abroad or
b) exemptions from duties or charges, including taxes, on the use of services related to conference events located in your country.

c. Tourist guides services
CPC 7472

* Remove nationality requirements

11. TRANSPORT SERVICES

A. Maritime Transport Services

International shipping services

Bind all measures that affect
a) the crossborder supply of international shipping services,
b) the purchase abroad by national consumers of international shipping services and
c) the commercial presence of providers of international shipping services
at the existing level of market access and national treatment.

Make a binding commitment to eliminate all measures that restrict market access or condition national treatment for
a) the crossborder supply of international shipping services and
b) the purchase abroad by national consumers of international shipping services
within three years after the entry into force of the Agreement.

Maritime transport auxiliary services

Bind all measures that affect
a) the crossborder supply of maritime transport auxiliary services,
b) the purchase abroad by national consumers of maritime transport auxiliary services and
c) the commercial presence of providers of maritime transport auxiliary services
at the existing level of market access and national treatment.

Definition of terms, used above:

International shipping services:
transportation of passengers or goods between ports located in different states, including passenger cruise traffic outside a Party's territorial waters.

Maritime transport auxiliary services:
all maritime transport related services within the confines of the port or sea environment, limited to those which provide an immediate, interactive, supporting role to the primary function of the maritime transport industry, which is the transportation of goods and/or passengers between ports.

B. Internal Waterways Transport

Make a binding commitment on the present level of Market Access and National Treatment in this sector concerning:
* commercial presence
* cross-border supply and
* consumption abroad.

기 ~ 기

0014

C. Air Transport Services

Make a binding commitment on the present level of Market Access and National Treatment in this sector concerning:

* commercial presence
* cross-border supply and
* consumption abroad.

E. Rail Transport Services

Make a binding commitment on the present level of Market Access and National Treatment in this sector concerning:

* commercial presence
* cross-border supply and
* consumption abroad.

F. Road Transport Services

Make a binding commitment on the present level of Market Access and National Treatment in this sector concerning:

* commercial presence
* cross-border supply and
* consumption abroad.

경 제 기 획 원

우 427-760 / 경기도 과천시 중앙동1 정부제2청사 / 전화 503-9149 / 전송 503-9141

문서번호 통조삼 10502-*//o*
시행일자 1991. 11. 8.

수신 수신처 참조
　　　(외무부 통상기구 2)
참조

선결			지시	
접수	일자시간	91. 11. 8 :	결재·공람	
	번호	37331		
처리과				
담당자				

제목　UR 서비스협상관련 각국 Request에 대한 대응방안 제출

　　1. 통조삼 10502-697('91.10.5)와 관련입니다.

　　2. UR서비스협상은 11월 11일부터 서비스 일반협정(GATS)에 대한 협상을 재개하여 11월하순까지 동 협정을 마무리짓고 12월 9일 시작주에는 양허협상을 할 예정으로 있으며 전반적인 UR협상의 진행이 순조로울 경우 국내서비스시장의 개방수준을 결정하는 양허협상이 집중적으로 진행될 가능성이 크다고 판단됩니다.

　　3. 동 양허협상과 관련하여 '91년 10월말 현재 미국, EC, 일본, 캐나다, 호주, 스위스, 스웨덴, 핀랜드등 8개국이 Request List를 제시한 바(주제네바 대표부가 전문으로 각 부처에 이미 발송) 각 부처는 소관분야의 Request에 대한 대응방안을 별첨 양식에 따라 작성하여 경제기획원(통상조정3과)에 11월 13일까지 제출해 주시기 바랍니다.

　　4. 아울러 지난 10.31~11.1일간 개최된 미국, 캐나다, 호주와 양자협의결과와 EC와 호주가 새로운 양허표 작성방식에 따라 자국의 Initial Offer를 수정한 Offer List 및 각국의 Initial Offer List(Ⅳ)를 송부하니 서비스협상 대책추진에 만전을 기해 주시기 바랍니다.

0015

첨부 : 1. 각국 Request List에 대한 대응방안 작성양식 및 요령 1부.

2. EC 및 호주의 수정 Offer List 1부.

3. 각국의 Initial Offer List 1부.   끝.

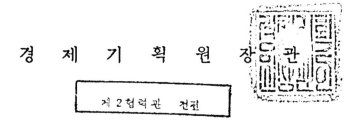

경 제 기 획 원 장 관

제 2협력관 전결

수신처 : 외무부장관, 내무부장관, 재무부장관, 법무부장관, 교육부장관, 문화부장관,

농림수산부장관, 상공부장관, 보건사회부장관, 건설부장관, 교통부장관,

노동부장관, 동자부장관, 체신부장관, 체육청소년부장관, 과학기술처장관,

환경처장관, 공보처장관, 특허청장, 해운항만청장

0016

관리
번호 : P1-
1P0

외 무 부

종 별 :

번 호 : GVW-2288

일 시 : 91 1108 1900

수 신 : 장관(봉기,경기원,재무부,법무부,농수부,문화부,상공부 건설부,

발 신 : 주 제네바 대사 보사,노동,교통,체신,과기처,공보처,항만청)

제 목 : UR/TNC DUNKEL 총장 보고서 협상 분야별 분석 평가(서비스)

연: GVW-2220

일반문서로 재분류(1081 . 12 . 31 .)

연호 서비스분야 DUNKEL 총장 보고서에 대한 당관 분석 평가를 하기 보고함.

1. FRAMEWORK

O FRAMEWORK 35 개 조문중 미결 상태에 있는 조문이 많이 남아 있으나 대부분 기술적 사항에 불과한 것으로 보고 있으며 협상 진전에 큰 장애가 되지 않는 것으로 평가 하고 있음

- 다만 중요한 결정이 필요한 조문으로서 BOP, 예외, 협정 부적용 조항을 지적하고 있는바, 예외조항과 관련 많은 예외 사유가 거론되고 있으나 CULTURAL VALUE만 본질적 의견 대립이 있는 사항으로 부각시키고 있음

2. 분야별 MFN 일탈

O 서비스 협상최 최대정치적 과제는 분야별 MFN 일탈을 최소화 하는 문제라고 전제하고 이는 INITIAL COMMITMENT 협상과 연계되는 문제임을 거듭 강조하고 있음

- 한편, 해운, 기본통신 분야에 대한 미국이 입장변경과 AUDIO VISUAL 분야에 대한 EC 의 입장 변경없이는 서비스 협상이 타결될 수 없음을 암시하고 있음

- 기타 항공, 육운, 내수로 운송, 인력이동 분야는 MFN 일탈을 최소하 하는가운데 각국의 문제를 해결할 수 있는 법률적 기술문제를 토의중임을 언급

3. 분야별 부속서

O 인력이동 부속서 및 통신 부속서에 대해서는 일부 이견이 남아있으나 사실상 완료단계에 있는 것으로 파악

- 금융부속서에 대하여는 중요한 결정이 필요한 상태라고 지적하고 특히 시장접근과 대우를 의무로 규정하는 문제(TWO TRACK APPROACH)를 주요 잇슈로 요약하고 있음

통상국	장관	차관	1차보	2차보	외정실	분석관	정와대	안기부
법무부	보사부	문화부	교통부	체신부	경기원	재무부	농수부	상공부
건설부	노동부							

PAGE 1

91.11.09 07:14

외신 2과 통제관 BD

0017

4. INITIAL COMMIMENT

0 지금까지 제출된 OFFER 숫자 및 현재까지 진행된 양자 협의에 대하여 대체로 긍정적인 평가를 내리는 한편 MFN 일탈 문제의 중요성을 재차 강조하고 있음. 끝

(대사 박수길-국장)

예고:91.12.31. 까지

PAGE 2

<table>
<tr><td>문</td><td>화</td><td>부</td></tr>
</table>

영 읍   35100-14718   720-4967   1991. 11 .   .

수 신   외무부장관

참 조   통상국장

제 목   UR/서비스협상 회의 참가결과 보고서 송부

　　　　1. 영읍 35100-14570 ('91.10.26) 및 통기 20644-52940

('91.10.29)의 관련입니다.

　　　　2. 별첨과 같이 UR/서비스협상 회의참가 결과 보고서를

송부하오니 참고하시기 바랍니다.

첨　　부 :　UR/서비스 한.미양자 협의 결과 1부. 끝.

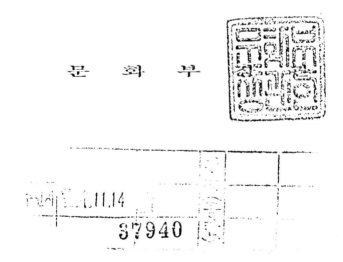

문　　화　　부

87940

0019

UR/서비스 한·미 양자협의 결과

1. 협의개요

   o 일   시 : '91. 11. 1 (금), 14:30 ~ 18:30

   o 장·소 : USTR 제네바 사무소 (스위스)

   o 참   석

      - 한국측 : 경제기획원 이윤재국장등 10명 (8개부처)

           (경제기획원, 법무부, 농림수산부, 문화부,
             상공부, 건설부, 노동부, 과기처)

      - 미국측 : 무역대표부 부대표보 MS. BONNIE RICHARDSAN 등 4명

   o 협의진행

      - UR/서비스 협상에 대한 의견 교환

      - 미국 REQUEST 사항에 대한 질의 응답

      - 통신 금융 서비스에 대한 이견이 있었으나 AUDIO VISUAL부문에

        대해서는 이해

0020

2. UR/서비스 협상에 대한 의견 교환

○ UR/서비스 양허협상은 20개 주요국의 비공식으로 진행

○ FRAMEWORK 제8조 (조화 및 인정), 제14조(예외) 협의

- 제8조 (조화 및 인정)의 자격,표준은 다자간 조화, 상호인정뿐만
  아니라 일방적 인정도 반영

- 제14조 (예외) 자국의 관심사항(CULTURAL VALUE등 예외사유)을
  반영하는 경우 구체적이며 한정적으로 접근

○ 금융부속서

- 내국민 대우규정은 FRAMEWORK 과부속서초안과 똑같이 적용

○ AUDIO VISUAL 서비스

- FRAMEWORK에 CULTURAL EXCEPTION조항의 반영 주장국가는 우리나라,
  캐나다, 인도, 부속서 제정 주장국가는 EC, 북구, 호주, 이 두가지를
  모두 반대한 국가는 미국, 일본 - 서로가 주장

0021

3. UR/서비스 중 AUDIO VISUAL 분야

가. 개 항

o 미국으로부터 우리나라에 대한 REQUEST을 2종 제출하였으며 이에 성의 있게 답변을 바람 (영화상영제한 철폐 및 영화프린트 수입벌수 재한 철폐)

o 미국은 한국에 대해 이 분야를 쌍무적 관계로 생각하며 비중이 아주 크게 다루고 있음.

나. REQUEST에 대한 답변

o 스크린쿼타제도 운영 철폐는 언제나 할 것인가?

- 현재로는 계속 존속할 방침임.

- 세계 각국에서도 자국문화 보존 및 자국영화 산업을 위해서 시행 (영국, 이태리 : 3/10, 멕시코 : 1/2)

o 영화프린트의 수입벌수에 대한 철폐는 언제할 것인가?

- 외화 프린트벌수에 대한 제한도 계속 유지함. 다만, '88 한·미 영화협정에 따라서 단계적 시행을 하고 있음.

- 미국이 한국영화산업에 대한 무리한 요구는 오히려 불리함을 자초 하는 경우가 될 것이며 일본 역시 개방을 더 심하게 요청할 것임.

- 미국 대표는 한국실정을 충분히 이해하며 솔직히 말한데 대해서 고마움 표시

0022

4. 평가 및 전망

o 금번 UR/서비스 협상에 우리나라에 대해서 일본도 REQUEST 했었으나 한국과의 협상은 보류함.

  - 여타 국가와의 협상결과에 따라서 대응할 눈치 예상 (극영화,비디오,음반 수입 개방 요청)

o 미국측은 우리의 실정을 이해하려는 눈치는 보이나 아주 세밀한 분야까지 파악하려 함.

o UR/서비스협상을 11.3일까지 마무리 지으려했으나 통신,금융 여타 분야의 물리적 양에 따라 지연 (12월중까지 타결 예정)

o 우리부의 협상참여는 여타부서에 대해 주요한 문화예술분야임을 인식 시켜주었음.

o 대외 문화예술교류분야에대해 꾸준한 효과적인 대응 대처가 요망됨.
  - 일본등 대응책 요구

0023

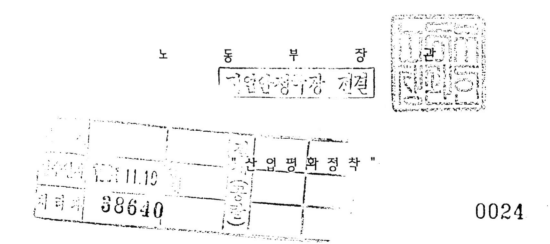

"노 사 관 계 안 정"

노   동   부

해고 32482-1661°   503-9750   1991. 11. 18.

수신 외무부장관

참조 통상국장

제목 해외출장 결과보고서 제출

    1. 통기 20644-52940(91.10.29)의 관련입니다.

    2. '91.10-11.2 기간중 제네바에서 개최된 UR/ 서비스협상
회의참석 결과를 별첨 보고서와 같이 제출합니다.

첨 부 : UR/ 서비스 협상참석 등 해외출장 결과보고서 1부.   끝.

노   동   부   장

" 산 업 평 화 정 착 "

0024

┌─────────────────────────────────┐
│ ── UR / 서비스 협상참석 등 ── │
│ 해 외 출 장 결 과 보 고 │
└─────────────────────────────────┘

1991. 11.

보 고 자

노 동 부
직 업 안 정 국

해외고용과장 서기관 신제면
해외고용과 행정사무관 김규하

0025

UR / 서비스 양자협의 참석 및 부속서 제정동향

- 노동력 이동분야 -

1. 총 괄

o 출장기간 : '91. 10. 30 - 11. 3.

o 출장지역 : 스위스 (제네바)

o 참석자 명단 (10개부처 13명)

경 제 기 획 원	제 2 경협관 국 장	이 윤 재	(수석대표)
"	통상조정 2과 사무관	신 호 현	
"	통상조정 3과 사무관	김 용 준	
법 무 부	국제법무심의관실 검사	김 영 철	
문 화 부	영상음반과장	이 돈 중	
노 동 부	해외고용과장	신 재 면외 1명	
건 설 부	해외협력과 사무관	방 재 영	
과 학 기 술 처	기술용역과 기 좌	송 우 근	
제네바 대표부	경제기획원 사무관	한 철 수	
대외경제정책연구원	박 사	성 극 제	
한국개발연구원	박 사	김 지 홍	
김 & 장 법률사무소	변 호 사	신 희 택	

0026

2. 미국과의 양자협의

가 . 일   시 : '91.11.1 (금)   14:30 - 18:00

나 . 장   소 : USTR 빌딩 2층 회의실 (제네바 소재)

다 . 미국 대표단

USTR Ms. Bonnie Richardson (Head of Delegation Coordinator for UR

Services Bilaterals)

연방통신위원회 (FCC) John Copes

상   공   부   F. T. Elliott

노   동   부   H. R. Dobson

라 . 협의내용

(아측) : 미국은 인력이동에 대해 어떤 정책을 갖고 있는지 궁금함

특히 미국의 인력이동에 관한 입장이 Canada와 어떻게 다른가

또한 전문가 (Specialist)에 대한 어떤 정의를 갖고 있는가 ?

(미측) : 미국은 전문가의 정의에 대해 Canada와 비슷한 개념을 갖고 있슴

단 카나다는 서비스 판매와 관계된 판매인을 포함하고 있슴.

그러나 sellers of service는 이미 거의 제한이 없는 상황이기

때문에 반드시 포함시키지 않아도 된다고 봄.

서비스 trade는 약 80%가 상업적주재를 통해 일어나기 때문에 그를

위한 기본적인 인력이동의 보장이 매우 긴요함

(아측) : 각 분야별 전문가의 정의가 매우 어려운데 최종 해석의 책임은

누가지게 되는가

0027

(미측) : 그 문제의 최종책임은 이민국이 지게될 것임

현재 UR/서비스하에서 concession과 이민법 사이의 경계가 불분명한 상황임.

그러난 현행 이민법에서는 전문가는 각 회사 고유의 지식을 가진 사람으로 정의하고 있으며 이 정의는 잘 적용이 되고 있음

(아측) : 한국의 입장도 상업적주재와 관련된 기본적인 관리자,임원,전문가의 이동을 허용하자는 것이며 그외 인력은 양허협상에서 논의하자는 것으로 미국과 큰 차이가 없슴. 다만 어떤 방식으로 binding할 것인가에 의문이 있슴

3. 카나다와의 양자협의

가. 일 시 : '91. 10. 31 (수) 16:30 - 18:00

나. 장 소 : GATT 2012 호

다. 카나다 대표단

대외무역성 J.L. MacNeil, D. Roseman. 산업,과학,기술성 N. Shaw.

기타 관계부처 실무자 2인

라. 협의내용

ㅇ 카나다측 노동관계 전문가가 부속서 협상으로 불참

ㅇ '91.11.11 부터 2주간 양자협의시 거른 전망

0028

4. 호주와의 양자협의

가. 일 시 : '91. 11. 1 (금) 11:30 - 13:00

나. 장 소 : GATT 의 F 회의실

다. 호주 대표단

· 대외무역성 Peter Gray (수석대표)

재무성, 채신부, 항만청, 대외무역성의 실무자 각 1인

라. 협의 내용

호주측에서 인력이동에 대한 국제 및 카나다의 접근방식을 기본적으로 채택

하고 있음을 설명하므로 공감을 표시함

5. 노동력이동 부속서 제정 동향

o GATT 사무국에서 작성, 배부한 초안 (10.30자)에 토의 하였는바,

- 노동력의 종류에 관한 예시표 제정 첨부조항 삭제

- 모든 범주의 노동력이 양허협상이 된다는점 명시

- MFN 일탈문제는 기본협정 제2조 (MFN) 제14조 (예외)에서 다루기로 함

o 따라서 각본야중 노동력이동 부속서에 대하여는 상당한 진전이 있었으나

다만 오직 일부사항에 대하여만 법률적 관점에서 이견을 보이고 있음

6. 전망 및 대책

o 노동력이동부속서 초안상의 문제점을 제외하기로 합의에 도달함으로써 조기에

타결될 전망임

o 노동력이동허용범위도 당초 필수인력 (관리자, 중역, 전문가)에 한해 자유화하고

기타인력은 양허협상에서 결정하자는 종래의 입장을 완화하여 모두 양허협상에

위임함으로써 향후 쌍무 양자협상이 중요한 현안으로 대두됨

o 상업적주재에 따른 필수인력은 원칙적으로 허용하되 국내에서 대체할 수 없는

전문적, 독점적지식을 가진 전문가에 한해 이동이 허용되도록 적극 대처

0029

외 무 부

종 별 :

번 호 : GVW-2320　　　　　　　　　　　일 시 : 91 1113 1830

수 신 : 장 관(수신처 참조)

발 신 : 주 제네바대사

제 목 : UR/GNS 협상

　　11.13(수) 오전 개최된 JARAMILLO 의장 주재 주요국비공식 협의에서 향후 협상계획을결정하였는 바, 하기 보고함.

　　1. FRAMEWORK

　　- 하기와 같이 구분하여 주요국 비공식 협의를 계속하되 각 잇슈별로 특별히 문제가 있는 국가와 의장의 개별 접촉 또는 이행 당사국간 협의 결과를 주요국 비공식협의에 회부(11.18주까지 FRAMEWORK에 대한 작업을 완료할 계획)

　　O SCHEDULING 관련 조문(6조, 7조, 14조, 16조, 17조 및4부) : 11.14(목) 부터 매일 오전 주요국 비공식 협의개최(HAWES 호주대사 주재)

　　O 기타 모든 조문: 11.14(목) 부터 매일 오후 주요국비공식 협의 개최(JARAMILLO 의장 주재)

　　O MFN 일탈(항공, 해운, 육운, 내수로 운송,기본통신, AUDIO VISUAL) : 11.18주에 비공식 협의개최(JARAMILLO 의장 주재)

　　2. 분야별 부속서

　　- 금융부속서 : FRAMEWORK 협상 결과를 참조할 수 있도록 11.25.부터 HAWES 대사 주재로 주요국비공식 협의 개최(동 주간에 금융전문가 현지출장 필요)

　　- 통신부속서 : 당분간 ROBERT TRITT 공동의장이 각 잇슈별로 개별접촉(FAX 또는 전화 이용),그이후 전체 협의 개최 시기는 미정

　　- 인력이동 부속서: JARAMILLO 의장 주재의 FRAMEWORK 조문에 대한 협의에 포함

　　- 해운분야 공통자유화 및 해운보조 서비스 접근보장 문제: 11.18주에 협의.끝

　　(대사 박수길-국장)

통상국　　2차보　　경기원　　재무부　　농수부　　상공부

주 제 네 바 대 표 부

제네(경) 20644-985   1991. 11. 14.

수신 : 외무부장관

참조 : 통상국장, 경제기획원장관, 체신부장관   91. 11. 15

제목 : UR/서비스 협상 문서 송부

　　　　UR/서비스 협상 관련 통신분야 공동의장이 작성한 통신부속서 초안

(11.8자)을 별첨 송부합니다.

　　　첨부 : 통신부속서 초안 1부.　　　끝.

　　　　　　　　　　주　제　네　바　대　사

65678

0031

주 제 네 바 대 표 부

제내(경) 20644-984   1991. 11. 14.

수신 : 외무부장관

참조 : 통상국장, 경제기획원장관, 재무부장관   91. 11. 15

제목 : UR/서비스 협상 문서 송부

　　　UR/서비스 협상 관련 금융분야 공동의장이 작성한 금융부속서 초안

(11. 8자)을 별첨 송부합니다.

　　　첨부 : 금융부속서 초안 1부.　　　끝.

주 　 제 　 네 　 바 　 대

0032

주 제 네 바 대 표 부

제네(경) 20644-983   1991. 11. 14.

수신 : 외무부장관

참조 : 통상국장, 경제기획원장관

제목 : UR/서비스 협상 문서 송부

91. 11. 1 5

　　　UR/서비스 협상 관련 Framework 각 조문에 대하여 현재 토의되고 있는
대안들을 함께 모은 작업문서를 별첨 송부합니다.

첨부 : UR/서비스 Framework 작업문서 1부.　　끝.

주　　제　　네　　바　　대　　사

선결			견 재 (공 람)	
접수일시	1991.11.1			
처리과	65676			

0033

외 무 부

종 별 :

번 호 : GVW-2339

일 시 : 91 1115 1200

수 신 : 장 관(수신처참조)

발 신 : 주 제네바대사

제 목 : UR/GNS 회의(1)

11.14(목) 개최된 주요국 비공식 협의 내용을 하기보고함.

1. SCHEDULING 관련 조문(11.14 오전, HAWES 대사주재)

가. 제 6조(국내 규제)

- 2항 III) 의 자격 기준 및 기술적 표준의운영과 관련하여 ITU 등 국제기구에서제정된 표준을 채택하는 경우에는 자동적으로 서비스협 정상의 의무에 합치하는 것으로 간주하도록 하는 조항의 규정 문제가 제기되어(인도, 알젠틴) 대상 국제기구의 정의, 국제기구 제정 표준의 범위(구속력이 없는 권고사항등의 포함여부)등에 대하여추가 협의키로 함.

- 6항의 출입국 관리 절차에 의한 인력 이동 약속의 침해 금지 규정은 일단 삭제하고 인력이동 부속서의 관련 조항이 부적당하게 될 경우에는 재 논의키로 합의함.

나. 제 7조 (조화 및 인정)

- 사무국 작성 초안에 자격 및 표준 이외에 REGULATION 이 추가된대 대하여 많은 나라가 동조항의 범위가 너무 확대되는 것이며, MFN관련 중대한 문제가 발생하게 된다고 우려를 표명함.

다. 제 16조 (시장접근)

- 일부 자귀 수정이 있었음.

2. 분쟁해결(11.14 오후 JARANILLO 의장 주재)

- NON-VIOLATION CASE 에 대하여만 논의하였는바 인도는 이의 삭제를, 알젠틴은갓트 23조와 동일하게 규정할 것을 주장하였으나 그외 모든국가는 동 조항을 보다 구체적으로 명확하게 규정하는 접근 방법을 지지하였음.

- NON-VIOLATION CASE 의 범위와 관련 캐나다, 호주는 SPECIFIC COMMITMENT 의 침

통상국 농수부	2차보 상공부	법무부 노동부	보사부 과기처	문화부 해항청	교통부 공보처	체신부	경기원	재무부

PAGE 1

91.11.16　07:58 WH

외신 1과 통제관

0034

해 뿐만 아니라GENERAL OBLIGATION 의 침해까지도 포함하여야 한다고한 반면 갓트법률국은 GENERAL OBLIGATION 의 경우에는 동 OBLIGATION 에 따른 혜택만 침해하는사례는 예상하기 어려우며, OBLIGATION자체의 위반이 될것이라고 함.

  - NON-VIOLATION CASE 의 구제와 관련 당해 조치의 철회의무는 없으며, 본 조항의 규정 목적은 보상문제에 있다는데에는 이의가 없었으나 불가피한 경우에는 당회 조치 자체의 철회도구제조치에 포함될수 있도록 규정하자는 의견과 PANEL 또는 패소국의 결정에 맡기면 된다는 의견이 대립하였음. 끝

  (대사 박수길-국장)

  수신처:(통기, 경기원, 재무부, 법무부, 농림수산부, 문화부, 상공부, 건설부, 보사부, 노동부 ,교통부, 체신부, 과기처, 공보처, 항만청)

외 무 부

종 별 :

번 호 : GVW-2374   일 시 : 91 1120 1500

수 신 : 장관(수신처참조)

발 신 : 주 제네바 대사

제 목 : UR/GNS 협상

　　　1.18(월) 미 USTR 은 당관에 별첨과 같이 12.10(화) 서비스 분야(금융, 증권제외)에 대한 한.미 양자 협상 개최를 요청하여 왔는바, 별도 의견이 없을 경우 미측요청대로 합의코자 하니 양지 바람.

　　　첨부: USTR 서한 1부. (GVW(F)-516)

　　　(대사 박수길-국장)

　　　수신처:(봉기, 경기원, 재무부, 법무부, 농림수산부, 문화부, 상공부, 건설부, 보사부, 노동부, 교통부, 체신부, 과기처, 공보처, 항만청)

통상국	2차보	법무부	보사부	문화부	교통부	체신부	경기원	재무부
농수부	상공부	건설부	노동부	과기처	해항청	공보처		

91.11.21   08:24 DQ

외신 1과 통제관

0036

Guw(H)-576 11/20 1500
Guw-237K 언접

UNITED STATES TRADE REPRESENTATIVE
1-3 AVENUE DE LA PAIX
1202 GENEVA, SWITZERLAND
TELEPHONE: 732 09 70

November 18, 1991

Dear Mr. Han:

Ms. Bonnie Richardson from USTR/Washington has requested an
appointment with you on Tuesday, December 10 at 9:30 a.m. to
discuss initial requests and offers as part of the Group of
Negotiations on Services. She proposes meeting at USTR, 1-3
Avenue de la Paix, in the second floor conference room. She is
prepared to discuss all services sectors, except for banking
and securities. This latter sector is being handled by an
official from the US Treasury Department, who will be
contacting your delegation separately.

Given the necessity of meeting with so many delegations in a
short time period, we would appreciate confirmation from your
mission as soon as possible. You may contact me or Ms. Brita
Lineburger at 749-5280 or 749-5310. Our fax number is
749-4885.

Thank you for your consideration. I look forward to hearing
from you.

Sincerely,

Christina Lund
Attache, USTR Geneva

/—/   0037

外 務 部

종   별 :

번   호 : GVW-2377   일   시 : 91 1120 1500

수   신 : 장관(수신처 참조)

발   신 : 주 제네바 대사

제   목 : UR/GNS 회의(2)

　　11.18(월) 및 11.19(화) 오전 HAWES 대사 주재로 개최된 주요국 비공식 협의는 11.15(금) 협의에이어 예외조항(14조)에 대하여 논의하였는바, 주요내용은 하기 보고함.

　　1. 협의 개요

　　- HAWES 대사는 현 서비스 협상 초안에 열거된 사유를 최소화 할 목적으로 각 항목별로 포함을 원하는 국가를 확인하고 그 이유 및 협정상의 다른 조문(국내 규제,시장 접근 및 내국민 대우에대한 협상등)에 의하여 동 문제가 해결될수있는지 여부에대하여 토의하였는바, 각국 입장에 변화는 없었으나 대세에 의하여 협의안을 도출할가능성을 보이고 있음.

　　2. 주요 토의 내용

　　가. 인력 이동등에 따른 국가안보

　　- ASEAN 및 홍콩이 동 사유 포함 입장을 계속 견지하였으나 'PUBLIC ORDER' 조항의 정의 규정을 보다 넓게 하면 해결될수 있다는 의견이 대세를 이루어 'PUBLIC ORDER'의 정의에 대하여 추가 토의키로 함.

　　나. SAFETY

　　- SAFETY 는 결국 인간 동식물의 생명을 보호하기 위한 것이기 때문에 상호 중복되므로 삭제키로 합의함.

　　다. 환경

　　- 캐나다, 스위스, 오지리등이 환경 보호를 위한 조치에 MFN 일탈 피요성이 있는경우가 많음을 들어 동항목의 포함을 주장하였으나, 대부분의 국가가 정부간 협정에의한 의무 이행을 위한 경우에 한하여 예외 조항에 반영할 것을 주장하였음.

　　0 한편, 캐나다, 스위스등은 GATT 에서 논의되고있는 환경과 무역과 관련하여 GATS

통상국 경기원	2차보 재무부	정와대 농수부	안기부 상공부	법무부 건설부	보사부 노동부	문화부 과기처	교통부 해항청	체신부 공보처

91.11.21   09:01 DQ

외신 1과 통제관

0038

에서도 UR 이후 추가 작업 계획을 설정하자고 제의함.

　라. 유한 자원 보호

　- 캐나다, 멕시코가 동 항목의 포함을 주장하였으나, 갓트 법률국은 GATS 에서는 수출 통제가 허용된다는 점을 들어 회의적 견해를 표명함.

　마. 소비자 보호

　- 대부분의 국가가 인간, 동식물의 생명보호, 기만행위의 방지등에 의하여 동문제가 규율될수 있다는 의견을 제시함.

　바. 문화적 가치

　- 아국, 인도, 태국, 말련등이 동 항목의 포함을 주장하였으나 대부분의 국가가 문화적 가치의 의미가 애매하고 너무 광범위하여 남용 가능성이 많을뿐만 아니라 시장접근 및 내국민 대우에 관한 약속에 의하여 해결될수 있다는 입장을 표명함.

　O 한편 종전에 동 항목의 포함을 주장하던 카나다는 이의 범위를 구체적으로 좁혀 다른 조항에 규정할 것을 제의함.

　사. 개인적 자료의 보호

　- EC 는 동 항목이 국내규제(제 6조)에 의하여 COVER 될수도 있으나 시장접근과 내국민 대우에 관한 약속도 침해할 필요가 있는 경우가 있으므로 제6조만으로는 불충분하다고 하고 다만 협정 규정에 위배되지 않는 국내 법규의 이행을 위해 필요한 경우에 한하여 예외 조항에 반영하는 방안도 고려 가능하다고 함. (스위스, 오지리, 북구 동조)

　아. 세금 부과 문제

　- 미국은 세금 자체가 내.외국인간 차별적인 경우는 SCHEDULE 에 기재되어야 하나 동일한 세금을 징수하는 방법이 내.외국인간에 다를 경우(예: 외국사업자에게만 세금을 원천 징수하는 경우)가 있으므로 이를 예외 조항에 반영하여야 한다고 하였으며, 다른 나라로부터 동 개념자체에 대한 반대는 없었으나 구체적 사례를 추가 검토키로 함.

　3. 향후 협의 계획

　- 사무국에서 11.15-11.19 간 토의 결과를 반영하여 새로운 초안을 작성 11.21(목) 재토의키로 함. 끝

　(대사 박수길-국장)

수신처:(봉기, 경기원, 재무부, 법무부, 농림수산부, 문화부, 상공부, 건설부, 보사부, 노동부
,교통부, 체신부, 과기처, 공보처, 항만청)

0040

외 무 부

종 별 :

번 호 : GVW-2425

일 시 : 91 1122 1900

수 신 : 장 관(수신처 참조)

발 신 : 주 제네바 대사

제 목 : UR/GNS 회의(3)

11.21(목) 속개된 주요국 비공식 협의 내용을 하기보고함.

1. SCHEDULING 관련 조문 (11.21 오전, HAWES 대사주재)

가. 14조 (예외)

- 11.19(수) 토의 결과를 바탕으로 사무국에서 재작성한 초안을 배부하였으나, 11.22(금) 토의예정

0 동 초안은 공중도덕 및 질서, 인간.동.식물의 생명, 환경 관련 정부간 협정상의 의무 이행,서비스 협정규정에 합치하는 국내 법규의 이해등은 합의가 형성되고 있는 사항으로 분류하고 문화적 가치를 조합한 기타 사유는 이견이 많거나 소수의견인사항으로 분류하였음.

나. 6 조 (국내 규제)

- 사무국에서 재작성한 초안을 배부, 토의하였는 바, 국제기구에서 설정한 국제표준의 사용시 서비스협정상의 의무와 일치하는 것으로 추정하는 문제에 대하여 미국, EC, 카나다등이 국제기구 및국제 표준의 범위가 애매모호 하다고 지적함.

다. 제 16조(시장접근)

- 16조 2항(D) 의 서비스 공급에 필요한 자연인의 숫자에 대한 제한과 관련 동 항목이 특정 서비스분야 또 세부분야에 종사하는 인력에 대한 QUOTA와 개별 서비스 공급 기업별로 고용 가능한 서비스공급 인력수에 대한 제한을 모두 포함한다는데에는합의가 형성되었으며, 다만 이를 명확히 표면할 문안에 대하여 추가 협의키로 함.

- 16조 2항(E)의 상업적 주재 형태에 대한 제한에 대하여는 일본, 홍콩, 오지리만 이외국인에 대한 차별적 제한만 기재되야 한다는 입장을 취하였으며, 기타 모든 국가는 내.외국인 무차별적 제한도 기재되어야 한다고 함.

라. ADDITIONAL COMMITMENT

| 통상국 | 2차보 | 경기원 | 재무부 | 농수부 | 상공부 | 법무부, 문화부 건설부 보사부 노동부 |

PAGE 1

91.11.23   09:23 WH

외신 1과   통제관

0041

- 아국 및 오지리, 알젠틴, 브라질, 인도, 이집트등은 동 조항의 규정 여부 자체에 대하여 유보의사를 표명하였으나, EC, 카나다, 북구, 호주등은 동조항이 무차별적 질적 규제, 보조금등에 대한 시장접근 약속 여부를 예단하는 것이 아니며 서비스분야의 특성상 이에 대한 근거조항이 필요하다고 하였으며, 특히 호주는 이를 명문 규정함으로서 공개주의 원칙하에 협상되어 양자 협상 결과에 MFN 원칙이 적용될수 있으며, 그렇지 않을경우 밀실에서 협상되어 차별적으로 운영될 것이라고 언급함.

2. 서비스 분야별 토의(11. 21 오후, MARAMILLO 의장주재)

가. 해운

- 아국을 포함한 홍콩, 싱가폴등 많은 나라가 북구제안 6항의 해운 보조 서비스에 대한 접근보장 의무를 규정하는데 지지의사를 표명하였으나, 인도는 이에 대한 주석 규정을 발전시키기에는시간이 부족하다고 함.

- 한편, 카나다, 호주, 뉴질랜드, EC, 일본등은 보조서비스 접근 의무 뿐만 아니라 국제해운의 공통자유화, CABOTAGE 및 보조 서비스 공급 사업에 대한 STANDSTILL도 일괄하여 규정되어야 한다는 입장을 표명하였으나, 미국은 해운 분야의 특수한상황 때문에 일방조치도 사용할 필요가 있다고 하였으며, 인도는 부속서가 자유화 약속을 규정하여서는 안된다고 함.

- 갓트 법률국은 해운 보조서비스 접근 보장문제가 대부분 FRAMEWORK 제 2조(MFN), 제 8조(독점), 제 17조(내국민 대우)에 의하여 COVER 될수있다고 지적함.

나. 항공

- EC 는 브랏셀 각료회의시 초안이 많은 점에서 낡은 것이 되었다고 전제하고 지상 조업 서비스등 SOFTRIGHT 도 물리적 제약 때문에 MFN 적용이 어려운 점을 감안,항공 보조 서비스에 대한 접근보장에 관한 제안을 제출할 예정이라고 하였는 바, 동제안 제출 이후 내주초에 재토의키로함.

다. 육운

- 오지리만이 MFN 일탈을 주장하였으나, 기타국가는 동 문제는 다자간 규칙 차원이 아닌 다른방법으로 자체적으로 해결 하여야 할 것이라고 함.끝

(대사 박수길-국장)

원 본

외 무 부

종 별 :

번 호 : GVW-2417

일 시 : 91 1122 1540

수 신 : 장 관(수신처참조)

발 신 : 주 제네바 대사

제 목 : UR/GNS 협상

11.22(금) 당관에 전달된 인도의 대아국 서비스 분야 REQUEST LIST 를 별첨송부함.

첨부: 인도의 REQUEST LIST 1 부.

(GVW(F)-0526)

수신처: 봉기, 경기원, 재무부, 법무부, 농림수산부, 문화부, 상공부, 건설부, 보사부, 노동부, 교통부, 체신부, 과기처, 공보처, 항만청

(대사 박수길-국장)

예고:91.12.31. 까지

통상국	장관	차관	1차보	2차보	분석관	정와대	안기부	법무부
보사부	문화부	교통부	체신부	경기원	재무부	농수부	상공부	건설부
노동부	과기처							

PAGE 1

91.11.23   04:27

외신 2과 통제관 FI

0043

G.VW(R)-0526   111 I 1540

" 첨부 "

B K.Zutshi
Ambassador/PR to GATT

भारत का स्थायी मिशन
जेनेवा
PERMANENT MISSION OF INDIA
TO THE UNITED NATIONS OFFICES
9. RUE DU VALAIS
1202 GENEVA
TELEPHONE : 732 08 59

No:GEN/PMI/GATT/204/12/91   November 22, 1991

Dear Mr.Ambassador,

      In accordance with procedures agreed upon by
the Group of Negotiations on Services, India submits
its request list to all participants in the Services
negotiations. The list contains requests for
liberalization commitments in sectors, and sub-sectors
of particular interest to India and removal of barriers
to trade by way of restrictions on movement of
relevant categories of personnel in these specific
sectors.

2.   This request list may be modified or amended
and additional requests may be made in the light of the
negotiations.

3.   India would appreciate the opportunity to
discuss these requests with your Government, at your
earliest convenience.

4.   India has separately submitted its conditional
offer on initial commitments to the GATT Secretariat.

Regds,,

Yours sincerely,

(B.K.Zutshi)

H.E.Mr.Soo Gil Park,
Ambassador,
Permanent Representative to GATT,
Permanent Mission of Korea,
Geneva.

0044

5-1

INDIA'S INITIAL REQUESTS IN THE
SERVICES NEGOTIATIONS

India requests commitments from all participants in Market Access in the following sectors:-

1. Professional Service

    (i)   Accounting, auditing and book-keeping
    (ii) Taxation Services
    (iii) Architectural Services
    (iv) Integrated engineering services
    (v)   Medical and dental services
    (vi) Services provided by mid-wives, nurses
    (vii) Physiotherapists and para-medical personnel

2. Computer and related services

    (i)   Installation of computer hardware
    (ii)   Software implementation service
    (iii) Data processing service
    (iv) Data base service
    (v)   Maintenance and repair services of office machinery and equipment including computers.

3. Other Business Services

    (i)   Technical testing and analysis services
    (ii) Placement and supply services of personnel
    (iii) Maintenance and repair of equipment
    (iv) Building cleaning services.
    (v)   Investigation and security services
    (vi) Services incidental to agriculture
    (vii) Services incidental to fishing

0045

2

4. Health Related and Social Services

    (i)   Hospital services
    (ii) Other human health services
    (iii) Social Services

5. Tourism, Travel and Leisure Services

    (i)   Hotels and Restaurants
    (ii) Travel agencies and tour operators services
    (iii) Entertainment services (not covered under audiovisual services)
    (iv) Other road transport services related to tourism.

6. Education Services

    (i)   Primary education services
    (ii) Secondary education services
    (iii) Adult education services

7. Transport Services by railways

    - Operation and maintenance of railsways.

The main impediment that India encounters in Market Access in these sectors is restriction on movement of natural persons. India requests relaxation of these restrictions with a view to enabling Indian services operators to move in certain categories of skilled personnel for temporary residence of 3-5 years.

An illustrative list of categories of personnel in

0046

5-3

3

respect of which a general flexibility for free movement wouldbe required on the above basis is given below:

1. Computer and related services

  - Computer scientist;
  - System analyst;
  - Programmer;
  - Software Documenter;
  - Field Engineer;
  - Data Entry Operator
  - Drawing Digitizer

2. Health related Services

  - Physician/Surgeon
  - Psychologist/Psychiatrist
  - Physiotheparist
  - Occupational therapist
  - Optometrist
  - Radiographer
  - Laboratory Technician (Pathology;
          Bio-Chemistry,Microbiology,Electron
          Microscopy, Radiology)
  - Pharmacist/Dispenser
  - Dietician
  - Nurses

3. Hotel and Restaurant Services

  - Manager
  - Housekeeper
  - Chambermaid
  - Chef (including Executive Chef & SOUS Chef)

0047

5-4

4

- Restaurant Hostess
- Lobby Hostess
- Steward /waiter
- Horticulturist/Florist
- Maintenance Engineer (Civil & Electrical)
- Laundryman
- Lifeguard

0048

5-5

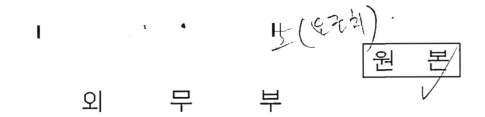

외 무 부

종   별 :

번   호 : GVW-2430   일   시 : 91 1125 1500

수   신 : 장 관(수신처 참조)

발   신 : 주 제네바대사

제   목 : UR/GNS 회의(4)

11.22(금) 개최된 주요국 비공식 협의 내용을 하기보고함.

1. 예외조항(11.22.오전 HAWES 대사주재)

- 각 항목별로 기술적, 법률적 문제에 대한 의견교환이 있었으나 실질적 문제인각항목의 포함 여부에 대하여는 별다른 진전은 없었음.

0 특히 유한자원의 보호 항목에 대하여 카나다, 멕시코, 베네주엘라는 수산자원, 광물자원등의 생산봉제 조치가 광업자문 서비스등 관련 서비스 공급활동에 영향을미칠수 있으므로 예외조항에 반영되어야 한다고 하였으나 기타 모든 국가 및 갓트법률국은 유한 자원의 생산봉제 조치가 사실상관련 서비스의 영업 기회를 축소하게 되는 경우가 있으나 법률적으로 제 16조(시장접근) 관련약속을 위배하는 것은 아니기때문에 예외조항이 필요없다고 반박함.

0 문화적 가치에 대하여 HAWES 대사는 특정국가의 문화적 동질성 보존을 위해 외국서비스의 시장접근 제한하는 사례는 예상 가능하나 국가간에 차별하는 것은 정당화 되기 어려울것이라고 지적하고 예외조항중 특히 문화적 가치문제에 DEADLOSK 이 있다고 언급함. 한편 캐나다는 문화적 가치 보존 문제관련 서비스분야의 범위를 좁혀구체적으로 규정하는 접근방법을 제시함.

2. MFN(11.22오후 JARAMILLO 의장 주재)

- 사무국에서 작성 배부한 별첨(FAX 송부)배경문서를 기초로 토의하였는바, 아국포함 많은 나라가 MFN 일탈이 개별적으로 양허 협상과정에서 정해지기 보다는 사전에 DISCIPLINE이 마련되어야 한다고 지적함.

- 한편 의장은 사무국 문서상의 세가지 범주별로(MFN 일탈 대상 구체적 조치, 한시적MFN 일탈, 시한이 없는 MFN 일탈) 각국이 관련 정보를 조속히 제출할 것을 요구하였으며11.25.주에 사무국에 LEGAL ANNEX 초안을 작성 재토의키로 함.

통상국	2차보	법무부	보사부	문화부	교통부	체신부	경기원	재무부
농수부	상공부	건설부	노동부	과기처	해항청	공보처		

PAGE 1   91.11.26   09:55 WH

외신 1과 통제관

0049

3. 건의

- MFN 일탈과 관련 해운분야등 아국이 MFN일탈을 요청할 사항이 있는 경우 상기 GNS의장의 요청대로 MFN 일탈 대상 구체적 조치, 일탈 요청 사유, 일탈 시한등을 명시하여 조속 봉보바람.

첨부: MFN 일탈 관련 사무국 문서 1부

(GVW(F)-0532).끝

(대사 박수길-국장)

수신처:봉기, 경기원, 재무부, 법무부,농림수산부,문화부, 상공부, 건설부, 보사부, 노동부 ,교봉부, 체신부, 과기처, 공보처, 항만청

GW(저)-532 11/25/ *(handwritten)*
GW-2430 관련 *(handwritten)*

EXEMPTIONS FROM M.F.N. FOE EXISTING MEASURES → Pour memoire Para. 2er 상치됨 *(handwritten)*

Steps to be taken before the GATS enters into force:

(A) For any exemption for measures which do not conform to the m.f.n. obligation, a Party must provide information relating to:

- the precise measure for which the exemption is sought;

- in the case of a sector specific exemption; the sector, sub-sector and activity for which the measure is relevant;

- in the case of horizontal measures, the subject matter for which the measure is relevant (e.g. labour, investment, <u>double taxation</u>, legal assistance); and

- the purpose of the non-conforming measure.

(B) In the case of time a bound exemption, information additional to (A) should be provided relating to:

- the time period for which the exemption is sought; and

- modalities for the phase-out.

(C) In the case of an open-ended exemption, information additional to (A) should be provided relating to:

- justification for a need for an open-ended exemption as compared to option (B).

532-3-1

M-MFN

0051

Steps to be taken after the GATS enters into force:

(i) Short-term exemption (i.e. phase-out in less than 3 years):

- Notification at the end of the specified period that the phase-out has taken place according to the modalities.

(ii) Longer-term exemption (i.e. phase-out after more than 3 years):

- Review (timing to be decided by the PARTIES) to assure that the phase-out is taking place according to the modalities;

- Notification that the phase-out has taken place.

(iii) Non-time bound exemption for all participants:

ex: Traffic rights

- Review after 5 years to reconsider the possible application of m.f.n;

- Review after 5 years to evaluate the degree of liberalization in specific sectors.   ex: Basic Telecommunication

(iv) Non-time bound exemption for individual participants:

- Review (timing to be decided by the PARTIES) to establish whether conditions that provided the justification for the exemption still prevail.

M-MFN

$532 - 3 - 2$

0052

Pour mémoire:

1. If non-conforming measures are to be taken in the future, or a particular measure is not phased out under the terms specified, or the conditions justifying the non-time bound exemption no longer prevail, then normal procedures established in GATS would apply.

2. Notification of the intention to possibly introduce non-conforming measures in a specified sector <u>after</u> the entry into force of the GATS, without having to resort to the normal GATS procedures, has also been proposed.   ex: basic telecom. 그때 이것이 가능하게되면 새로운것에 의해 MFN 공약을 규제하는 Annex가 있기가 힘들것이나

3. It has been proposed by some participants that in the case of non-time bound exemptions, other parties should be free to decide as to whether they extend m.f.n. treatment in the sector concerned to those participants seeking such exemptions.

✓ 4. At the completion of the Uruguay Round, <u>a decision will be taken individually/collectively with respect to the acceptability of the exemptions/liberalization commitments undertaken.</u>

✓ 5. There is a need to develop at a later date the nature and content of the Review; for example, an evaluation of the level of liberalization achieved in a particular sector over the period since the exemption was taken.

6. While individual participants appear to be prepared to indicate a <u>minimum</u> of intended exemptions, some have made it clear that the final composition of the list will depend on the nature and extent of exemptions requested by other participants.

7. Some participants have indicated that the final initial commitments made in a particular sector will depend on the extent of m.f.n. exemptions by other parties in the same sector.

532 — 3 — 3

M-MFN

0053

외 무 부

종 별 :

번 호 : GVW-2431
일 시 : 91 1125 1500

수 신 : 장 관(수신처참조)

발 신 : 주 제네바대사

제 목 : UR/GNS 회의(5)

11.24(일) JARAMILLO 의장 주재로 개최된 주요국비공식 협의는 11.25(월)의 금융부속서 논의에앞서 이사회 및 그 하부기구에 관한 규정(FRAMEWORK제 25조)에 대하여 토의하였는바 주요 내용 하기보고함.

1. 접근 방법

- 갓트 법률국에서 제시한 방법대로 FRAMEWORK 제25조에는 이사회 및 하부기구의설치구성에 관한 근거 조항만 규정하고 서비스 분야별 위원회의 임무및 금융서비스위원회의 설치는 별도로 각료들이 결정 형태로 하는데 합의함.,

2. FRAMEWORK 규정

- 이사회와 그 하부기구를 설치하도록 규정하는 한편 이사회는 모든 서비스 협정체약국이 회원국이 되도록 하되 하부기구는 이사회가 달리 결정하면 참가자격이 제한될수도 있도록 규정하는데 합의 함.

3. 각료들의 결정

- 서비스 분야별 위원회의 설치 및 임무에 관한다음 각료들의 권고안을 마련하여서비스 협정발효이후 첫번째 이사회에서 승인하도록 하는데 합의함

0 금융 서비스 위원회의 설치

0 기타 서비스 분야별 위원회의 임무

I) 당해서비스 분야에 관계되는 협정 규정의적용에 관한 검토 및 감시

II) 이사회에 대한 구체적 제안

III) 분야별 부속서의 수정 또는 추가

IV) 당해 분야에 대한 기술적 작업

V) 개도국에 대한 기술지원

VI) 관련 국제기구와의 협력

통상국 농수부	2차보 상공부	법무부 건설부	보사부 노동부	문화부 과기처	교통부 해항청	체신부 공보처	경기원	재무부

91.11.26   11:12 WH

외신 1과 통제관
0054

VII) 기타 이사회에서 부여하는 임무

4. 상기 합의사항을 사무국에서 문서로 작성하여 11.25(월) 금융부속서 논의시 재토의할 예정임.끝

(대사 박수길-국장)

수신처:통기, 경기원, 재무부, 법무부, 농림수산부, 문화부, 상공부, 건설부, 보사부, 노동부,교통부, 체신부, 과기처, 공보처, 항만청

외 무 부

종 별 :

번 호 : GVW-2437   일 시 : 91 1125 1900

수 신 : 장 관(수신처참조)

발 신 : 주 제네바대사

제 목 : UR/GNS 회의(6)

　　1. 11.25(월) 오후 개최된 금융 부속서에 대한 주요국 비공식 협의는 HAWES 대사가 SCHEDULING 관련조문(제 6조, 7조, 14조, 16조, 17조)의 최근 초안과 11.24(일) 비공식 협의를 거친 이사회 및 하부기구에 대한 초안(별첨 FAX 송부)을 배부하고그 배경을 설명하는데 그쳤으며 부속서 내용에 대한 토의는 11.26(화) 오전에 진행할 예정임.

　　2. 한편 미국 금융 전문가는 미국정부의 입장이라고 전제하고, 10.14 자 금융 분야 공동의장 초안과유사한 내용의 금융 서비스기구 및 분쟁해결에 관한 비공식 제안을 제시하였음.

　　첨부: 이사회 및 하부기구에 대한 사무국 초안 1부, 끝

　　(GVW(F)-0535)

　　(대사 박수길-국장)수신처:(봉기, 경기원, 재무부, 법무부, 농림수산부, 문화부, 상공부, 건설부, 보사부, 농동부, 교통부, 체신부, 과기처, 공보처, 항만청)

통상국	2차보	법무부	보사부	문화부	교통부	체신부	경기원	재무부
농수부	상공부	건설부	노동부	과기처	해항청	공보처		

91.11.26   10:18 WH

외신 1과 통제관

0056

GV(二)-0535   11년 5 1800

"GUN-2437 첨부"

Article IV

Council

1. The PARTIES shall establish a Council which will perform such functions as may be assigned by them to facilitate the operation of this Agreement and further its objectives. The Council may establish such subsidiary bodies as it considers appropriate for the effective discharge of its functions.

2. The Council and, unless the Council decides otherwise, its subsidiary bodies shall be open to participation by representatives of all Parties to this Agreement.

3. The Chairman of the Council shall be elected by the PARTIES. The Council shall establish its own rules of procedure.

COMMENTS:

Paragraph 1:   The reference to creation of subsidiary bodies has been moved so as to precede paragraph 2. Its language parallels the GATT CONTRACTING PARTIES Decision creating the GATT Council ("The Council may establish such subsidiary bodies as it considers appropriate to carry out its functions in relation to the examination of questions placed before it, consultations with governments, and the drafting of reports to the CONTRACTING PARTIES..." --BISD 9S/7). A "body" may include committees, working parties, working groups, groups of experts or the like. For instance, the GATT Council has established a Committee on Tariff Concessions and various other committees.

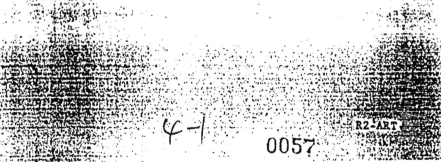

4-1

0057   R2-ART

- 2 -

Paragraph 2: This provision would make participation in the Council or in any of its sub-bodies open in principle to any party to the GATS, while reserving the option of the Council to create limited-participation subsidiary bodies if it decides to do so. Examples of limited-participation subsidiary bodies in the GATT include the Balance-of-Payments Committee and various wise men's groups.

0058

R2-ART

DRAFT

MINISTERIAL DECISION ON INSTITUTIONAL ARRANGEMENTS
FOR THE GENERAL AGREEMENT ON TRADE IN SERVICES

Ministers recommend approval by the Council of the General Agreement on Trade in Services at its first meeting of the decision on subsidiary bodies set out below.

INSTITUTIONAL ARRANGEMENTS FOR
THE GENERAL AGREEMENT ON TRADE IN SERVICES

The Council of the General Agreement on Trade in Services, acting pursuant to Article XXV with a view to facilitating the operation and furthering the objectives of that Agreement,

Decides as follows:

1.   Any subsidiary bodies the Council may establish shall report to the Council annually or more often as necessary. Each such body shall determine its own rules of procedure, and may set up its own subsidiary bodies as appropriate.

2.   Any sectoral committee shall carry out responsibilities as assigned to it by the Council, and shall afford Parties the opportunity to consult on any matters relating to trade in services in the sector concerned and the operation of the sectoral annex to which it may pertain. Such responsibilities shall include:

(a)   to keep under continuous review and surveillance the application of the Agreement with respect to the sector concerned;

4-3   0059   R2-ART

(b) to formulate proposals or recommendations for consideration by the Council in connection with any matter relating to trade in the sector concerned;

(c) if there is an annex pertaining to the sector, to consider proposals for amendment of that sectoral annex, and to make appropriate recommendations to the Council;

(d) to provide a forum for technical discussions, to conduct studies on measures by parties and to conduct examinations of any other technical matters affecting trade in services in the sector concerned;

(e) to provide technical assistance to developing country parties and developing countries negotiating accession to the Agreement in respect of the application of obligations or other matters affecting trade in services in the sector concerned; and

(f) to cooperate with any other subsidiary bodies established under this Agreement or any international organizations active in any sector concerned.

3. There is hereby established a Committee on Trade in Financial Services.

발 신 전 보

분류번호 | 보존기간

번 호 : WGV-1711   911127 1846 FH   종별 : _____

수 신 : 주 제네바 대사. 총영사

발 신 : 장 관 (통 기)

제 목 : UR 서비스 협상 (Request List)

~~UR 정부선우대표단 귀지 방문시 귀관에 전달한 UR 서비스협상~~
~~1.20 귀지에서 개최된 UR 대책 실무위원회에서~~ 검토 결정된 아국의 Request List를

갓트 및 해당국에 제출하기 바람.   끝.   (통상국장 김 용 규)

보 안
통 제

앙고재 | 91년11월27일 통기과 | 기안자성명 조천 | 과장 | 심의관 | 국장 전결 | 차관 장관 회람

외신과통제

0061

경 제 기 획 원

우 427-760 / 경기도 과천시 중앙동1 정부제2청사 / 전화 503-9149 / 전송 503-9141

문서번호 봉조삼 10502-841

시행일자 1991. 11. 기.

선결			지시		
접수	일시	자시간	˙: ˙	결재·공람	
	번 호				
	처 리 과				
	담 당 자				

수신 외무부장관
참조

제목 UR서비스분야의 상대국에 대한 Request List 제출

    11월 20일 제네바에서 개최된 UR대책실무위원회의 결정에 따라 별첨과 같은 UR서비스분야의 상대국에 대한 Request List가 상대국 및 GATT에 즉시 제출되어 12월 8일주에 개최 예정인 양자협의과정에서 협의될 수 있도록 조치하기 바랍니다.

별첨 : 상대국에 대한 Request사항(국·영문).   끝.

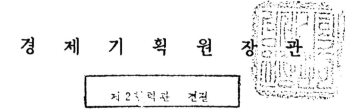

경 제 기 획 원 장 관

제2협력관 견결

0062

외 무 부

종 별 :

번 호 : GVW-2465

일 시 : 91 1127 1100

수 신 : 장 관(수신처 참조)

발 신 : 주 제네바 대사

제 목 : UR / GNS 회의(7)

11.26(화) 속개된 주요국 비공식 협의 내용을 하기보고함.

1. 금융부속서 (11.26 오전 HAWES 대사 및 FRANKSWEDLOVE 공동 주재)

가. 협의 개요

- 11.8 자 의장 작성 부석서 초안 제 1조 부터 제6조까지 토의 하였는바, 대체적으로 합의가형성된 제 1조(SCOPE AND DEFINITION)및 제2조(DOMESTIC REGULATION)에대하여는 FRANK SWEDLOVE공동의장이 특별히 문제가 있는 국가 및 법률전문가와 함께문안 정리 작업을 하기로하였으며, 제 3조(조화및 인정)에 대하여는 금일미국이 제안한 초안을 기초로 제토의키로 하였음.

O 제 5조 (INSTITUTIONAL MACHINERY)에 대하여는 11.8의장 초안과, GNS 의장이 제시한 11.25 자 제 25조(COUNCIL) 및 각료들의 결정초안, 미국제안등3개 초안의 비교표를 작성 11.27 재토의키로 하였으며

O 제 6조 (DISPUTE SETTLEMENT)에 대하여는 사무국에서GATT 의 분쟁해결 체제 GATS 의 분쟁해결규정, UR/분쟁해결 그룹의 논의 동향등에대한 배경문서를 작성 이를 기초로 토의키로하였음.

나. 주요 토의 내용

- 제 2조(DOMESTIC REGULATION)

O 제 1항에 대하여 EC, 스웨덴, 스위스등은 현초안이 균형을 잃고 있다고 지적하였으며

O 제 2항의 '인가결정에 필요한 구체적 정보제공의무'에 대하여 인도, 이집트등은 FRAMEWORK 제 6조4항에 인가신청인이 언제든지 동 인가문제 처리상황에 대한 정보를 요청할수 있으므로 별문제가 없다고 한 반면 미국, 카나다는 동 의무가FRAMEWORK 또는 금융 부속서에 반영되어야 한다고함.

통상국 체신부 공보처	1차보 경기원	외정실 재무부	청와대 농수부	안기부 상공부	법무부 건설부	보사부 노동부	문화부 과기처	고통부 해항청
PAGE 1								

91.11.28   23:11 FO

외신 1과 통제관

0063

- 제 3조(HARMONIZATION AND RECOGNITION)

0 미국이 규제조치의 인정 및 조화협정, 상호 협력협정등에 관한 초안을 배부하였는바, 카나다가지지의사를 표명하였으며, 인도는 FRAMEWORK 제7조(인정)가 자격이나표준의 인정만을 다루기때문에 규제의 인정, 정보교환, 협력협정등일부 금융 부속서에 추가할 요소가 있다고 언급함.

- 제 6조(DISPUTE SETTLEMENT)

0 분쟁해결 절차를 자세하게 규정한 미국제안에대하여 많은 나라가 특정 분야에대하여만 구체적절차를 정하는 것은 시기 상조이며 FRAMEWORK 상의일반적인 분쟁해결절차가 선결되어야 한다고지적하였는바, 미국 역시 일반적인 분쟁해결절차가 선행되어야 한다는 점에는 동의하나 동절차 토의 과정에서 금융 분야에 관한미국제안이 고려되어야 한다고 언급함.

2. 제 8조 (독점) 및 제 30조(협정 부적용) (11.26 오후JARAMILLO 의장 주재)

가. 제 8조(독점)

- 독점 서비스 공급자의 의무 부담 범위에 대하여 제2조(MFN) 및 협정 제 3부(SPECIFIC COMMITMENT)에한정하기로 하는등 동 조항 각부분에 대하여완전히 합의하였음.

나. 제 30조(협정 부적용)

- 주요 쟁점이었던 분야별 부적용은 삭제하기로합의하였으나 부적용 조항의 원용요건 및감시등에 대하여는 각국이 종전 입장을 견지하여재 토의키로 하였음. 끝

수신처   :
봉기, 경기원, 재무부, 법무부,농림수산부, 문화부, 상공부, 건설부, 노동부,교통부, 채신부, 과 기처, 공보처, 항만청

(대사 박수길-국장)

PAGE 2

0064

외 무 부

종   별 :

번   호 : GVW-2489   일   시 : 91 1129 0900

수   신 : 장관(수신처 참조)

발   신 : 주 제네바 대사

제   목 : UR/GNS 회의(8)

11.27(수) 속개된 주요국 비공식 협의 내용을 하기보고함.

1. FRAMEWORK 제 7조(인정) (11.27. 09:30-11:30, HAWES대사 주재)

- 제 1항

O 서비스 공급자의 자격 관련 인정대상이 학력,경험, LICENSE, CERTIFICATION 또는 기타 REGUIREMENT임을 분명히 하도록 초안을 재작성하기로 함.

- 제 4항

O 상호 인정에 관한 협상에 관심 국가가 협상초기부터 충분히 참여할수 있도록 문안을 재작성하기로 함.

2. 금융 부속서 중 INSTITUTIONAL MACHINERY(11.27,11:30-13:30, HAWES 대사 및 FRANK SWEDLOVE 공동주재)

- 사무국에서 작성한 3개 초안 비교표를 기초로 토의하였는바, SEACEN 을 제외한 대부분의 개도국들은 11.25 자 FRAMEWORK 제 25(이사회) 및 각료들의 결정 초안에의한 접근 방법을 지지하고 다음과 같이 논평함.

O 최고의사 결정기관으로서 이사회와 그 하부기구로서 분야별 위원회간에 분명한 계층 구조가 설정되어야 함.

O 금융 서비스 기구만 그 기능과 책임등을 달리규정할 아무런 특성이 없음

O 금융 서비스기구 참가 자격을 제한하는 것은 타분야기구에도 영향을 미침으로써 서비스 협정의 분산을 초래하며 참가자격을 모든 서비스 협정 회원국에 개방함으로써 어떤 문제 발생 가능성이 있는것도 아님.

- 스웨덴, 스위스, 카나다, EC 등 선진국은 금융서비스 기구가 이사회의 하부 기구라는 점에는 이의가 없으며, 11.8 자 의장초안 및 미국제안도 그와 같은 전제하에작성되었다고 하고 다음과 같이언급함.(미국은 발언하지 않음)

통상국	장관	1차보	외정실	청와대	안기부	법무부	보사부	문화부
교통부	체신부	경기원	재무부	농수부	상공부	건설부	노동부	과기처
해항정	공보처							

PAGE 1

0 금융 서비스 기구에 대한 이사회의 권한 위임이 명확하게 규정되어야 함.

0 금융 서비스기구의 기능과 관련 FREMEWORK 제25조와 각료들의 결정 초안에는 일부 누락된요소가 있음.

. 금융분야 분쟁해결의 금융 서비스 기구 전담

. 금융분야 자유화 협상 GUIDELINE 개발등 자유화과정에의 참여

. 금융부속서 규정의 해석 및 자문

. 이사회와의 공동 행위 준비등

- HAWES 대사는 각료들의 결정 초안 3항(금융서비스 기구 설립)에 동 기구에 대한 권한 위임을명확히 하고 제 2항(분야별 위원회 기능)에필요사항을 추가하여 재토의하겠다고 함.

3. 금융 부속서중 제 1조 및 2조(11.27, 15:00-17:00,FRANK SWEDLOVE 주재)

- 제 1조(SCOPE/DEFINITION) 3항과 관련 의장이재작성한 초안에 대하여 대체로 합의가 형성됨.

- 제 2조(DOMESTIC REGULATION)와 관련 의장이 재작성한 초안에 대하여 아국, 홍콩, 인도가 PRUDENTIAL MEASURE 는 결과적으로 협정상의 의무나 시장 접근 및 내국민 대우에 대한 SPECIFIC COMMITMENT 도 침해할수 있는바 이점에 대하여 새로운 초안이 불명확하다는 점을 지적하여 재토의키로 함.

4. 분쟁해결(11.27, 17:00-18:00 JARAMILLO 의장주재)

- 개도국들은 구체적인 분쟁해결 절차는 서비스협정 발효이후 분쟁해결 그룹 협상 결과를 감안하여 결정하여야 한다는 입장을 견지하였으나 EC, 카나다, 일본등은 금융 분야에서 구체적 절차문제가 제기되었을 뿐만 아니라 일부 절차적 사항은 실체적규정과 함께 UR 에서 다룰필요가 있다고 주장하여 11.28 다음 사항에 대하여토의키로 함.

0 NON-VIOLATION

0 패널, 상소, 의사결정등 절차 문제

0 CROSS(SECTORAL) RETALIATION 및 보복배제대상(ACQUIRED RIGHTS 등)

0 제 1조, 5조, 6조, 15 및 인력이동 분속서등 타조문관련 사항. 끝

(대사 박수길-국장)

PAGE 2

0066

외　무　부

종　별 :

번　호 : GVW-2491　　　　　　　　　　　　일　시 : 91 1129 0900

수　신 : 장 관(수신처 참조)

발　신 : 주 제네바대사

제　목 : UR/GNS 회의(9)

　11.28(목) 속개된 주요국 비공식 협의 내용을 하기보고함.

　1. 금융부속서(11.28 오전 HAWES 대사 및 FRANKSWEDLOVE 공동주재)

　가. INSTITUTIONAL MACHINERY

　- HAWES 대사는 11.8 자 의장부속서 초안 및 미국제안에는 규정되어 있으나 FRAMEWORK 에 따른 각료들의 결정초안(11.25자)에는 누락된 금융서비스 기구의 기능중에서 다음 세가지는 각료들의 결정 초안이나 금융부속서에 반영될 수있을 것이라고 언급함.(분쟁해결 담당 기구문제는 당분간 유보)

　0 이사회와 서비스 분야별 기구와의 공동행동준비(각료들의 결정에 반영)

　0 자유화 협상 GUIDELINE 개발등 점진적 자유화과정에의 참여(각료들의 결정에 반영)

　0 부속서 규정의 해석(의사 결정기구에 대하여 추가검토 필요)

　- 미국 및 스위스, 카나다의 금융대표는 이사회의 기능과 분야별 기구의 기능이불명확하다고 전제하고 이사회의 기능중에서 금융서비스 기구에 위임되는 상황이 분명하게 규정되어야 하며 다음사항에 대하여 금융서비스 기구가 의사 결정권한을 행사하여 야 한다고 함.

　0 금융부속서 규정의 해석

　0 금융부속서 분쟁해결

　- GATT 법률국 및 EC의 GNS 대표, 개도국들은 협정규정(부속서 포함)의 해석에 대한 의사 결정권한은 체약국단에 귀속되는것이나 체약국단의 위임을 받아 이사회가 최종 결정을 하는 것이며 분야별 기구는 자문역할에 한정하여야 한다고 함.(각분야별기구가최종 결정을 할 경우 혼란 초래)

　- HAWES 대사는 토의 결과를 다음과 같이 요약함.

통상국 농수부	2차보 상공부	법무부 건설부	보사부 노동부	문화부 과기처	교통부 환경처	체신부 공보처	경기원	재무부

91.11.30　09:11 WH

외신 1과 통제관

0067

0 이사회는 무엇이든지 체약국단으로부터 모든 사항을 결정할 수 있으며 하부기구역시 이사회로부터 위임된사항은 무엇이든 할 수 있음.

0 협의,협상,권고안 작성등 1차적 실질문제는 분야별 기구의 고유 기능임

0 공식적인 결정, 협정 개정등의 담당기구가 문제인 바, 갓트 법률국 및 EC 견해와 같이 GATT 방식에 따라 구성할 필요가 있음.

나. 분쟁해결

- 사무국에서 미국제안과 의장 부속서초안, UR/분쟁해결 그룹초안의 비교표를 작성11.29(금) 토의키로 함

다. 조화 및 인정

- 미국제안에 대하여 HAWES 대사, EC 의 GNS대표 및 많은 나라가 동 제안 제 2항은 'LIKECIRCUMSTANCES' 를 구체화하였다는 점에서 긍정적으로 평가함.

0 그러나 제1항에 조화 및 인정대상을 'MEASURE'로 규정하는 것은 너무 광범위하다고 지적하고MEASURE 의 범위에 대하여 질의함.

- 미국 금융대표는 FRAMEWORK 에서 정의된 MEASURE 즉 모든 형태의 정부 규제가조화 및 인정 대상이라고 하였으며 EC 금융대표는 조화의 주요대상은 PRUDENTIAL MEASURE 라고 한바 미국은 동 PRUDENTIAL MEASURE 의 정의가 매우어려울 것이나 ILLUSTRATIVE LIST 작성은 유용할것이라고 함.

2. FRAMEWORK 상의 분쟁해결(11.28 오후 JARAMILLO의장 주재)

- '91.11.27 자 UR/분쟁해결 그룹의 협상 초안에 대하여 서비스 분야의 특성상 수정할 필요가 있는 사항만 검토하였는바 각국이 지적한 사항은 다음과 같음

0 패널 리스트의 자격 및 ROSTER 관련 서비스분야의 경험도 언급되어야 함

0 사무총장에 의한 PANELIST 선임시 이사회뿐 아니라 서비스 분야별 기구와의 협의도 필요

0 분쟁해결 관련 개도국 우대조항 재검토요(EC)

0 서비스 분야 전문가와의 협의를 단순한 자문에 한정할 것인지 재검토요

0 패널보고서 채택기관을 이사회로 한정할 것인지 재 검토요(분야별 기구에의 위임 여부)

0 의사결정 관련 이사회의 기능을 축소하고 자동화하는 것을 서비스 분야에도 그대로 적용할 것인지재검토요(인도, 멕시코)

0 상소기구의 필요여부 재검토요(인도)

PAGE 2

0 상소기구에 갓트 및 국제무역 전문가 뿐만 아니라 서비스 분야 전문가도 참여필요

0 CROSS-RETALITION 에 대하여 계층 구조(1차적으로 같은 서비스분야, 그다음에타서비스 분야, 최종적으로상품, 서비스간 보복허용) 설정 필요(EC)

3. 향후 협상 계획

- 11.29(금) 오전: 금융부속서 비공식 협의오후: GNS 공식회의(지금까지 협의 결과를 모든국가에 알리기 위한 것이며 FULL CLEAN TEXT 는 배부하지 못함)- 12.5(목) 부터 비공식 협의 속개(11월중 협의와 같은 형태)

0 12.5-6 및 주말: 해운 및 기타 운 송분야,분쟁해결(JARAMILLO 의장 담당분야)OHAWES 대사 담당분야 11.29 회의에서 결정 예정- 12.9 주부터 양자협의가 계획되어있는바 개도국뿐만 아니라 EC,카나다, 호 주등 선진국들도 FRAMEWORK 및 부속서에 대한 협상 때문에 현실적으로 양자협의 개최가 어렵다고 문제를 제기하였으나 JARAMILLO 의장은 FRAMEWORK 에대한 협상과 병행할 수 있을 것이라고 하여 결론을 내리지 못함.끝(대사 박수길-국장)수신처: 봉기, 경기원, 재무부,법무부,농림수산부,문화부,상공부,건설부,보사부,노동부,교통부,체신부,과기처, 공보처,환경처

외 무 부

종 별 :

번 호 : GVW-2516   일 시 : 91 1129 1930

수 신 : 장 관(수신처 참조)

발 신 : 주 제네바대사

제 목 : UR/GNS 회의(10)

　　11.28(금) 오전 속개된 주요국 비공식 협의와 동일오후 GNS 공식회의 내용을 하기
보고함.

　　1. 금융부속서에 대한 비공식 협의(HAWES 대사및 FRANK SWEDLOVE 공동주재)

　　가. 인정

　　- FRAMEWORK 제 7조(인정)의 상호인정 대상인 LICENSE, CERTIFICATION, 학력, 경
험등과는 달리MEASUR 를 조화 및 인정대상으로 하는 미국제안을 수정하여 금융분야의
PRUDENTIAL MEASURE만을 인정대상으로 추가하는 내용의 의장 초안이 새로 배부되었는
바

　　O 금융부속서에 PRUDENTIAL MEASURE 를 인정대상으로 추가하는데에는 별다른 이견
이 없었으나

　　O 동 의장 초안 1항에 FRAMEWORK 제 7조2항(이해관계국에 상호인정에 관한
협상참여기회제공) 및 4항 B) (상호인정에 관한 협상사전통지)를 배제하고 있는점과
관련금융분야에 동 조항의 적용을 배제할 이유가 없다는 의견이 제시되어 문안을
재작성 하기로 함.

　　나. 분쟁해결

　　- 미국, EC, 카나다, 스위스, 스웨덴, 말련등의 금융대표는 순수한 절차적 문제에
관한한 금융분야를 특별 취급하고자 하는 것은 아니며 금융서비스가 경제전체에
미치는 영향을 고려하여 동 분야의 분쟁해결이 금융전문가에 의해서 처리되어야
한다고 함.

　　O 또한 이들은 PRUDENTIAL MEASURE 의 경우 법률문제와 사실 문제의 구분이
어렵다는 이유로 상소기구의 역할을 법률심에 한정하는 것은 문제가 있다고 함

　　O 특히 EC 는 무엇이 PRUDENTIAL MEASURE 인가를 결정하는 것이 금융분야

통상국 상공부	2차보 건설부	법무부 노동부	보사부	문화부 해항청	교통부	경기원 공보처	재무부	농수부

PAGE 1   91.11.30   09:51 WH

외신 1과 통제관

0070

분쟁해결의 핵심문제가 될것이라고 지적하는 한편 최종 의사 결정기구는 일반적인 제도적규정에서 다룰수 있을 것이라고 함

  - 인도등 개도국들은 금융분야를 특별 취급할 특성을 발견하기 어렵다고 전제하고 다음과 같이논평함.

  0 관련 기구에의 대표임명은 개별국가 가자국 이익을 고려하여 각자 결정할 주권사항이며 이를 다자간 규칙을 설정하여 제한 하는 것은 부당함.

  0 분쟁해결 과정에 금융전문가의 참여도 일반적 분쟁해결 절차에 보장되어 있음.

  - 한편 개별과정의 분쟁해결 배제는 HORIZONTALISSUE 로서 추가 논의되어야 할 사항이라는 점과 서비스 분야간 보복과 관련 원칙적으로 동일분야에 한정하여야 한다는 점, 보복의 경우에도 기설립된 서비스 공급기업등 ACQUIRED RIGHTS 는 보호되어야한다는 점에는 별다른 이견이 없었음.

  다. 향후 작업계획

  - HAWES 대사는 다음주 중반 서비스의 특성을 고려한 분쟁해결 절차, 금융분야관련 특별취급이 예상되는 요소등에 관한 문서를 작성 배부하겠다고 함.

  0 차기 금융부속서 회의는 12.16 주에 개최예정(FRAMEWORK 토의를 우선하기 위한 것임)

  - 한편, INSTITUTIONAL MACHINERY 와 관련해결되어야 할 문제를 서면(FAX)으로 배부함.

  2. GNS 공식 회의

  - 필리핀, 알젠틴, 호주, 스위스, 인도가 INITIALOFFER 및 수정 OFFER 제안 설명을 함

  0 특히 알젠틴, 호주는 자국 OFFER 가 MFN 등 서비스협상 문제뿐만 아니라 타협상 그룹 특히 농산물 분야의 만족스러운 결과를 조건으로 하는것이라고 함.

  0 인도는 자국 OFFER 가 인력이동에 대해 무조건적인 COMMITMENT 를 하였다고 강조함

  - JARAMILL 의장 및 HAWES 대사는 각각 그간 비공식 협의를 거친 조문 초안을 배부함

  0 JARAMILL 의장 담당분야 : 제 6조, 7조, 14조, 16조,17조, ADDITIONAL COMMITMENT

  - 북구는 해운분야에 대한 비공식 초안(FAX송부)을 제출(12.12. 협의예정) 하였으

며 사무국에서는 예외 조항관련 조세문제에 관한 배경문서(FAX)를 배부함.

첨부: 1. 금융분야 INSTITUTIONAL MACHINERY 관련쟁점사항 1부

2. 해운분야 북구 비공식 제안 1부

3. 조세문제에 관한 사무국 배경문서 1부.

(GVW(F)-0563)끝

(대사   박수길-국장)수신처:

봉기, 경기원, 재무부, 법무부, 농림수산부, 문하부상공부, 건설부, 보사부, 노동부, 교통부, 채신부, 과기처, 공보처, 항만청)

Gvw(b)-563   1112P1P00
Gvw-2516 원본

<u>Informal Statement by Ambassador Hawes</u>

<u>Co-Chairman of the Group of Negotiations on Services</u>

<u>on 29 November 1991</u>

<u>Summary of outstanding issues: Institutional Machinery</u>

It appears widely agreed that there should be a committee on financial
services. This committee should be established by the Council of the GATS
as a subsidiary body with responsibilities assigned by the Council.

Regarding the assignment of responsibilities, the three texts under
consideration (Article XXV and the draft Ministerial Decision, the
Co-chairman's text, and the United States' proposal) appear to be
consistent in key respects. They all call for the assignment of a variety
of deliberative responsibilities as well as an advisory role to such a
committee on matters relating to the sector.

There remain, however, certain issues that need to be identified and
reflected upon further. These issues are in many respects linked to
outstanding questions about what may be the hierarchical relationship among
the PARTIES of the GATS, the GATS Council, and its subsidiary bodies. (It
is possible that these issues might also be affected by decisions on
Uruguay Round instruments overall.) Such questions relate to the
distribution of authority among the various bodies to be established and
the nature of weight and influence that the activities of these bodies will
exercise on one another. Some of the principal issues that may require
further consideration are listed below.

<u>Joint Action</u>

It is not agreed what authorities a financial services or other
sectoral committee may have in decision making or the taking of joint

8-HAW

563-12-1   0073

- 2 -

action by the PARTIES when it is related to the sector. The draft
Ministerial decision indicates that a committee would make recommendations
or proposals to the Council, and, as such, the Council would consider and
take appropriate action. The Co-chairman's text calls for an approach in
which the PARTIES and the committee would cooperate (the committee would
"participate in the preparation of joint action"). These two proposals
could be viewed as consistent; the first indicates the way in which
cooperation between the two bodies would be undertaken and the second is
open regarding how "participation" would be defined, but essentially
underlines the importance of this function to the committee's activities.
The United States' proposal calls for the delegation of the
responsibilities of the PARTIES for joint action to the committee for
matters relating to financial services. The United States' proposal also
indicates that prior to adopting decisions, the committee "shall consult
with other relevant bodies", presumably including the Council.

Dispute settlement

There also remains disagreement regarding what role a financial
services or other sectoral committee should play in dispute settlement. As
it stands, the draft Ministerial Decision is silent on the question of
dispute settlement. Both the text of the Co-chairman and that of the
United States call for the responsibilities of the PARTIES with respect to
dispute settlement to be delegated to the committee when the obligations
and commitments involved relate to financial services; one difference is
that the text of the Co-chairman's text limits this role to disputes which
"exclusively" involve financial services.

Progressive liberalization

The text of the United States explicitly assigns a role for a
financial services committee in progressive liberalization. It calls for
"participation" of the committee in the process, rather than for an
outright delegation of the responsibilities of the PARTIES. It also
specifies that the committee would participate in the elaboration of

S-HAW

0074

- 3 -

negotiating guidelines for the sector. While not explicitly granting such a role in progressive liberalization to sectoral committees, the draft Ministerial Declaration could be viewed as envisioning ways in which a committee could contribute to the process, partly under item (d) on technical activities, but also under item (b) in which the scope of proposals and recommendations that the committee may forward to the Council is open-ended.

Interpretation of the Agreement

Under item (b), the United States' proposal calls for the financial services committee to undertake "examination of technical issues" including advisory opinions and interpretation of specific provisions of the financial services annex. In view of item (e) of that text, the committee would presumably have the authority to adopt these as binding opinions and interpretation. The provision indicates that interpretations relating to financial services of the application of the provisions of the Agreement (parts other than the annex) would be undertaken in consultation with the Council. Again, an advisory and interpretive role of the committee is possible under item (b) of the draft Ministerial Decision, but the Council retains the authority to adopt such advisory opinions or interpretive notes.

Possible points for further consideration

The four issues cited above are interrelated to a significant degree. Wherever the boundaries among bodies are drawn, it is clear that such a committee would have a comprehensive and important deliberative role with respect to matters relating to financial services. Moreover, dispute prevention comes before dispute settlement; the deliberations if a financial services committee would facilitate the development of rules that reduce uncertainty and help prevent disputes. Therefore, possible points to consider with respect to these issues, whether addressed in a Ministerial or an Annex, include:

B-HAW

0075

563-12-3

- 4 -

- To what extent should a subsidiary body be delegated authorities
  that will result in obligations that are binding on all Parties.

- To what extent might the exercise of these authorities by a
  sectoral body incur obligations that bind Parties in other
  sectors as well.

- Are there certain types of instruments or issues that a sectoral
  body should be permitted to decide or adopt on its own authority
  (e.g. reports on technical matters), and others which it should
  not, even if the sector may be affected?

8-HAW

5/3 -12- 4

0076

COMMUNICATION FROM THE NORDIC COUNTRIES

Explanatory notes to paragraphs 3, 5 and 6
MTN/GNS/W/135

International Shipping (paragraph 3)

Paragraph 3(b) foresees commitments by Parties to undertake in particular the following actions:

- Elimination of cargo sharing agreements, as being inconsistent with the m.f.n. discipline;

- Progressive elimination of unilateral cargo reservation schemes and opening of access to non-military government cargoes, as measures to open market access;

- Progressive elimination of discriminatory measures affecting foreign shipping companies in the supply of international shipping services as compared with national companies. This does not extend to support systems falling within the scope of Article XV of the framework.

The priorities to achieve in these actions, as well as the conditions under which flexibility can be provided to developing countries in this programme, should be further discussed and detailed at a later stage.

Auxiliary services as supplied by maritime transport operators (paragraph 5)

Paragraph 5 aims at ensuring a progressive liberalization of auxiliary services which normally are, or may be, offered by suppliers of international shipping services (see illustrative list).

0077
37-MISC4

- 2 -

Auxiliary services may be provided by the maritime transport operator directly, or sub-contracted with a local company.

Each Party shall commit itself not to impose new restrictions on such auxiliary services which are supplied or offered by maritime transport operators, relating to cargoes which are transported on vessels.

The kind of liberalization foreseen may for some services induce shipping companies to request the right to establish locally a subsidiary and/or an agency in order to supply these auxiliary services. The issue of establishment is, however, also to be covered directly by the framework agreement.

In the case of loading/unloading the emphasis may be on the possibility for the vessel to use its own equipment when practicable, or for the local agency/subsidiary to rent or use its own equipment.

The standstill set out in paragraph 5a shall be implemented. In addition, Parties should make commitments to remove existing restrictive measures with respect to certain items.

Illustrative list of auxiliary services relevant to paragraph 5

- Loading and unloading;
- Cargo handling within the port or inland terminal confines;
- Stevedoring, warehousing and storage;
- Clearing cargo with customs, including making cargo available for inspection when required;
- [Customs brokerage];
- Onward transport on a through bill of lading;
- [Freight forwarding].

37-MISC4 0078

- 3 -

Auxiliary services as required by maritime transport operators (paragraph 6)

Each Party shall ensure that access to and use of publicly available port infrastructure services (see illustrative list) offered within or from its territory is accorded to maritime transport services and suppliers of such services of other Parties on reasonable and non-discriminatory terms and conditions.

In this view, Parties shall ensure that when such services are supplied by monopolies or exclusive service providers, these providers operate in accordance with commercial considerations and shall not act in a manner inconsistent with the Parties commitments under this agreement.

When port infrastructure services for the provision of maritime transport services are supplied by private operators, Parties shall not prevent any services supplier under its jurisdiction from acting in accordance with the principle set out above, nor prevent maritime transport service suppliers of other Parties to choose freely among available services suppliers.

Reasonable terms and conditions commit each Party to ensure that rules and practices governing access to and use of such facilities shall be administered in an objective, impartial and transparent manner, including as regards the charges collected for the use of these services. However, Parties will not be required to construct new or expand existing port infrastructure services in order to meet the commitments referred to above.

Non-discriminatory terms and conditions commit each Party to accord to services and service providers of any other Party, in respect of all measures affecting the access to and use of port infrastructure services treatment no less favourable than it accords to its own like services and like service providers.

Repair of ships and related equipment is not covered by this commitment.

0079

37-MISC4

경 제 기 획 원

우 427-760 / 경기도 과천시 중앙동1 정부제2청사 / 전화 503-9149 / 전송 503-9141

문서번호 봉조삼 10502-844

시행일자 1991. 11. 28.

선결			지시		
접수	일자시간	91.11.20 :	결재·공람		
	번호	40036			
처리과					
담당자					

수신 수신처참조

참조 통상기구과

〈기 FAX 시행〉

제목 UR서비스 양자협의를 위한 관계부처 회의개최

────────────────────────────────────

　　　1. 현재 우리나라에 Request를 한 국가는 미국, EC, 일본, 캐나다, 호주, 스위스, 스웨덴, 노르웨이, 핀랜드, 인도등 10개국이며 12월 8일주에 이들 국가들과 스위스 제네바에서 양자협의를 할 예정이며 미국과는 12월 10일로 협상일자가 확정되었습니다.

　　　2. 이에 따라 상대국의 Request 사항에 대한 대응방안과 우리의 상대국에 대한 Request 사항에 대한 요구논리등을 논의하기 위한 관계부처회의를 별첨과 같이 개최코자 하니 분야별 협상대책자료를 지참하고 반드시 참석하여 주기 바랍니다.

　　　첨부 : UR서비스 양자협의 추진대책 1부.　　끝.

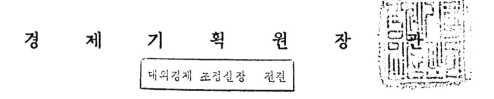

경 제 기 획 원 장

대외경제 조정실장 전결

수신처 : 외무부장관, 내무부장관, 재무부장관, 법무부장관, 교육부장관, 문화부장관,
　　　　농림수산부장관, 상공부장관, 보건사회부장관, 건설부장관, 교통부장관,
　　　　노동부장관, 동자부장관, 체신부장관, 체육청소년부장관, 과학기술처장관,
　　　　환경처장관, 공보처장관, 특허청장, 해운항만청장, 대외경제정책연구원장,
　　　　한국개발연구원장

0080

UR/서비스 兩者協議(12월 8일주) 推進對策

Ⅰ. 兩者協議概要

1. 協商對象國家 및 日程

- 美國 : 12월 10일(火)

- EC, 日本, 캐나다, 濠洲, 스위스, 스웨덴, 노르웨이, 핀랜드,
  印度등 9개국 : 未定

2. 場所

- 대부분 GATT 會議室에서 진행할 것으로 예상

3. 議題

- Request를 바탕으로 各國의 서비스市場 開放에 대한 구체적
  인 협상진행

Ⅱ. 推進對策

1. 協商代表團의 構成

가. 出張期間(暫定) : 12.8∼12.14

나. 代表團構成
  - 首席代表 : 經濟企劃院 第2協力官
  - 代　　表
    ○ 財務部, 商工部, 建設部, 交通部, 遞信部등 상대국에게
      Request한 部處는 반드시 참석하고 기타 關聯部處도
      가급적 참여
    ○ KIEP, KDI의 專門家도 참석

0081

2. 關係部處會議 開催

- 場　　所 : 經濟企劃院 小會議室(과천청사 1동 721호)

- 參席對象 : 經濟企劃院 第2協力官(會議主宰)
　　　　　　 關係部處의 擔當課長
　　　　　　 KIEP 성극제博士, 김태준博士
　　　　　　 KDI　김지홍博士

- 持參資料

　① 相對國의 Request에 대한 對應方案

　　ㅇ Request 事項이 중복되더라도 國別로 각각 별도의
　　　 자료를 항목별로 旣 通報한 作成樣式(통조삼 10502-
　　　 790<'91.11.8>)에 따라 작성

　② 우리의 Request에 대한 要求論理

　　ㅇ 相對國에게 Request한 財務部, 商工部, 建設部,
　　　 交通部, 遞信部등 5개부처는 各 項目別로 相對國의
　　　 規制事項이 포함된 要求論理를 다음과 같은 양식에
　　　 따라 國·英文으로 작성

Request	要　求　論　理

　　· A4용지를 옆으로 뉘여서 作成하되 國文을 먼저
　　　 쓰고 그 아래에 英文으로 기재

0082

- 各 部處別 會議日程 및 所管業種

日　時	對象部處	業　種
12. 3(火) 10:00-12:00	科技處	엔지니어링, 기술테스트 및 분석, 과학 및 기술컨설팅, 컴퓨터관련서비스
	建設部	도시계획 및 조경, 장비임대, 장비의 유지 및 수선, 건설, 부동산관련서비스
	內務部	부동산관련서비스, 건물청소
	農林水産部	농업, 임업, 수렵, 어업관련서비스
	動資部	광업 및 유전에 부수되는 서비스
14:00-17:00	法務部	법무서비스
	文化部	시청각서비스, 사진, 번역 및 통역, 인쇄 및 출판
	公報處	광고, 시장조사 및 여론조사
	勞動部	인력배급 및 공급, 印度가 요구한 인력이동사항(보사부, 교통부, 과기처, 관련사항 취합)
	環境處	하수처리 및 위생
	文敎部	기술및 직업교육, 초등.중등.성인교육
12. 4(水) 10:00-12:00	遞信部	전기통신
	交通部	육운, 항공, 장비임대, 장비의 유지 및 수선, 상업서류송달, 관광
	海運港灣廳	해운
14:00-17:00	商工部	유통, 제조업관련 컨설팅, 건설이외의 설치 및 조립, 포장
	財務部	은행, 보험, 증권, 회계, 장비임대, 경영컨설팅

0083

경 제 기 획 원

우 427-760 / 경기도 과천시 중앙동1 정부제2청사 / 전화 503-9149 / 전송 503-9141

문서번호 봉조삼 10502-892

시행일자 1991. 12. 3.

수신 수신처참조

참조

선결			지시		
접수	일자시간	91.12.5	결재·공람		
	번호	40532			
	처리과				
	담당자				

제목 UR/서비스 협상관련 각국의 Offer List 배포

　　　최근에 각국이 GATT에 제출한 인도의 Initial Offer List와 스위스의 수정 Offer List를 별첨과 같이 배포하니 UR/서비스협상 대책추진에 만전을 기해 주시기 바랍니다.

　　　아울러 '91년 11월말 현재 Offer를 제출한 국가는 43개국이며 이중 EC, 호주, 스위스는 새로운 양허표 작성방식에 따라서 수정 양허표를 제출하였음을 알려 드립니다.

별첨 : 1. 각국의 Initial Offer List(V)
　　　 2. 각국의 수정 Offer List(Ⅱ). 끝.

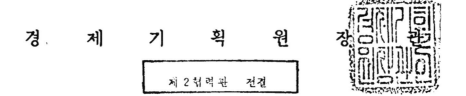

경 제 기 획 원 장

제2협력관 전결

수신처 : 외무부장관, 내무부장관, 재무부장관, 법무부장관, 교육부장관, 문화부장관,
　　　　농림수산부장관, 상공부장관, 보건사회부장관, 건설부장관, 교통부장관,
　　　　노동부장관, 동자부장관, 체신부장관, 체육청소년부장관, 과학기술처장관,
　　　　환경처장관, 공보처장관, 특허청장, 해운항만청장, 대외경제정책연구원장,
　　　　한국개발연구원장

0084

외 무 부

원 본

종 별 :

번 호 : GVW-2561   일   시 : 91 1205 1700

수 신 : 장 관(수신처 참조)

발 신 : 주 제네바 대사

제 목 : UR / 서비스 양자협의

1. 12.9 주간에 개최 예정인 표제 양자 협의 관련현재까지 마련된 잠정 일정을 하기 보고함.

- 12.10(화) 09:30: 미국

- 12.11(수) 09:30 EC

15:00: 스웨덴

- 12.12(목): 카나다 (시간미정)

- 12.13(금) 09:00: 핀랜드

2. 상기 협의는 금융.증권을 포함한 전분야를대상으로 할 예정임. 끝

(대사 박수길-국장)

수신처:(봉기, 경기원, 재무부, 법무부, 농림수산부, 문화부, 상공부, 건설부, 보사부, 노동부 ,교통부, 체신부, 과기처, 공보처, 항만청)

| 통상국 | 법무부 | 보사부 | 문화부 | 교통부 | 체신부 | 경기원 | 재무부 | 농수부 |
| 상공부 | 건설부 | 노동부 | 과기처 | 해항정 | 공보처 | | | |

PAGE 1   91.12.06   04:40 FO

외신 1과 통제관

0085

외 무 부

110-760 서울 종로구 세종로 77번지 / (02)720-2188 / (02)725-1737

문서번호 통기 20644-

시행일자 1991.12. 6.(   )

수신 내부결재

참조

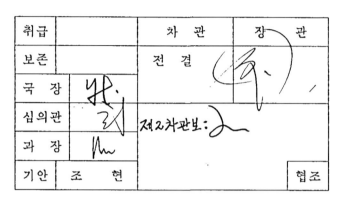

제목 UR/서비스 협상 정부대표 임명

91.12.9-13간 제네바에서 개최되는 UR/서비스 협상 주요국간 양자협의 참가할 정부대표단을 "정부대표 및 특별사절의 임명과 권한에 관한 법률"에 의거 아래와 같이 임명코자 건의하오니 재가하여 주시기 바랍니다.

- 아   래 -

1. 회 의 명 : UR/서비스 협상, 주요국간 양자협의

2. 회의 개최기간 및 장소 : 91.12.9-13, 제네바

3. 양자협의 대상국

   ㅇ 미국, EC, 일본, 캐나다, 호주, 스위스, 스웨덴, 노르웨이, 핀랜드, 인도

4. 정부대표단

   ㅇ 수석대표 : 경제기획원 제2협력관   이윤재

   ㅇ 대   표 : 경제기획원 통상조정3과 사무관   김용준

                재 무 부 국제금융과 사무관   윤여권

                       보험정책과 사무관   임승태

                법 무 부 국제법무심의관실 검사 김영철

                교 통 부 국제협력과 사무관   황성연

0086

채 신 부 정보산업국 사무관   김명룡

건 설 부 국제경제과 사무관   박기풍

ㅇ 자   문 : KIEP 연구위원   성극제

김태준

KDI 연구위원   김지홍

5. 출장기간 : 91.12.8-14 92. 1. 26 - 2. 2

6. 소요경비 : 해당부처 소관예산

7. 훈   령 :

ㅇ 아국에 대해 Request list를 제출한 국가들과의 양자협의를 통해
  상대국의 Request 사항을 명료히 하고, 아국이 이미 전달한 offer
  list 범위내에서 이들의 요구를 수용한다는 원칙으로 대응토록 함.

ㅇ 아국이 상대국에 제출한 Request list의 내용과 배경을 설명,
  상대국측의 이해와 협조를 요청토록 함.

ㅇ UR/GNS 협상의 주요쟁점에 관한 각국의 입장등 관련 정보를 파악토록 함.

끝.

외 무 부 장 관

0087

건 설 부

우 427-760 경기 과천 중앙 1 / 전화 (02) 503 - 7396 / 전송 503 - 7409

문서번호 해외 30600-33722

시행일자 1991. 12. 3   (1년)

선결			지시	
접수	일자시간	91·12·5	결재·공람	
	번호	40531		
	처리과			
	담당자			

수신 수신처 참조

참조

제목 UR/서비스 협상회의 참가에 따른 협조 요청

'91. 12. 10 ~ 13간 스위스 제네바에서 개최되는 UR/서비스 건설분야 양허협상의 정부
대표단의 일원으로 우리부 관계관을 다음과 같이 참석시키고자하니, 필요한 조치를 취하여
주시기 바랍니다.

다   음

1. 회 의 명 : UR/서비스 양자협의

2. 회의기간 및 장소 : '91. 12. 10 ~ 12. 13. 스위스 제네바

3. 참가자 소속 및 직.성명

   ○ 건설부 건설경제국 건설경제과 행정사무관   박 기 풍
   (자 문)

   ○ 국토개발원 건설경제연구실 수석 연구원   김 흥 수

4. 출장기간 : '91. 12. 8 ~ 12. 14.

건   설   부   장

건설경제국장 전결

수신처 : 경제기획원 장관, 외무부 장관

0088

재 무 부

우 427-760 경기도 과천시 중앙동 1 / 전화 (02)503-9266 / 전송 503-9324

문서번호 국금 22251-1748

시행일자 '91. 12. 4 ( )

수신 수신처 참조

참조

선결			지시		
접수	일자시간	91.12.6	결재·공탐		
	번호	40685			
	처리과				
	담당자				

제목 UR 서비스 양자협상 참석자 통보

1. 등조삼 10502-844('91.11.28)와 관련입니다.

2. UR 서비스협상과 관련 스위스 제네바에서 '91.12.9~13간 개최되는 양자협상에 참석할 당부대표를 아래와 같이 파견코자 하오니 필요한 조치를 취해주시기 바랍니다.

아   래

소 속	성 명	기 간
국제금융과 사무관	윤 여 권	'91.12.8 ~ 15
보험정책과 사무관	임 승 태	"

첨부 : 회의 참석 대책.   끝.

재 무 부 장

차 관 전 결

수신처 : 경제기획원장관, 외무부장관   0089

UR 서비스 양자협상 참여

1. 협상 개요

- 일시 및 장소

  o 1991. 12. 9 ~ 13, GATT

- 협상대상국

  o 미국, EC, 일본, 캐나다 등 Request 제출 10개국

- 의 제

  o Request를 제출한 국가간의 양자협상

- 대표단 구성

  o EPB 제2협력관외 관계부처 실무자 및 KIEP, KDI 전문가

  o 당부는 사무관 2인 참석

2. 협상 대책

- 아국은 미국, EC 등 주요국으로부터 Request를 받았으나 대부분
  한·미 금융정책회의시 제기된 사안들로서

  o 미국과는 그간 양자협의를 통하여 아국금융현안에 대하여 충분히
    논의하였으며, 이에 대한 양국간의 상호이해가 존재

  o EC 등 여타국에 대해서도 이를 기본 position으로 양허협상에 대처

- 또한, 아국이 제출한 Request를 제기함으로 상대국의 금융장벽을 부각
  시키고 아국의 금융여건 및 금융시장 개방정책을 설명

0030

3. 아국에 대한 Request 검토

가. 제출 국가

- '91.12 현재 <u>10개국</u>이 금융분야에 대해 <u>Request List</u>를 제출

    o 이중 미국, EC, 일본, 호주, 스위스, 카나다 등 <u>6개국이 구체적인</u>
      <u>개방요구</u>를 하였으나,

    o 핀란드, 노르웨이, 스웨덴, 인도 등은 <u>현존 규제조치의 동결</u> 또는
      선진국이 제시한 <u>Negative 방식의 자유화 추진 수용</u>을 요구

나. 주요 요구사항

- 외국금융기관의 <u>국내진출 형태에 대한 규제 완화</u>
    o 현지법인 설립 요구

- <u>외국은행의 영업기반 확충</u>
    o Call 시장, CD 발행제도 개선
    o 본점자본금 인정
    o 신상품 도입 규제 완화

- 외국인의 <u>국내 주식투자 규제 완화</u>

- <u>보험중개업 허용</u>

0091

4. 주요국가에 대한 Request

가. 대상 국가

- 선진국을 위주로 작성하였으며 ASEAN 등 선발개도국의 경우 SEACEN 국가의 일원으로 금융부속서 협상시 공동보조를 취한 것을 감안하여 추후 양자협의시 고려

  o 미국, EC, 일본, 캐나다, 스위스, 호주 등 6개국

나. 대상분야 및 주요 요구사항

- 현재 우리 금융기관이 기진출하여 영업을 하고 있는 은행. 보험업을 위주로 함.

- 은 행
  o 은행 진출형태 제한 폐지(미), BOJ의 재할인한도 확대(일), 복수점포장제도 폐지(독), 한국계은행의 여신한도규제 폐지(불), 이사의 국적요건 완화(스), 지점형태 진출 허용(카), Trading banks 설립 요구(호) 등 37개 사항

- 보 험
  o 주별 면허제 폐지(미), 역외국에 대한 지불능력요구 차별 폐지(영), 보험사 주식투자 제한 폐지(불). 외국보험사 광고제한 폐지(네) 등 9개 사항

0092

경 제 기 획 원

우 427-760 / 경기도 과천시 중앙동1 정부제2청사 / 전화 503-9149 / 전송 503-9141

문서번호 통조삼 10502- 867
시행일자 1991. 12. 6.

수신 외무부장관
참조 통상국장

선결			지시		
접수	일자 시간	. . :	결재·공람		
	번호				
처리과					
담당자					

제목 UR/서비스 양자협의 참석

1. 스위스 제네바에서 개최되는 UR/서비스 양자협의 및 UR전반의 마무리협상에 다음과 같이 참석코자 하니 협조하여 주기 바랍니다.

- 다 음 -

가. 출장자

① UR/서비스 양자협의(12.8~12.14)

- 수석대표 : 경제기획원 제2협력관 이윤재

- 대 표 : 경제기획원 통상조정3과 사무관 김용준
  재 무 부 국제금융과 사무관 윤여권
  보험정책과 사무관 임승태
  법 무 부 국제법무심의관실 검사 김영철
  교 통 부 국제협력과 사무관 황성연
  체 신 부 정보산업국 사무관 김명룡
  건 설 부 국제경제과 사무관 박기풍

- 자 문 관 : KIEP 연구위원 성극제
  김태준
  KDI 연구위원 김지홍

0093

② UR전반의 마무리협상(12.15~12.21)

　　　- 경제기획원　제2협력관　　　　　이운재
　　　　　　　봉상조정3과 사무관　김용준

나. 출 장 지 : 스위스 제네바

다. 경비부담 : 경제기획원, 각부처, KIEP, KDI등

첨부 : 출장일정 1부.　끝.

경　제　기　획　원　　장　

0094

出 張 日 程

'91. 12. 8(日)   12:40   서울발(KE 901)
                18:10   파리착
                20:45   파리발(SR 729)
                21:45   제네바착

12. 9(月) ┐
          ├   UR/서비스 兩者協議
~12.14(土) ┘

12. 15(日) ┐
           ├   UR全般의 마무리協商 參席
~12. 19(木) ┘

12.20(金)   18:05   제네바발(AF 960)
            19:10   파리착
            20:30   파리발(KE 902)

12.21(土)   17:40   서울착

0095

교　　　통　　　부   [도사전송]

우100-162 서울 중구 봉래동2가 122   / 전화 (02) 392-7396 / 전송 (02)392-9809

문서번호	국협10502-/3234		선견			지시	
시행일자	1991. 12. 6 ( )		집	일자	· ·	결	
(경유)				시간	:	재	
			수	번호		공	
수　　신	수신처참조(외무부)		처 리 과			람	
참　　조	통상기구과		담 당 자				
제　　목	UR/서비스협상 양자협의 참가						

　　　'91.12.10 - 13 개최예정인 미국, EC, 스웨덴등과의 UR/서비스협상 양자협의와

관련, 당부 참석자 명단을 아래와 같이 통보하오니 필요한 조치를 취하여 주시기 바랍니다.

- 아　　　래 -

소　　속	직　급	성　명
수송정책실 국제협력과	행정사무관	황성연 (Hwang, Sung Yeon)

교　　통　　부　　장

[차 관 전 결]

0096

- 알뜰한 엄마 검소한 아빠 건강한 사회 -

체 신 부

110-777 서울 종로구 세종로 100   /(02) 750-2341   /(02) 750-2915

문서번호 통협 34400-8963

시행일자 1991. 12. 5

수신 외무부장관

선결			지시		
접수	일자시간	91 . 1ｙ. 6 :	결재·공람		
	번호	40687			
처리과					
담당자					

제목 UR.GNS양허협상 참가

1. 경제기획원 통조삼 10502-844 (91.11.28) 관련

2. 위 관련 UR/GNS한.미 양허협상 및 우리나라에 Request 를 제출한 EC,일본등 기타 국가와의 공식.비공식 협상이 91.12.10(화-12.13(금) 스위스 제네바에서 개최되는 바, 동 협상에 대한 통신분야 전문가를 아래와 같이 참석케 하고자 하오니 적극 협조하여 주시기 바랍니다.

　　　가. 참가자 및 출장기간

　　　　O 출 장 자 : 체신부 행정사무관 김명룡

　　　　O 출장기간 : 91.12.8(일)-12.15(일) (8일간). 끝.

체 신 부 장

차 관 전결

0097

법   무   부

국심 20411- **27159** (503-9505)   1991. 12. 7

수신 외무부장관

제목 UR 서비스 양자협의 참석대표 추천

91년 12월 스위스 제네바에서 개최되는 우루과이라운드 서비스 양자
협의 본부일원으로 아래 사람이 참석할 수 있도록 협조하여 주시기 바랍
니다.

아   래

0 소 속 : 국제법무심의관실

0 출장자 : 김 영 철

0 직 위 : 검사

0 생년월일 : 1959. 2. 27

0 출장지 : 스위스 제네바

0 경 비 : 당부 부담

첨부 : 국·영문 이력서 1부.   끝.

법   무   부

외 무 부

110-760 서울 종로구 세종로 77번지 / (02)720-2188 / (02)725-1737

문서번호 통기 20644- **61387**

시행일자 1991.12. 7.( )

수신 수신처 참조

참조

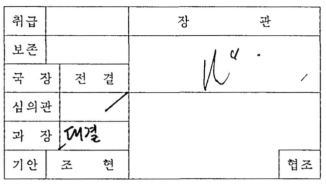

취급		장 관
보존		
국 장	전 결	
심의관		
과 장	대결	
기안	조 현	협조

제목 UR/서비스 협상 정부대표 임명 통보

91.12.9-13간 제네바에서 개최되는 UR/서비스 협상 주요국간 양자협의 참가할
정부대표단이 "정부대표 및 특별사절의 임명과 권한에 관한 법률"에 의거 아래와 같이
임명 되었음을 통보합니다.

- 아 래 -

1. 회 의 명 : UR/서비스 협상, 주요국간 양자협의

2. 회의 개최기간 및 장소 : 91.12.9-13, 제네바

3. 양자협의 대상국

  ㅇ 미국, EC, 일본, 캐나다, 호주, 스위스, 스웨덴, 노르웨이, 핀랜드, 인도

4. 정부대표단

  ㅇ 수석대표 : 경제기획원 제2협력관   이윤재

  ㅇ 대   표 : 주 제네바 대표부 관계관

            경제기획원 통상조정3과 사무관   김용준

            재 무 부 국제금융과 사무관   윤여권

                  보험정책과 사무관   임승태

            법 무 부 국제법무심의관실 검사 김영철

            교 동 부 국제협력과 사무관   황성연

0099

I

체 신 부 정보산업국 사무관   김명룡

건 설 부 국제경제과 사무관   박기풍

ㅇ 자　문 : KIEP 연구위원   성극제

김태준

KDI 연구위원   김지홍

5.　출장기간 : 91.12.8-14

6.　소요경비 : 해당부처 소관예산

7.　출장 결과 보고 : 2주일이내.   끝.

수신처 : 경제기획원장관, 재무부장관, 법무부장관, 교통부장관, 체신부장관,

건설부장관.

외　무　부　장　관

0100

2

분류번호	보존기간

발 신 전 보

번 호 : WGV-1785   911207 1151 DU   종별 :

수 신 : 주   제네바   대사. 총영사

발 신 : 장 관 (통 기)

제 목 : UR/서비스 협상

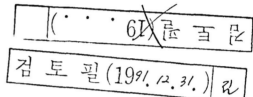
검 토 필 (1991. 12. 31.) 김

대 : GVW-2561

　　　대호 12.9 주간에 개최 예정인 UR/서비스 협상 양자협의에 참가할 정부대표가 아래 임명되었음.

- 아 　　　　 래 -

1. 정부대표단

　　ㅇ 수석대표 : 경제기획원 제2협력관　　　　　이윤재

　　ㅇ 대　　표 : 주 제네바 대표부 관계관

　　　　　　　　경제기획원 통상조정3과 사무관　김용준

　　　　　　　　재 무 부 국제금융과 사무관　　윤여권

　　　　　　　　　　　　보험정책과 사무관　　임승태

　　　　　　　　법 무 부 국제법무심의관실 검사 김영철

　　　　　　　　교 통 부 국제협력과 사무관　　황성연

　　　　　　　　체 신 부 정보산업국 사무관　　김명룡

　　　　　　　　건 설 부 국제경제과 사무관　　박기풍

보 안 통 제	

앙고재	91년 12월 7일	통기과	기안자 성명	조현	과 장	심의관	국 장 전결	차 관	장 관	외신과통제

0101

o 자   문 : KIEP 연구위원   성극제

                                           김태준

   KDI 연구위원   김지홍

   국토개발원 건설경제연구실 수석연구원   김흥수

2. 출장기간 : 91.12.8-14

3. 훈   령 :

   o 아국에 대해 Request list를 제출한 국가들과의 양자협의를 통해 상대국의
     Request 사항을 명료히 하고, 아국이 이미 전달한 offer list 범위내에서
     이들의 요구를 수용한다는 원칙으로 대응토록 함.

   o 아국이 상대국에 제출한 Request list의 내용과 배경을 설명, 상대국측의
     이해와 협조를 요청토록 함.

   o UR/GNS 협상의 주요쟁점에 관한 각국의 입장등 관련 정보를 파악토록 함.

                                 끝.   (통상국장   김 용 규)

0102

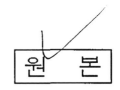

외 무 부

종 별 :

번 호 : GVW-2589　　　　　　　　　일 시 : 91 1210 1230

수 신 : 장 관(수신처 참조)

발 신 : 주 제네바 대사

제 목 : UR / GNS (1)

12.9(월) 오후 JARAMILLO 의장 주재로 개최된 주요국 비공식 협의 내용 을 하기보고함.

　　1. 협의 진행 계획(잠정)

　　- 12.9(월) 오후: 분쟁해결 (JARAMILLO 의장 주재)

　　- 12.10(화) 오후: 제 7조(인정), 제 14조(예외),(HAWES 대사 주재)

　　12.11(수) 오전: 제 7조(인정), 제 14조(예외), (HAWES대사 주재)

　　오후: 제 10조(세이프가드), 제 11조(지급 및 이전), 제12조(BOP), 제13조(정부조달), 제 15조(보조금),(JARAMILLO 의장 주재)

　　- 12.12(목) 오전: 해운, 항공등 운송분야(JARAMILLO 의장 주재)

　　오후: MFN (JARAMILLO 의장 주재)

　　- 12.13(금) 오전: 제 6조(국내규제), 제16조(시장접근), 제 17조(내국민대우),(HAWES대사 주재)

　　오후: 제 5조(경제통합), 제 34조(용어의 정의),(JARAMILLO 의장 주재)

　　- 12.15 주에는 금융, 봉신 부속서를 협의할예정이며, 의장은 동 부속서 협의 개시 이전에FRAMEWORK 의 대부분의 조문을 완료하기 바란다고함.

　　2. 분쟁해결에 관한 협의 개요

　　- 갓트 사무국에서 11.28 주요국 비공식 협의 결과를 감안하여 갓트 분쟁해결 절차의 서비스 분야원용시 수정이 필요한 다음 사항을 정리 문서로배부 토의함.

　　0 전문가의 역할, 각 기구간 관할권, 개별결정의 분쟁해결 의뢰 여부, NON-VIOLATION,상소절차, 보상및 양허의 정지(보복)

　　- 각 잇슈별로 각국의 기본 입장에는 변동이없었으나 상기 요소들의 법적 규정 방법에대하여는 개별 결정의 분쟁해결 의뢰여부 및NON-VIOLATION, 서비스 분야간

통상국	법무부	보사부	문화부	교통부	체신부	경기원	재무부	농수부
상공부	건설부	노동부	과기처	해항정	공보처			

PAGE 1　　　　　　　　　　　　　　　　　　91.12.11　00:39 FO

　　　　　　　　　　　　　　　　　　　　外신 1과　통제관

　　　　　　　　　　　　　　　　　　　　　　　　0103

보복문제를제외하고는 FRAMEWORK 에 반영하기에 부적합한절차적 규정이라는데 대체적으로 합의가 형성됨.

- 이에 따라 사무국에서 FRAMEWORK 이외의 곳에반영할 절차적 규정들을 DRAFT DECISION 형태로작성하여 재토의키로 함.

3. MFN 예외

- 사무국에서 MFN 일탈 협상 절차, MFN 일탈신청양식, MFN 일탈에 관한 부속서 등의 초안(FAX 송부)을 작성 배부함. (12.12 토의예정)

0 동 초안중 MFN 일탈 신청 양식에 따라 아국이요청할 사항을 작성, 송부 바람.

첨부: MFN 일탈 절차에 관한 사무국문서 1부. 끝

(GVW(F)-590)

수신처: 통기, 경기원, 재무부, 법무부, 농림수산부, 문화부, 상공부, 건설부, 보사부, 노동부 ,교통부, 체신부, 과기처, 공보처, 항만청)

(대사 박수길-국장)

PAGE 2

0104

주 제 네 바 대 표 부

번 호 : GVW(F) - 570   년월일 : 11210   시간 : 1200

수 신 : 장   판 (총기. 경제원. 재무부. 법무부. 농림수산부. 문화부. 상공부. 건설부. 보사부. 노동부
밤 신 : 주 제네바대사   교통부. 체신부. 농수부. 과기처. 공보처. 공법청)

제 목 : GVW-258P 첨부

총   매(표지포함)

보 안 봉 제	

| 외신과 동 제 | |

MFN EXEMPTION PROCEDURES

Note by the Secretariat

Attached to this note are draft texts designed to implement the m.f.n. exemption procedures discussed by negotiators:

(A) **Agreed Negotiating Procedure**: This procedure applies to the phase of negotiations prior to the adoption of the text of the Agreement. It will not form part of the final text of the Agreement. It details how requests should be made, and how exemptions should be agreed.

(B) **Request Form**: This form is to be used by participants in making requests for exemptions under Article II:2. It will not form part of the final Agreement.

(C) **Annex on M.f.n. Exemptions**: This Annex, which will be attached to the GATS, is applicable to the period after the entry into force of the Agreement. It lists the specific m.f.n. exemptions accorded, and sets out the general rules applicable to them.

(D) **Amendment to Article II:2**: This is a technical change proposed for Article II designed to provide a clearer link between the Agreement and the Annex on m.f.n. exemptions.

Attachment "A"

AGREED NEGOTIATING PROCEDURE

Requests for Article II Exemptions

Scope

1.   This procedure applies to requests by GNS participants, made prior to
the adoption of the text of the GATS, for specific exemptions from the
obligations of Article II:1 of the Agreement.

Request

2.   A Party may request, prior to the adoption of the text of the GATS, an
exemption from its obligations under Article II:1 with respect to a specific
measure. The request shall contain the following information:

   (a) the name or description of the measure;

   (b) the service sectors affected by the measure;

   (c) the countries, or category of countries, which receive less
      favourable treatment as a result of the measure;

   (d) the policy objective of the measure;

   (e) the treatment, inconsistent with Article II:1 of the Agreement,
      provided for under the measure;

   (f) a legal reference to the text of the measure;

MFN

0107

(g) the intended duration of the exemption;

(h) where the intended duration of the exemption is more than 3 years,

    (i)   a timetable for the progressive phase-out of the measure, or the reason why a progressive phase-out is not possible;

    (ii)   the reason why the policy objective stated above cannot be achieved through measures which are consistent with the Agreement;

    (iii) the conditions which, when they occur, will make unnecessary the continued exemption of the measure.

(i) any further remarks on the requested exemption.

Approval

3.   If GNS participants approve of a Party's request for exemption, the exemption, subject to any conditions attached, shall be incorporated in the Annex on Article II Exemptions, and form part of the GATS draft text for adoption.

Attachment "B"

Date: _____

REQUEST FORM

Exemptions under Article II

COUNTRY "A" hereby requests that, with regard to the following measures, exemptions from obligations under Article II:1 be inscribed in the Annex on Article II Exemptions attached to the draft text for adoption of the GATS.

Name of Measure:

1. Service sectors affected by the measure:

2. Countries, or category of countries, which receive less favourable treatment as a result of the measure:

3.   Policy objective of the measure:

4.   Treatment inconsistent with Article II:1 of the Agreement provided for under the measure:

5.   Legal reference to the text of the measure:

6.   Intended duration of the exemption:

- 6 -

7.   Where the intended duration of the exemption is more than 3 years,

   (a)   Timetable for the progressive phase-out of the measure or reason why a progressive phase-out is not possible:

   (b)   Reason why the policy objective stated above cannot be achieved through measures which are consistent with the Agreement:

   (c)   Conditions which, when they occur, will make unnecessary the continued exemption of the measure:

8.   Any further remarks on the requested exemption:

Attachment "C"

ANNEX

Article II Exemptions

Scope

1. This Annex specifies the conditions under which a Party is exempted from its obligations under Article II:1 of the Agreement.

A. Conditions Applicable to All Exemptions

Review

2. The PARTIES shall review all exemptions granted for a period of more than 3 years. The first such review shall take place no more than 5 years after the entry into force of the Agreement.

3. The PARTIES in a review shall:

   (a) examine whether a phase-out of the measure, if stipulated, has proceeded according to the agreed timetable;

   (b) examine whether the exemption continues to be justified and, in particular, whether conditions sufficient for the elimination of the exemption, as set out in the Annex to Article II Exemptions, exist; and

   (c) determine the date of any further review.

Termination

4.   The exemption of a Party from its obligations under Article II:1 of the Agreement with respect to a particular measure terminates on the date provided for:

(a) under the conditions of the exemption, or

(b) in a decision by the PARTIES.

5.   A Party shall notify the PARTIES at the termination of the exemption period that the inconsistent measure has been brought into conformity with Article II:1 of the Agreement.

Decisions

6.   All decisions by the PARTIES taken under this Annex shall be taken on the basis of a two-thirds majority of the votes cast, comprising more than half of the Parties to the Agreement.

B. Conditions Applicable to Individual Exemptions

PARTY "A"

1. Name or category of measure No. 1

(a) the service sectors affected by the measure;

(b) the countries, or category of countries, which receive less favourable treatment as a result of the measure;

(c) the policy objective of the measure;

MFN · 0113

(d) the treatment, inconsistent with Article II:1 of the Agreement, provided for under the measure;

(e) the legal basis of measure;

(f) the duration of the exemption;

(g) where the intended duration of the exemption is more than 3 years:

(i) a timetable for the progressive phase-out of the measure, or the reason why a progressive phase-out is not possible;

(ii) the reason why the policy objective stated above cannot be achieved through measures which are consistent with the Agreement; and

(iii) the conditions which, when they occur, will make unnecessary the continued exemption of the measure;

(h) the date of the first review;

(i) any other conditions relating to the exemption.

2. Name or category of measure No. 2
(...) etc.

PARTY "B"

1. Name or category of measure No. 1
(...) etc.

Attachment "D"

Article II

Most-favoured-nation Treatment

New paragraph 2

2.   A Party may maintain a measure inconsistent with paragraph 1 provided
that it is listed in, and meets the conditions of, the Annex on Article II
Exemptions.

경 제 기 획 원

우 427-760 / 경기도 과천시 중앙동1 정부제2청사 / 전화 503-9149 / 전송 503-9141

문서번호 봉조삼 10502-*878*
시행일자 1991. 12. 9 .

수신 <u>외무부장관</u>, 문화부장관
참조

선결			지시	
접수	일자 시간	91. 12. 11	결재·공람	
	번호	**41236**		
	처리과			
	담당자			

제목 UR/서비스협상관련 MFN일탈

　　1. 봉조삼 10502-738('91.10.21)과 관련입니다.

　　2. '91년 12월 UR/서비스 양자협의를 위한 관계부처 회의('91.12.3)결과 영화의 제작 및 배급서비스분야는 다음과 같은 사유로 MFN일탈을 요청하지 않기로 결정하였음을 통보하니 양지하시기 바랍니다.

- 다　　　음 -

- 특정국가에 개별적인 MFN일탈사항은 다른 협상참가국가로 부터 동의를 받아야 하고 국제협정에 근거를 두고 있어야 한다는 등 제약요건이 있는바 영화제작 및 배급서비스분야의 MFN일탈은 이같은 요건에 비추어 실현가능성이 희박한 것으로 판단됨.

- 또한 MFN일탈을 요구할 경우 MFN의 다자화시한등에 대한 방침이 내부적으로 마련되어야 하는 바 영화분야에 있어서는 당분간 이러한 중기시간표의 마련도 어려운 상황임.

- 따라서 UR/서비스협상에서 공식적으로 MFN일탈문제를 제기하기 보다는 양국간 에 개별적으로 해결을 도모하는 것이 바람직함.　끝.

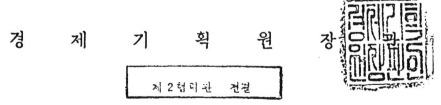

경 제 기 획 원 장

제 2 협력관　전결

0116

외 무 부

종   별 :

번   호 : GVW-2611   일   시 : 91 1212 1730

수   신 : 장 관(수신처참조)

발   신 : 주 제네바 대사

제   목 : UR/GNS 회의(2)

12.10(화), 12.11(수) 개최된 주요국 비공식 협의내용을 하기 보고함.

1. 예외조항 (12.10 오후 및 12.11.오전, HAWES대사주재)

가. 소비자 보호, 운송체계의 보전, 유한자원 보호, 문화적 가치

- 상기 사항들은 예외조항에서 삭제하기로 결론에 도달하였으며 특히 문화적 가치에 대하여는 아직 이견이 있으나 HAWES 대사는 동 문제는 시장접근 및 내국민 대우에 관한 낮은 수준의 COMMITMENT 또는 개별적인 MFN 일탈신청등의 방법으로 해결하여야 할것이라고 잠정적인 결론을 내림

나. 환경보호

- 14조 (B)항의 인간, 동.식물의 생명보호가 궁극적으로 환경문제를 포괄하기 때문에 환경보호를 별도 예외 사유로 명문규정화지는 않다는데 합의가 형성되었으나

0 동 14조 B)항으로서 포괄하지 못하는 요소가있는지 검토하기 위하여 서비스 협정 발효이후 WORKING PARTY 설치하는 문제와 관련 동작업반의 작업시한 및 위임 범위에 대하여 일부이견이 상존 재협의가 필요함.

다. PERSONAL DATA

- 14조 C)항의 서비스 협정 규정에 위배되지않은 법규의 시행을 위하여 필요한 예외적조치에 동 항목을 포함시키는데 대체적으로 합의가 형성됨.

라. 조세문제

- 조세부과.징수의 3단계 (기본세율, 평가,징수) 별로각각 MFN, 내국민 대우에 위배되는 사례의법률적 처리가 해결되어야 할 과제인바, 기본 세율자체가 내.외국민간차별적인 경우는 NATIONALSCHEDULE 에 기재되어야 할 사항이나 기타 문제에 대하여는

0 조세관련 양자협정으로 인한 MFN 위배문제는 제2조 (MFN)에 대한 FOOT

통상국	2차보	법무부	보사부	문화부	체신부	경기원	재무부	농수부
상공부	건설부	노동부	과기처	해항청	공보처			

PAGE 1   91.12.13   07:25 WG

외신 1과 통제관

0117

NOTE공통적으로 MFN 적용을 배제하고 내.외국인간 차별적인 조세평가.징수는 각국별로 NATIONAL SCHEDULE 의 HEAD NOTE 에 기재하거나 예외조항 (제 14조)에 반영하는 방법과

0 이들은 구분하지 않고 전부 예외조항에 반영하는 방법 (미국)이 대두되고 있으며 특히 미국의 접근방법에 대하여 LOOP-HOLE이 생길수 있다는 반론이 많이 제기되고 있음.

2. MFN 일탈 (12.11 오후 JARAMILLO 의장 주재)

- 사무국이 작성한 MFN 일탈 절차 (12.9 자 기 FAX송부)에 대하여 논의하였으나 미국의 강력한반대로 결론을 내리지 못하고 재협의키로 함.

- 미국은 사무국 문서에 대하여 다음사항을 이유로 근본적 문제점이 있다고 강력한 반대 의사를 표명함.

0 갓트는 MFN, 내국민 대우, 수량제한 금지가 모두의무사항인 반면 GATS 는 자유화 추진에 보다 중요한 내국민 대우 및 수량제한 금지는 의무가아닌 양허협상 대상에 불과하고 MFN 만이 의무로되어 있으며 동 MFN 조항의 중요성이 과장되고있음.

0 사무국 접근 방식은 UR 협상 결과를 자국국내업계 및 의회에 제시할 수 있는 능력을 침해하여 특히 서비스 발효이후 MFN 일탈연장결정에 2/3이상 동의를 요건으로 한 것을 국내 업계에 전달할 수 없음.

- 이에 대하여 기타 모든 국가는 MFN 원칙이없이는 다자협정이 성립할 수 없으며 사무국문서상에 시한이 없는 MFN 일탈도 허용받을수있는 길이 있음을 지적하고 사무국 접근 방식지지 입장을 견지함.

- 한편 MFN 일탈 신청 대상과 관련 이중과세방지 협정, 부자 협정등의 HORIZORTAL AGREEMENTS와 항공협정등 모든 국가에 공통되는 사하오 사무국 문서상의 방법대로 MFN 일탈 신청을 하여야 하는지 여부는 결정되지 않았으며 신청시한도 12.20 또는 1.13. 또는 그이후등의 3개대안이 있으나 구체적으로 토의되지 않았음.

0 따라서 아국의 MFN 일탈신청은 사무국 작성양식에 따르되 우선 해운등 아국의 개별적문제에 대하여만 준비하기 바라며 제출시기는 추후보고하겠음.끝

(대사 박수길-국장)

수신처:통기, 경기원,재무부,법무부,농림수산부,문화부,상공부,건설부,보사부, 노동부 , 교통부,체신부,과기처, 공보처, 항만청

외 무 부

종 별 :

번 호 : GVW-2639   일 시 : 91 1213 1630

수 신 : 장관(수신처 참조)

발 신 : 주제네바대사

제 목 : UR/GNS 회의(3)

12.12(목) 속개된 주요국 비공시 협의 내용을 하기보고함.

1. 운송분야(12.12.오전 JARAMILLO 의장 주재)

가. 해운

- 국제해운 분야 공통자유화(COMMON APPROACH)에 대하여는 이를 지지하는 아국 및 선진국들과 이에 반대하는 미국 및 개도국들의 입장이 계속 대립하였으며

0 해운 보조서비스의 사용 및 접근 보장문제는 그 기본 취지에 대하여는 합의가형성됨

- 의장은 국제해운 공통 자유화문제는 합의를 이룰수가 없다고 전제하고 다만 해운 보조서비스 사용및 접근보장에 관한 ANNOTATION 초안작성을 사무국에 의뢰할 것을 제의함.

0 미국은 동 ANNOTATAION 을 작성하여 협상 GUIDELINE 으로 쓰는 것은 무방하나폐쇄동맹이 무역에 미치는 영향도 함께 검토되어야 한다고 하였으며 인도는 동 ANNOTATION 이 해운분야에 시장접근 약속을 한 국가에만 적용되어야 하며 그이상은 수용할 수 없다고 하여 합의를 이루지못하고 재협으키로 함.

나. 항공

- EC 가 항공운수권 및 이와 직접 관련된 보조서비스는 협정적용으로 부터 배제하되 항공기수선.유지, CRS 포함 항공 서비스판매등 보조서비스를 협정(MFN 포함) 적용대상으로 하고 공항설비 이용.접근 보장문제에 대하여 동사항이 양자협정에 의해규정 된다는 점을 들어 동문제의 포함에 반대입장을 견지함.

2. FRAMEWORK 조문(12.12.오후 JARAMILLO 의장 주재)

가. 지급 및 이전

- IMF 규정에 의하여 인정된 경우를 제외하고는 시장접근 약속에 관계된 경상거래

통상국	2차보	외정실	분석관	정와대	안기부	법무부	보사부	문화부
체신부	경기원	재무부	농수부	상공부	건설부	노동부	과기처	해항정
공보처								

PAGE 1

의 제한을 금지하는 의무만 제11조 조문에 반영하고 자본이동에 대하여는 시장접근에 관한 약속을 함과 동시에 관련 자본이동도 허용하는 것으로 약속하는 것임을 INTERPRETATIVE NOTE 에 반영하는 것으로 합의가 형성됨.(일부 자구 정리필요)

　　나. BOP 조항

　- 브랏셀 TEXT 1안에 비하여 BOP 조항 원용조건을 일부 강화하되 BOP 를 이유로한 조치대상은 지급 및 이전뿐만 아니라 서비스 무역전체를 대상으로 하는데 합의가 형성됨 (EC는 조치대상을 지급 및 이전에 한정할 것을 계속 주장)

　- 기타 BOP 조항 원용시 제한조건 (무차별적 적용, 한시정, 점진적 폐지등) 및 BOP 협의절차 (GATT/UR 협상 결과 원용)에 대하여 합의를 도출함.끝

　　(대사 박수길-국장)

　　수신처:　　　　　봉기, 경기원, 재무부, 법무부,　　　　　농림수산부, 문화부, 상공부, 건설부, 보사부, 노동부, 교통부, 체신부, 과기처, 공보처, 항만청

외 무 부

종 별 :

번 호 : GVW-2656　　　　　　　　일 시 : 91 1215 1830

수 신 : 장 관(수신처참조)

발 신 : 주 제네바 대사

제 목 : UR/GNS 회의(4)

　　12.13(금) 속개된 주요국 비공식협의 내용을 하기보고함.

　　1. 제 21조, 양허수정(12.13 오전 HAWES 대사 주재)

　　- 미국은　　TNC/W/35　　상의　　현초안이　　서비스무역의특성(대부분　　상업적 주재에의하여이루어짐)　상양허수정에 따른 보상이　MFN　원칙하에제공되도록 보장하지 못하는 결함이 있다는전제하에 다음과 같은 내용의 수정안을 제시함

　　0　MFN　원칙하에　보상이　제공되어야　하며　이를위하여　다른　서비스분야 뿐만아니라서비스 이외의다른 분야까지도 보상제공 대상이 되어야 함

　　0 양허 수정 통지후 90일 이내에 모든 이해관계국간합의에도 도달하지 못하면 중재절차에 회부되어야하며 중재인은 양허수정에 따른 무역액을측정하여야 함

　　0 양허 수정 통지국가는 중재결과에 따른보상제공 전까지는 양허수정을 실시할 수 없음.또한 동국가가 중재결과에 따르지 않을 경우관계국은　NON-MFN　하에 보복할 수있음

　　- 이에 대하여 많은 국가가 다음과 같은 문제점을지적하여 추후 재협의키로 함

　　0 서비스 이외분야까지 보상 대상으로 하는 것은수용불가(개도국)

　　0 무역액을 측정하는 것은 현실적으로 어려움

　　0 NON-MFN 하의 보복허용은 협정의 INTEGRITY 를저해함

　　2. 분쟁해결 절차(12.13.오후 , JARAMILLO 의장주재)

　　- 사무국에서 분쟁해결 절차에 반영되어야 할요소를 문서로 정리하여 토의하였으나 다음사항에대하여 의견 대립이 계속되어 협상이 교착상태에빠짐

　　0　이사회　하부기구의　분쟁해결　과정　참여여부(사무총장이　PANELIST　선임시 분야별기구의장과의 협의 의무화 여부 포함)

　　0 PANEL 보고서 채택방법 및 상소기구 설치 여부,동 상소기구의 업무 범위

통상국	2차보	청와대	법무부	보사부	문화부	고통부	체신부	경기원
재무부	농수부	상공부	건설부	과기처	해항청	공보처		

O 서비스 분야간 보복의 원칙적 제한 여부등.끝

(대사 박수길-국장)

　수신처:통기, 경기원, 재무부, 법무부, 농림수산부, 문화부, 상공부, 건설부, 보사부, 교통부, 체신부, 과기처, 공보처, 항만청

0122

외 무 부

종 별 :

번 호 : GVW-2651

일 시 : 91 1215 1830

수 신 : 장 관(수신처 참조)

발 신 : 주 제네바 대사

제 목 : UR/GNS 회의(5)

12.14(토) 속개된 주요국 비공식 협의 내용을 하기보고함.

1. 항공부속서(12.14.09:00-10:30)

   - 8개국(아국,카나다,EC, 호주,스위스,스웨덴,일본,뉴질랜드)이 다음과 같은내용의 부속서 초안에 합의 다음주 초 GNS비공협의에 상정키로 함.

   0 항공 운수권 및 이와 직결된 보조서비스의협정적용 배제 및 양자간 분쟁 해결

   0 항공기 수선유지, 항공서비스 판매, CRS 에의협정규정(MFN 포함) 적용

   0 시장접근 약속을 한 보조서비스와 관련 공항서립 접근 이용의 수차별적 보장

   0 항공부속서의 주기적(최소한 매 5년) 재검토

2. FRAMEWORK 조문(12.14.10:30-13:00, JARAMILLO의장 주재)

   가. 정부조달(제 13조)- 동 규정의 범위를 PUBLIC PROCUREMENT 보다 좁은개념인 GOVERNMENT PROCUREMENT 로 하는데 합의함.

   - UR 이후 협상계획과 관련 작업 계획설정자체에 대하여는 대체적으로 합의가 형성(일본은반대입장)되었으나 다음사항에 대하여 의견이대립하여 재협의키로 함.

   0 카나다는 UR 이후 협상 대상조문(국내규제, 세이프가드, 보조금, 예외조항의 환경)을 일괄하여 FRAMEWORK 아 아닌 각료들의 결정에 반영할것을 주장

   0 EC 등 선진국은 정부조달 협정에서 서비스분야도 협상이 진행중임을 들어 정부조달 서비스의담당기구를 예단하지 말아야 한다고 한 반면 인도,싱가폴,유고등은 UR이후 협상이 GATS 하에서 이루어져야 한다고 주장

   나. 보조금(제15조)

   - 미국이 보조금에 대하여 제 16(시장접근), 제17조(내국민 대우) 를 완전 배제하는 제안을제시하였는바, 대부분의 나라가 서비스 무역의 경우외국기업이 국내에 서비스 공급기업을 설립하기때문에 일부 외국인 서비스 공급기업도 보조금지급대상인

통상국	2차보	청와대	보사부	문화부	교통부	체신부	경기원	재무부
농수부	상공부	건설부	노동부	과기처	해항청	공보처		

PAGE 1

91.12.16 06:00 FO

외신 1과 통제관

0123

국내기업에 해당하기 때문에 미국문안에 의하면 MFN 위배 문제도 제기된다는문제점을지적함.

- 한편, 많은 나라가 현초안(MFN/TNC/W/35)에의하면 보조금은 SCHEDULE 에 기재할 필요가없다고 해석하였으나 갓트 법률국은 현 초안상에보조금 지급을 금지하는 규정은 없으나 보조금지급에 의하여 내.외국인 서비스 공급자간경쟁조건이 변화될 경우에는 제17조 위배사항이되므로 SCHEDULE 에 기재되어야 한다고 함.

3. SCHEDULING 관련 조문(12.14, 14:30-19:00, HAWES대사 주재)

가. 국내규제(제 16조)

- 제1항을 서문에 규정할 것인지 제 6조에 규정할것인지에 대하여 선.개도국간 의견을 좁히지못하였으며

0 제2항의 국내규제의 합리적, 개관적, 공평한운영 의무를 모든 서비스 분야에 적용할 것인지시장접근 약속을 한 분야에만 적용할 것인지에대하여도 합의를 이루지못하였으나 우선 현초안(시장 접근 약속을 한 분야에만 적용)의괄호를 삭제하기로 함.

나. 시장접근(제 16조)

- 2항의 E) 의 상업적 주재 형태의 제한의경우 외국인에 대한 차별적 제한 뿐만아니라내.외국인 무차별적 제한까지 포함하기로 합의함.

다. 내국민 대우(제 17조)

- 3항 괄호안의 'SIGNIFICANTLY'에 대하여 일본이동 17조가 금융 부속서에도 적용되어야 한다는조건하에 동용어를 삭제하는데 동의할 용의가있다고 함.

라. ADDITIONAL COMMITMENT

- 동 조항의 삭제를 주장하는인도,멕시코,브라질등 개도국과 선진국의 입장이맞서 의견을 좁히지 못함.

0 HAWES 대사는 참가국간 합의를 이루지 못할경우 자신이 판단하여 CLEAN TEXT 를 12.20 TNC에 제출하겠다고 함.끝

(대사 박수길-국장)

수신처:롱기, 경기원, 재무부,농림수산부,문화부, 상공부, 건설부,보사부, 노동부,교롱부 ,체신부,과기처,공보처,항만청

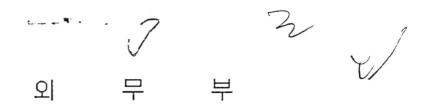

외 무 부

종　　별 :

번　　호 : GVW-2671　　　　　　　　　　일　　시 : 91 1216 1600

수　　신 : 장관(수신처참조)

발　　신 : 주제네바대사

제　　목 : UR/서비스 양자협의

　　12.10-13간 미국,EC,스웨덴,캐나다,핀란드,스위스와 진행한 표제 양자협의 결과를 하기 보고함.

　　1. 전반적인 사항

　　- 대부분의 국가와 상호간의 구체적인 REQUEST를 바탕으로 금융분야를 포함한 전분야에 대하여 양자협의를 진행

　　- 상대국의 요구사항에 대하여는 정식협상(NEGOTIATION) 이 아닌 만큼 우리가 OFFER한 내용에 대한 국내 규제제도를 보다 명확히 설명하고 상대국의 요구사항을 수용할 수 없는 논리와 국내 산업 여건을 설명하는 선에서 대응

　　- 이과정에서 대부분의 상대국은 요구 사항의 우선순위를 제시하거나 자국민간 업계의 관심사항을 밝힘.

　　- 한편 우리가 상대국에게 REQUEST 한 사항에 대해서도 사실 유무의 확인등 1차적인 검토결과를 듣고 필요시 우리 REQUEST 의 배경등을 설명

　　2. 국가별 협의내용

　　1) 미국

　　- 12.10일 오전 주 제네바 USTR 대표부에서 은행및 증권을 제외한 전분야에 대해서 협의를 갖고 오후에는 GATT 회의실에서 금융분야에 대한 협의를 가짐.

　　- 미측은 92년 2월까지 최초의 자유화 약속에 대한 양허협상을 완료한다는 가정하에 내년 1월말 이후 약 2주일간씩 두세차례의 양자 협상이 앞으로 필요할 것이라는의견을 표명

　　- 또한 현재 5개 양자 협상팀이 각국과 협의를 하고 있으며 자신이 이끄는 협상팀을 6개국가와 협의를 가질 예정이라고 밝힘.

　　- 미측은 수정 OFFER 작업이 거의 마무리 되었으며 12월 20일까지 각국에 배포할

롱상국	2차보	보사부	문화부	교통부	체신부	경기원	재무부	농수부
상공부	건설부	노동부	과기처	해항정	공보처			

PAGE 1　　　　　　　　　　　　　　　　　　　91.12.17　　08:09 DQ

　　　　　　　　　　　　　　　　　　　　　　외신 1과　통제관

　　　　　　　　　　　　　　　　　　　　　　　　　　　0125

계획이라고 언급하고 INITIAL OFFER 와의 차이점등을 설명

- 미측은 의료시설의 경영, 회계, 법률 서비스,금융분야에 대하여 상당히 높은 관심을 표명하고 광고, 인력이동 엔지니어링,건설, 프랜차이링,보험,통신분야에 대해서도 계속 국내규제 내용을 구체적으로 문의

- 우리가 REQUEST 한 통신, 건설,금융,유통,운송및 관광분야에 대하여 미측은 1차적인 검토결과를 설명

2) EC

- 12월 11일 오전에 GATT 회의실에서 양자협의를 가짐

- EC 는 이번기간중에 15개국가와 양자협의를 가질 예정인바 한국은 주요한 협상 대상국가라고 밝히고 양허 협상을 종료하기 위해서는 두번이상의 종합적인 협상이필요하며 분야별 협상도 추가적으로 필요하다고 언급

- EC는 모든 국가에 공통적인 요구 업종 중에서 광고, 회의용역, 건축 설계 서비스가 중요하다고 밝히고, 우리에 대한 개별요구 사항중 주로 법무서비스, 회계서비스, 금융서비스에 논의를 집중했으며 인력이동에 대한 우리의 입장에도 관심을 표명

- 우리가 REQUEST 한 통신, 건설,금융,유통 분야에대하여 아직 충분히 검토가 되어있지 않다고 밝히고 1차적인 검토 결과를 설명함.

3) 스웨덴

- 스웨덴과는 12월 11일 오후 GATT 회의실에서 양자협의를 가진바 스웨덴은 17개국가에게 REQUEST 를 했으며 이번에 6개국과 양자협의를 진해하고 있다고 밝힘.

- 스웨덴은 통신,금융,엔지니어링,유통,보험분야에 주로 관심을 표명하고 트럭킹및 철도운송업 분야의 한.미 협상 결과에 MFN원칙을 적용할 것인지를 확인

4) 캐나다

- 캐나다와는 12월 12일 오후 GATT 회의실에서 양자 협의를 가짐.

캐나다는 이번에 8개국과 협의를 하고 있으며, 수정 OFFER 를 92년 1월 중순경에는 각국에 배포할수 있을 것이라고 언급

- 캐나다는 공통 요청 사항중 특히 자국이 관심있는 분야를 제시한바 광업 및 자원관계 엔지니어링, 컨설팅, 프랜차이징(슈퍼마켓), 화물운송 주선업(FREIGHT FORWARDING), 육운 및 철도운송 서비스, R AND D 서비스 , 지질관련 서비스,환경관련 서비스, 금융서비스등을 열거

PAGE 2

0126

5) 핀랜드

- 핀란드와는 12월 13일 오전 GATT 회의실에서 양자협의를 가졌는바 92년 1월에최초의 자유화 약속에 대한 협상이 보다 본격화 될것이라고 언급하고 이번에 4-5개국가와 양자 협의를 진행중에 있다고 밝힘.

- 핀란드는 금융,광고,통신,엔지니어링,회계분야에 특히 높은 관심을 표명함.

- 우리가 REQUEST 한 통신분야와 관련하여 단순 데이타 전송 서비스는 기본 통신 서비스에 속한다고 설명함.

6) 스위스와는 12월 13일 오후 GATT 회의실에서 양자 협의를 가졌는바 본격적인양허 협상이 92년 1월말 부터 시작될 것이라고 언급하고 언제 끝나느냐가 문제가 아니고 실질적인 결과를 얻는것이 중요하다고 명백히 하고 이번에 동구 국가중 10개국가와 협의를 갖고 있다고 밝힘

- 스위스는 은행, 증권,보험, 유통분야에 깊은 관심을 표명하고 한국의 인력 이동에 대한 입장등을 문의함.

- 우리가 REQUEST 한 통신분야에 대하여 자국관련 제도를 설명.끝

(대사 박수길-국장)

수신처:통기,경기원,재무부,농림수산부,문화부,상공부,건설부,보사부,노동부,교통부,체신부,과기처,공보처,항만청

외 무 부

종 별 :

번 호 : GVW-2691　　　　　　　　　　　　일 시 : 91 1217 2000

수 신 : 장 관(수신처참조)

발 신 : 주 제네바대사

제 목 : UR/GNS회의(7)®

12.16(월) 속개된 주요국 비공식 협의결과를 하기보고함.

1. 금융부속서 (12.16 오전 및 오후 HAWES 대사 및 FRANK SWEDLOVE 주재)

가. 정의 및 범위

국내규제, 인정

- 정의 및 범위(제 1조)는 11.27자 초안에 국내규제(제 2조)는 10.30 자 초안에각각 합의가형성됨.

- 인정(제 3조)에 대하여는 의장이 새로이 제시한초안(12.16자)에 대하여 합의가형성되었으며, 다만 FRAMEWORK 제 7조중 4항 B)이외에는 4항 C)등 모든 내용이 금융부속서 제 3조(PRUDENTIALMEASURE 의 인정)에 적용된다는 점을 명문으로 규정하자는의견이 있었음.

나. INSTITUTIONAL MACHINERY, 분쟁해결

- HAWES 대사는 기구 및 분쟁해결 문제가 UR전체, 서비스 전체, 금융 서비스 등세가지 차원에서 논의되고 있는바 UR 전체 차원의 논의 동향을 알 필요가 있다고 전제 하고 제도분야협상 그룹 LA CARTE 의장의 설명을 요청

- LA CARTE 의장은 UR 협상 결과 전체를 한기구에 의하여 운영토록 하는 FINAL ACT 초안이 논의되고 있으며, 분쟁해결과 관련, 모든분야에 적용되는 단일 공통 분쟁해결절차를 수립하는 방안이 다수 의견이며, 2일내에 완전하고 자세한 TEXT가 나오게 될 것이라고 함.

0 또한 금융 부속서에서 제기된 분쟁해결과정에 금융전문가의 참여, NON-VIOLATION, 분야간 보복, 패널 보고서 채택의 자동화등 모든 문제가 일반분쟁해결 절차에 의하여 해결될수 있다고 함.

- 그러나 금융 부속서에 분쟁해결 관련 금융서비스 기구의 역할을 구체적으로

통상국	2차보	법무부	보사부	문화부	교통부	체신부	경기원	재무부
농수부	상공부	건설부	노동부	과기처	해항정	공보처		

PAGE 1　　　　　　　　　　　　　　　　　　　91.12.18　　09:05 WH

외신 1과 통제관

0128

명시코자 하는 선진국 입장은 변화하지 않았으며, HAWES대사는 FRAMEWORK 쪽에서 마련된 각료들의 결정 초안이상의 것을 2-3 일내에 합의할수는 없을 것이라고 하고 일반분쟁해결 절차 및 서비스협정 전체의 분쟁해결 절차가 합의된 이후(12.20 이후)에야 금융분야에 특수한 사항을 고려할수 있을 것이라고 함.

다. 자유화 추진 방식(협정 제 3부)

- 선.개도국간 입장이 전혀 좁혀지지 않았으며, HAWES 대사는 현 상태로서는 제 3 부에 관한 금융 부속서 초안을 12.20 TNC 에 제출할 TEXT중 FRAMEWORK 이나 금융 부속서에는 첨부할수 없으며, 다만 동 방식대로 자유화를 추진코자 하는 국가간에 NEGOTIATIATING GUIDELINE 으로 쓸수는 있을 것이라고 함.

2. MFN (12.16, 17:00 - 19:00, JARAMILLO 의장 주재)

- MFN 일탈 방식에 관한 12.9 자 사무국 문서에 대하여 토의하였는바, EC, 미국, 오지리, 스위스가 일부 유보의사를 표명하였으나 동방식을 기본 메카니즘으로 하는데 합의하고 다만 구체적 문안만 수정하여 12.17 재협의키로 함.

3. 항공 부속서 (12.16, 20:30-21:00 JARAMILLO 의장주재)

- 별첨 항공 부속서 안에 대하여 합의함.

0 다만 미국, 오지리는 동안에 대하여 원칙적으로 동의하나 본부 방침에 따라 의견을 제시할수도 있다고 함.

4. 경제 통합(12.16, 21:00-24:00 JARAMILLO 의장주재)

- 사무국 초안을 기초로 토의하였으나 전혀 의견이 좁혀지지 않아 재협의키로 함.

첨부: 항공부속서 초안 1부. 끝

(GVW(F)-639

(대사 박수길-국장)

수신처:(봉기, 경기원, 재무부, 법무부, 농림수산부, 문화부, 상공부, 건설부, 보사부, 노동부 ,교통부, 체신부, 과기처, 공보처, 항만청)

DRAFT
16.12.91

ANNEX ON AIR TRANSPORT SERVICES

1. All provisions of the General Agreement on Trade in Services shall apply to air transportation, scheduled and unscheduled, and ancillary services except where specifically reserved in paragraphs 2 and 5 below.

2. Except as set out in paragraph 3, no provision of the Agreement shall apply:

    (a) to traffic rights as covered by the Chicago Convention, including first and second freedoms, and by bilateral air services agreements;

    (b) to directly related activities which would limit or affect the ability of parties to negotiate, to grant or to receive traffic rights, or which would have the effect of limiting their exercise.

3. Notwithstanding the provisions of paragraph 2, all provisions of the Agreement shall apply immediately and unconditionally to:

    - aircraft repair and maintenance;

    - selling and marketing of air transport activities;

    - computer reservation systems.

4. Each Party shall ensure that access to and use of publicly available services offered within or from its territory, where commitments for such services have been made, is accorded to air services providers of other

0130

- 2 -

Parties on reasonable and non-discriminatory terms and conditions, unless otherwise specified in its schedule.

bed mention and CATS question ~~이리?가 to 이/s force

5. Dispute settlement procedures provided for in bilateral air service agreements or under the Chicago Convention shall apply with respect to traffic rights and directly related activities as covered by paragraph 2 above. The dispute settlement facilities of the Agreement may be invoked only where obligations or commitments have been assumed by the concerned Parties and where dispute settlement procedures provided for in bilateral air service agreements or under the Chicago Convention have been exhausted.

6. Air transport services and the provisions of this Annex shall be reviewed periodically or at least every 5 years.

7. Definitions:

   (a) aircraft repair and maintenance: activities required at a regular or ad hoc basis in order to guarantee the operational airworthiness of aircraft.

   (b) selling and marketing: opportunities for the air carrier concerned to sell and market freely its air transport services including all aspects of marketing such as market research, advertising and distribution.

   (c) computerized reservation system: computerized system that contains information about air carriers schedules, seat availability, fares and far rules, through which reservations can be made.

0131

2-2

16A-TRAN

재　무　부

우 427-760 경기도 과천시 중앙동 1　／ 전화 (02)503-9266　／ 전송 503-9324

문서번호 국금 22251-ㅇㅇㅇ

시행일자 '91. 12. 18　　( )

수신 수신처 참조

참조

선결			지시		
접수	일자시간		결재·공람		
	번호	**42056**			
처리과					
담당자					

제목　금융부속서에 관한 미국 제안 검토

　　1.　GVW-2516 ('91.11.29)와 관련입니다.

　　2.　금융부속서중 제도조항 및 분쟁해결 절차에 관한 미국 제안 검토의견을
별첨과 같이 송부합니다.

　　첨부 : 미국제안 검토.　　끝.

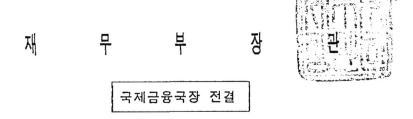

재　무　부　장

국제금융국장 전결

수신처 : 경제기획원장관(대조실장), 외무부장관(통상국장).

0132

금융부속서에 관한 미국제안 검토

1. 경 과

- 미국은 지난 금융부속서 회의시('91.11.25~29) 금융부속서에 대한 내용중 현재까지 구체적인 논의가 없었던 제도 조항(Institutional Machinery)과 분쟁해결절차(Dispute Settlement and Enforcement) 조항에 관한 자국안 제출

- 11월 회의시 미국제안에 대하여 논의를 하였으나 구체적인 합의를 못하고 12월 회의시 재론될 예정임.

2. 주요내용 검토

가. 제도 조항

```
─────────────< 미국 제안 내용 >─────────────

- 의장안에는 반영되어 있지 않은 다음의 기능을 금융서비스위원회
  (Financial Service Committee)의 역할에 추가
   o 금융부속서 및 서비스 일반협정중 금융부문 관련 조항 등에
     대한 유권해석
   o 금융서비스교역 자유화를 위한 각국간의 협상에 있어 협상
     Guideline 제시 등
```

0133

- 금융서비스 위원회의 기능중 특히 금융서비스위원회가 행하는 각종 자문, 결정 등의 구속력(binding) 여부에 대해 선진국과 개도국간에 의견이 대립

    o 개도국 : 금융서비스위원회는 이사회의 하부기구로서 자문역할만을 하며, 구속력있는 의사결정 권한은 모두 이사회가 가져야 함. (인도, 멕시코 등)

    o 선진국 : 금융서비스위원회는 일정범위내에서 구속력 있는 의사 결정을 할 수 있음. (미국, 스위스, 카나다 등)

- 검토 의견

    o 금융서비스위원회는 이사회의 하부기구로서 이사회가 위임하는 모든 사항들에 관한 결정을 할 수 있으나,

    o 동 결정사항이 구속력을 가지려면 금융서비스위원회의 참가자격을 일정국가(금융부문을 자유화하겠다고 공약한 국가)로 제한하지 말고 개방해야 할 것임.

나. 분쟁 해결 절차

┌─────────〈 미국 제안 내용 〉─────────┐

- 금융분야 분쟁해결을 위한 소위원회(panel)의 구성절차 등을 상세히 규정

- 분쟁해결 결과에 따른 최초의 보복은 당해 분야내로 함.

    o 그러나, 6개월 경과후 최초보복이 실효를 거두지 못했다고 판정될 경우 타부문(여타 서비스분야 및 상품교역)에 교차보복 가능*

    * 의장안에서는 분쟁해결 결과에 따른 보복은 원칙적으로(in principle) 당해 분야로 한정

- 각국의 금융감독관련 개별적 결정사항(individual prudential decision)에 관하여는 서비스 일반협정상의 의무와 이행약속을 위반한 경우에만 분쟁해결 절차에 의뢰 가능 (의장안과 동일)

└───────────────────────────────┘

0134

- 금융서비스에 대한 상세한 분쟁해결 절차 명시에 관하여 선진국과
  개도국간 의견대립 지속

    o 선진국 : 금융분야 분쟁은 금융전문가에 의해 처리되어야 하며
              이러한 원칙이 반영된 분쟁해결절차가 금융분야 부속서에
              구체적으로 규정되어야 함.

    o 개도국 : 금융분야 분쟁도 GATT의 일반적인 분쟁해결절차에 입각
              하여 처리할 수 있으므로 금융분야 부속서에서 별도로
              분쟁해결 절차를 상세히 규정할 필요가 없음.

    o 또한, 미국이 제안한 교차보복(cross retaliation)에 대하여는
       대부분의 국가가 반대

- 검토 의견

    o 금융분야 분쟁해결 절차는 금융분야의 특수성을 감안하여 금융
       전문가에 의해 처리되어야 하나, 분쟁해결절차는 GATT의 일반적인
       분쟁해결절차 및 Framework 규정에 명시하며 별도의 규정 불필요

    o 또한, 교차보복도 의장안에 따라 원칙적으로 당해분야로만 한정
       해야 하며, 당해 분야에 대한 보복이 불가능한 경우만 여타 서비스
       분야에 대한 보복을 검토해야 함.

0135

3. 항목별 검토

가. 제도 조항

금융분야 의장안	미국 제안	검 토 의 견
- 금융서비스위원회 참여 ㅇ 금융분야에 관한 commitment를 한 국가로 구성	좌 동	- 현재 offer를 제시한 43개국 중 일부국가를 제외하고는 금융분야 offer 제시 ㅇ 참가국 제한의 실익이 없으나 개도국들은 서비스 협정의 분산을 초래하므로 모든 서비스협정 회원국 에게 개방 요구 ㅇ Framework에도 보조기구에 대한 가입을 모든 회원국 에게 개방할 것을 명시 - 따라서, 금융서비스위원회가 선진국에 의해서 운영되지 않도록 하기 위해서 모든 회원국에게 개방이 바람직
- 위원회 구성 ㅇ 이사회 구성후 90일 이내에 금융서비스 위원회 설립	ㅇ 이사회 구성후 90일 이내 또는 이사회 첫 회의시 금융서비스위원회 설립	- 의견 없음.
- 금융서비스위원회 의무 ㅇ 금융서비스 이행 사항에 관한 내용을 이사회에 정기적으로 보고	ㅇ 금융서비스 이행 사항에 관한 내용을 이사회에 정기적으로 보고	- 의견 없음.

0136

금융분야 의장안	미국제안	검 토 의 견
o 업무수행에 필요한 rules와 procedures 제정 o 이사회와 공동 업무를 위한 절차 수립 - 금융서비스위원회 기능 o 금융부속서와 관련된 사항, 금융서비스와 연관된 서비스 협정 사항, 이사회가 위임한 기타사항으로 다음과 같은 내용을 포함. (a) 회원국이 제기한 사항 (b) joint action 에 관한 준비 (c) 금융서비스와 관련된 기술적 문제 검토 (d) 금융분야에 관한 국제기구 에 전문가와 협력 (e) 금융서비스의 의무와 약속에 관련된 분쟁 해결 절차	o 업무수행에 필요한 rules와 procedures 제정 o Chairman 선출 o 금융부속서와 관련된 사항, 금융서비스와 연관된 서비스 협정 사항, 이사회가 위임한 기타사항으로 다음과 같은 내용을 포함. (a) 회원국이 제기한 사항 (b) 금융서비스와 관련된 기술적 문제 . 검토의견 제시 . 금융부속서 조항 해석 . Framework 조항 의 금융부속서 적용 문제 - 기타 분야에 영향 을 미칠 사항을 결정하는 경우, 금융서비스위원회 는 관련 기구와 협의하며, 관련 기구도 금융서비스 이행에 영향을 미칠 사항 결정시 금융서비스위원회 와 사전협의 필요	- 의견 없음. o 원칙적으로 금융서비스위원 회의 기능은 금융서비스에 관한 모든 사항을 다룰 수 있으나, 이럴 경우 동 위원회의 구성을 모든 서비스협정 참가국에게 개방하는 것이 필수적임. o 다만, 금융부속서조항 해석에 관해서 EC, 개도국 들은 체약국단의 위임을 받아 이사회가 최종결정 하는 것이며, 분야별기구 는 자문역할에 한정할 것을 주장

0137

금융분야 의장안	미 국 제 안	검 토 의 견
	(a) 금융분야에 관한 국제기구 및 전문가와 협력 (b) 금융서비스와 관련된 분쟁 해결 절차 (c) 금융서비스의 자유화 추진 과정 참여 및 금융서비스협상 guideline 조정	
- 금융서비스위원회 구성 o 금융서비스 전문가(expertise in financial services)로 구성	o 금융서비스 전문가인 공무원 (official expert in financial services)으로 구성	- 금융서비스 전문가인 공무원 으로 한정하기 보다는 금융 서비스 전문가로 범위를 확대하는 것이 바람직

0138

나. 분쟁 해결 절차

금융분야 의장안	미 국 제 안	검 토 의 견
- 개별적 감독규제 조치에 대한 분쟁 해결 ㅇ 협정상의 자유화 의무 및 약속을 위반한 경우에만 분쟁해결 절차 의뢰 가능 - Panel 구성 - Panelist 자격 ㅇ 금융전문가로 구성 - Panel 설정 절차	ㅇ 협정상의 의무 및 약속을 위반했을 경우 제소 가능 ㅇ panel은 재고 권고만 할 수 있음. ㅇ 3인으로 구성 (의장 포함) ㅇ 금융전문가 ㅇ Panel 구성 신청후 14일 이내에 당사국 간에 합의가 이루어 지지 않을 경우 FSC 의장은 금융전문가로 구성된 Panelist 명부 에서 적의 선정 ㅇ 금융부문과 타부분이 모두 관계된 분쟁에 있어서는 FSC 의장과 Council의장이 각 부문 의 중요성을 감안하여 Panel을 구성 ㅇ 단, 금융관련 Panelist 는 모두 Panelist 명부에서 선정	- 금융분야에만 특수한 분쟁해결 절차를 정할 필요는 없으며, GATT 의 분쟁해결 절차와 Framework의 분쟁해결 절차를 준용하는 것이 바람직하나, ㅇ 다만, 금융분야의 특수성을 고려하여 panel의 구성을 금융전문가로 하며, ㅇ 분쟁해결에 따른 보상보복은 원칙적 으로 당해분야로 한정 해야 함.

0139

금 융 분 야 의장안	미 국 제 안	검 토 의 견
- Panel 보고서의 채택	o 당사국의 이의가 없을 경우 채택	
- 상소 기구 (Appellate body) o 상소기구는 panel 의 사실상 결정 (findings)을 번복하지 못함.	o FSC 의장이 선임하는 3인의 금융전문가로 구성	
- 상소 절차	o GATS Framework에 따름.	
- 상소결정의 채택	o FSC의 합의에 의해 부결되는 경우를 제외 하고 상소결정 채택 o 9개월내에 분쟁당사국 은 Panel 또는 상소 결정에 따라 시정조치 를 행하여야 함.	
- 보상 또는 보복 o 보상 및 보복은 원칙적으로 동일 분야로 한함.	o 최초 보복은 동일 금융분야로 한정 o 6개월후 최초 보복의 실효가 없을 경우 타분야에 교차보복 가능 o 타분야분쟁시에도 최초보복후 6개월경과 또는 FSC의 만장일치 에 의한 합의시 금융 분야에 교차보복 가능	

0140

경 제 기 획 원

우 427-760 / 경기도 과천시 중앙동1 정부제2청사 / 전화 503-9149 / 전송 503-9141

문서번호 봉조삼 10502-89?

시행일자 1991. 12. 18.

수신 수신처참조

참조

선결			지시	
접수	일자 시간	91. ㅣ~ㅣ)	결재·공람	
	번호	42129		
	처리과			
	담당자			

제목 UR/서비스 협상관련 추가 Request사항 제출

───

1. 지난 11월 29일 우리는 미국, EC, 일본, 캐나다, 호주, 스위스, 스웨덴, 핀랜드 등 8개국에 대하여 통신, 건설, 유통, 금융, 운송 및 관광분야를 Request한 바 있습니다. (각부처에 기송부, 봉조삼 10502-841('91.11.27))

2. 이에 추가하여 Request할 사항(추가대상국가, 추가대상분야)이 있는 부처는 12월 24일까지 경제기획원(통상조정3과)에 제출해 주기 바랍니다.

특히 우리민간업계의 진출 가능성이 큰 ASEAN, 중국등 개도국에 대한 Request사항 의 발굴에도 역점을 두기 바랍니다.   끝.

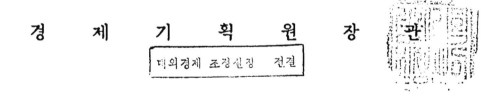

경 제 기 획 원 장

대외경제 조정실장 전결

수신처 : 외무부장관, 내무부장관, 재무부장관, 법무부장관, 교육부장관, 문화부장관,
         농림수산부장관, 상공부장관, 보건사회부장관, 건설부장관, 교통부장관,
         노동부장관, 동자부장관, 체신부장관, 체육청소년부장관, 과학기술처장관,
         환경처장관, 공보처장관, 경찰청장, 특허청장, 해운항만청장

0141

외 무 부

종 별 : 긴 급

번 호 : GVW-2695　　　　　　　　　　　일 시 : 91 1217 2100

수 신 : 장 관(봉기, 경기원, 항만청)

발 신 : 주 제네바 대사

제 목 : UR / GNS 협상(해운분야)

　　1. 12.17(화) CARLISLE 사무차장은 UR/서비스 해운분야 MFN 일탈 및 자유화 추진방식에 관한 미국의 비공식 제안(별첨 FAX 송부)을 본직에게 전달하고 의견을 문의하여 온바 지급검토 회시 바람.

　　2. 당관은 1차 검토 의견은 다음과 같음.

　　0 국제해운의 자유화와 해운 보조 서비스의 자유화를 상호 연계시키고 있는바, 이는 MFN 원칙을 조건부로 적용하는 개념으로서 근본적으로 수용 불가

　　0 서비스 협정 발효이후 10년간의 MFN 일탈은 너무장기간 임.

　　0 해운 항만서비스에 대한 접근 보장 의무를 협정발효 5년후에 부담할 것을 제안하고 있는바 이는협정 발효와 동시에 이루어져야 함.

　　첨부: 미국제안 1부. 끝

　　(GVW(F)-641)

　　(대사 박수길-국장)

통상국　　2차보　　경기원　　해항청

PAGE 1　　　　　　　　　　　　　　　　　91.12.18　　06:53 FO

　　　　　　　　　　　　　　　　　　　　외신 1과 통제관
　　　　　　　　　　　　　　　　　　　　　　　　　0142

주 제 네 바 대 표 부

번 호 : GVH(F) - 0641   년월일 : 11/17   시간 : 2100

수 신 : 장   관 (통기. 경기원. 공안청)

발 신 : 주 제 네 바 대 사

제 목 : GVW-2675 첨부

총   매(표지포함)

보 안 봉 재	

외신과 봉 재	

641 - 6 - 1

0143

15.12.91/20:00

Maritime Transport[*]

1.   So far the debate has been mainly focused on two options for resolving the problems relating to this sector. The first is an approach to liberalization which would be ambitious enough to obviate the need for exemptions from MFN. The second is to seek exemptions from MFN for individual countries.   This second option is based on the assumption that one cannot realistically expect to achieve the necessary level of liberalization by a "critical mass" of countries by the conclusion of this round of negotiations.

2.   A third option, which might be explored, is a combination of the first and second.   It could be envisaged along the following lines:

  (a)   Commitments to achieve the required level of liberalization, but to be implemented over a long period of time (e.g. 10 years);

  (b)   Exemptions from MFN for individual countries to be limited in scope and limited to the same time frame for the implementation of liberalization commitments.

3.   Commitments to liberalize could contain the following elements:

  (a)   A standstill commitment, on all international shipping restrictions by all developed countries and

---

[*]Cabotage is excluded.

HAL/maritime.not

641-6-2

0144

- 2 -

by certain key developing countries (mainly Far Eastern, South East Asian and Latin American countries);

(b) Commitments by the same countries to phase out progressively over a 10-year period (cargo sharing) arrangements and unilateral cargo reservation schemes;

(c) Commitments by the same countries that competition authorities would take measures so that after 5 years all international maritime routes would be open to competition from service providers of Parties to the Agreement;

(d) A standstill commitment by the same countries on the provision of ancillary services (Attachment A);

(e) A commitment by the same countries to phase out progressively over a 10-year period restrictions on the provision of ancillary services;

(f) A commitment by the same countries to ensure access, on reasonable and non-discriminatory basis, to port infrastructure services which are not covered by Article VIII after a period of 5 years (Attachment B);

4. Individual exemptions from MFN would be limited in scope and time bound in accordance with the time frame of implementation of commitments.

HAL/maritime.not

641 - 6 - 3

0145

- 3 -

Attachment A

Auxiliary Services

- Loading and unloading;

- Cargo handling within the port or inland terminal confines;

- Stevedoring, warehousing and storage;   stevedore 下投

- Clearing cargo with customs, including making cargo available for inspection when required;

- Onward transport on a through bill of lading;

- Marketing and sales of maritime transport services through direct contact with customers;

- Establishment of information services (subject to the provisions of the annex on telecommunications).

- 4 -

Attachment B

Port Services

- Pilotage;

- Towing and tug assistance;

- Anchorage, berths and berthing services;

- Lightening and water taxi services;

- Provisioning, fuelling and watering;

- Garbage collection and ballast waste disposal;

- Stevedoring and terminal services, including warehousing and storage;

- Port captains' services;

- Navigation aid services;

- Freight transport agency services;

- Cargo handling services (container and other cargo);

- Shore based operational services essential to ship operations including communications and electronic data interchange networks and water and electrical services;

HAL/maritime.not

6 41 - 6 - 5

0147

- 5 -

- Marine surveys and classification societies for the
  purpose of providing accurate documentation and
  certification of cargo and vessels;

- Customs agencies services.

AL/maritime.not

641-6-6

0148

외　무　부

종　별 :

번　호 : GVW-2706　　　　　　　　　일　시 : 91 1218 1500

수　신 : 장 관(봉기, 경기원, 항만청)

발　신 : 주 제네바대사

제　목 : UR/GNS 협상(해운분야)

　　　연: GVW-2695

　　　연호 해운분야 비공식 제안은 미국 제안이 아니라 해운분야 교착상태 타개를 위하여 가트 사무국이 작성한 초안이며, 92.1 토의 예정임. 또한 동자료를 대외적으로 공개되지 않도록 취급 바람.

　　　한편 동제안상의 PACKAGE APPROACH와 관련해운 보조서비스의 자유화 가능시기등각 보조 서비스별로 구체적 내용검토 회시바람. 끝

　　　(대사 박수길-국장)

통상국　　2차보　　경기원　　해항정

PAGE 1　　　　　　　　　　　　　　　　　91.12.19　　08:16 WH
　　　　　　　　　　　　　　　　　　　　외신 1과　통제관
　　　　　　　　　　　　　　　　　　　　　　0149

외 무 부

종 별 :

번 호 : GVW-2703   일 시 : 91 1218 1200

수 신 : 장관(수신처참조)

발 신 : 주제네바대사

제 목 : UR/GNS 회의(8)

12.17(화) 속개된 주요국 비공식 협의 내용을 하기보고함.

1. 금융부속서

- 분쟁해결 과정에 금융전문가의 참여와 관련패널 구성시 일반적인 서비스 무역전문가 및 서비스분야별 전문가로 구성하도록 각료들의 결정에 반영하되 금융분야의 PRNDENTIAL MEASURE 에 대한분쟁은 동 문제 전문가가 PANEL 구성원에 포함되도록 금융부속서에 규정하기로 합의함.

O 금융서비스 기구의 역할(분쟁해결 관련의사결정권등) 및 TWO-TRACK APPROACH 는 12.18(수)재협의 예정

2. FRAMEWORK 조문

- 제 9조(사기업자의 행위) 및 제21조(양허 수정)에대하여 합의함.

- 제34조(정의)에 대하여는 사무국 작성 초안(별도FAX 송부)을 기초로 토의하였으나 기술적 문제가 미진하여 12.20 이후 추가 작업이 필요한 상태

- SCHEDULING 관련 조문에 대해서는 그간 합의가 미진하였던 부문에 대하여 HAWES 대사가 다음과같이 정리할 예정이라고 일방적으로 통보함.

O 제 6조(국내규제) 1항은 서문에 규정

O 제7조(인정) 주석의 자격 검증 절차 제공 의무는제6조에 규정

O 제17조(예외) C에 PERSONAL DATA 포함

O 제 16조(시장접근) 2항 E 및 F 의 문안수정, 합작 부자 포함 명시

O 제 19조 삭제(제 18조 및 20조와 중복됨)

O ADDITIONAL COMMITMENT 조항은 추가 고려요3. 통신부속서

- JARAMILLO 의장은 통신분야 공동의장NOTE(별도 FAX 송부)를 배부하고 동 요소들을감안 최종문안을 정리 12.20 TNC 에제출하겠으며 참가국간 토의는

통상국	2차보	외정실	분석관	청와대	안기부	법무부	보사부	문화부
교통부	체신부	경기원	재무부	농수부	상공부	건설부	노동부	과기처
해항청	공보처							

PAGE 1

하지않겠다고함.

0 이에 아국, 일본, 인도, 이집트등이 유보 의사를표명하였으며 미국은 각국이 이에 대해 논평하기시작하면 협상을 완료할 수 없다고 전제하고 동사항들은 대부분 기술적 문제이며 기술적문제들은 12.20 이후에도 수정할 수 있을 것이라고함.

첨부: 1. 사무국 작성 34조(정의) 1부

2. 통신분야 공동의장 NOTE 1 부.

(GVW(F)-0646)끝

(대사 박수길-국장)

수신처:통기, 경기원, 재무부, 법무부, 농림수산부, 문화부, 상공부, 건설부, 보사부, 노동부 교통부, 체신부, 과기처, 공보처, 항만청

PAGE 2

0151

주 제 네 바 대 표 부

번 호 : GVR(F) - *0646*   년월일 : *11/218*   시간 : *1200*

수 신 : 장   관 (통기. 경기원. 재무부. 법무부. 농수산부. 상공부. 건설부. 보사부. 노동부.

교통부. 체신부. 문화부. 상공처. 과기처. 환경청)

발 신 : 주 제네바대사

제 목 : *GUW-2703 첨부*

총 *16* 매 (표지포함)

보 안 통 제	

외신과 통 제	

646-16-1

0152

DRAFT

14.12.91   *legal Division*

ARTICLE XXXIV: DEFINITIONS

Note by the Secretariat

1.   The Secretariat has drafted a revised Article XXXIV, encompassing definitions required or used elsewhere in the existing draft Agreement. Article I (Scope) was also examined and revised. Minor changes were made to Articles VIII (Monopolies), XXVIII (Accession) and XXXI (Denial of Benefits). The intent was to clarify the existing text, not to alter its meaning or effect.

2.   Two documents are attached:

   Attachment A: A side-by-side comparison of the existing text and the proposed revised text.

   Attachment B: Remarks on the revisions.

0153

646-16-2-

Attachment "A"

14.12.91

REVISED DEFINITION OF TERMS

EXISTING TEXT	REVISED TEXT	REM
Article I	Article I	
Scope and Definition	Scope	R1
1. This Agreement applies to measures by Parties affecting trade in services.	1. This Agreement applies to measures by Parties affecting trade in services.	
2. For the purposes of this Agreement, trade in services is defined as the supply of a service:	2. For the purposes of this Agreement, trade in services means the supply of a service: *where, by whom, How*	R2
(b) in the territory of one Party to the service consumer of any other Party;	a) outside the territory of a Party, to a service consumer of that Party, by a service provider of another Party ("consumer mode");	R3
(a) from the territory of one Party into the territory of any other Party;	b) into the territory of a Party, from the territory of another Party ("cross-border mode");	R4
(c) by natural persons of one Party in the territory of any other Party; and	c) inside the territory of a Party, by a service supplier of another Party, through presence of natural persons ("natural person mode"); and	R5
(d) through the [commercial] presence of [service providing entities] [juridical persons] of one Party in the territory of one Party in the territory of any other Party [, the provision of service being for a limited duration and a specified purpose].	d) inside the territory of a Party, by a service supplier of another Party, through commercial presence ("commercial presence mode")	R6

EXISTING TEXT	REVISED TEXT	REM

Article XXXIV

Definitions

Article XXXIV

Definitions

For the purpose of this Agreement:

"measure" includes any measure by a Party, whether in the form of a law, regulation, administrative action, rule, procedure, decision or any other form; (XXXIV:a)

(a) "measure" means any measure by a Party, whether in the form of a law, regulation, rule, procedure, decision, administrative action, or any other form;   R7

"measures by Parties" means measures taken by

(b) "measures by Parties" means measures taken by

(i) central, regional or local governments and authorities; and

(i) central, regional or local governments and authorities; and

ii) non-governmental bodies in the exercise of governmental powers [or in the grant of governmental benefits]" (Art I:3(a))

(ii) non-governmental bodies in the exercise of powers delegated by central, regional or local governments or authorities;   R8

"service" includes any service in any sector [except services supplied in the exercise of governmental functions]."(Art I:3(b))

(c) "service" means any service in any sector   R9

(handwritten notes in margin)

(d) "sector" of a service includes any subsector of that service;   R10

(handwritten notes)

"supply of a service" includes the production, distribution, marketing, sale and delivery of a service; (Art XXXIV:b)

(e) "supply of a service" includes the production, distribution, marketing, sale and delivery of a service;

"measures by Parties affecting the supply of a service" include measures in respect of

(f) "measures by Parties affecting trade in services" include measures in respect of   R11

(i) the purchase, payment, or use of a service;

(i) the purchase, payment or use of a service,

0155

-2-

EXISTING TEXT	REVISED TEXT	REM

(ii) the access to and use of distribution and transportation systems and public telecommunications transport networks in connection with the supply of a service; and

(ii) the access to and use of, in connection with the supply of a service,

    (a)   distribution and transportation systems, and

    (b)   public telecommunications transport networks ~~and services~~; and

presence of ~~juridical~~ natural person

(iii)   the commercial presence of natural and juridical persons of a Party supplying a service in the territory of another Party" (Art XXXIV:c)

(iii) ~~the commercial presence persons of a~~   **R12**
Party supplying a service in the territory of another Party; *Self Employed svc provider without commercial presence (own org?)*
(2) Commercial presence of natural person or ~~Coverage~~ two drafting ~~markers~~

physical presence

"commercial presence" means any type of business or professional presence within the territory of a Party for the purpose of supplying a service, whether through incorporation, the acquisition of existing enterprises, the creation of wholly- or partially-owned subsidiaries, joint ventures, ~~partnerships~~, branches, representative offices, or otherwise." (Art XXXIV:h)

(g) "commercial presence" means any type of   **R13**
business or professional presence, including through

    (i)   the constitution, acquisition or maintenance of a juridical person,

    (ii) the creation or maintenance of a branch or a representative office,

~~(iii) presence of natural person~~

within the territory of a Party for the purpose of supplying a service.

"service provider of another Party means any natural or juridical person of a Party that supplies a service, including any natural person of another Party employed by such a person (Art XXXIV:f)

(h) "service supplier" of another Party means any person of that Party that supplies a service;   **R14**

"service consumer of another Party means any natural or juridical person of a Party that receives or uses a service" (Art XXXIV:g)

(i) "service consumer" of a Party means any person of that Party that receives or uses a service;   **R15**

0156

·3· 646-16-5

EXISTING TEXT	REVISED TEXT	REM
	(j) "person" of a Party is either a natural or a juridical person of that Party	R16
"natural person of any other Party means any natural person who is a national of a Party under the law of that Party or, in the case of a Party to which Article XXVIII:3(b) applies, natural persons with the right of permanent residence in the territory of that Party" (Art XXXIV:d)	(k) "natural person" of a Party means (i) a natural person who is a national of the Party under the law of that Party, or (ii) in the case of a Party which does not have it own nationals, a natural person who has the right of permanent residence under the law of that Party, and who resides in the territory of a Party.	R17
		R18
"juridical person of any other Party means	(l) "juridical person" of another Party means any ~~corporation, partnership,~~ joint venture, ~~sole-proprietorship or association,~~ whether constituted for ~~profit or otherwise,~~ and whether ~~privately-owned or governmentally-owned,~~ which is	
i) any entity legally constituted under the law applicable in the territory of another Party and any partnership or association organized under such law, whether constituted or organized for profit or not and whether privately-owned or governmentally-owned; and	(i) constituted under the law of that Party, [and is engaged in substantive business operations in the territory of that or any other Party]; or }	
ii) any entity legally constituted or organized under the law applicable in the territory of a Party that is owned or controlled by natural persons identified in paragraph (d) or entities identified in paragraph (e)(i). (Art XXXIV:e)	(ii) owned or controlled by: 1) natural persons of that Party, or 2) juridical persons of that Party as defined under paragraph (i).	

·4·

EXISTING TEXT	REVISED TEXT	REM
	[(m) A juridical person is	R19

    i)   "owned" by persons of a Party if more than ████ of the equity interest in it is beneficially owned by persons of that Party;

    ii)   "controlled" by persons of a Party if such persons have the power ██████ ████████████████ or to otherwise ██████████████████

    iii)   "affiliated" with another person when it controls, or is controlled by, that other person; or when it and the other person are both controlled by the same person.]

0158

-5-   646-16-7

EXISTING TEXT	REVISED TEXT	REM

Article VIII

Monopolies and Exclusive Service Providers

2. ... an affiliated company, in the supply ...

Article VIII

Monopolies and Exclusive Service Providers

2. ... an affiliated company or other affiliated juridical person, in the supply ...

R20

Article XXVIII

Acceptance and Accession

1. This Agreement shall be open for acceptance until (...) by the governments whose schedules are contained in Annex (...).

2. Any government which does not accept this Agreement pursuant to paragraph 1 may accede to it on terms to be agreed with the PARTIES. Decisions of the PARTIES under this paragraph shall be taken by a two-thirds majority.

3. For the purposes of this Article and Article XXIX,

(a)   The European Economic Community, and

[(b)   any territory which possesses full autonomy in the conduct of its external economic relations and of the other matters provided for in the Agreement]

shall be deemed to be a government.

Article XXVIII

Acceptance and Accession

1. This Agreement shall be open for acceptance until (...) by the governments, and the European Economic Community, whose schedules are contained in Annex (...).

R21

2. Any government which does not accept this Agreement pursuant to paragraph 1 may accede to it on terms to be agreed with the PARTIES. Decisions of the PARTIES under this paragraph shall be taken by a two-thirds majority.

3. For the purposes of paragraph 2 and Article XXIX, any territory which possesses autonomy in the conduct of its external commercial relations and of the other matters provided for in the Agreement shall be deemed to be a government.

0159

-6-   646-16-8

EXISTING TEXT	REVISED TEXT	REM

Article XXXI

Denial of Benefits Clause

1. A Party may deny the benefits of this Agreement to services or service providers if it establishes that they originate from a country which is not a Party to this Agreement, or from another Party to whom the Party does not apply this Agreement pursuant to Article XXX.

Article XXXI

Denial of Benefits Clause

1. A Party may deny the benefits of this Agreement

  (i) to the supply of a service, if it establishes that the service originates in the territory of a country that is not a Party to this Agreement, or in the territory of a Party to which the denying Party does not apply this Agreement; and

  (ii) to a service supplier that is a juridical person, if it establishes that [ultimate] ownership or control of such person is held by persons of a country that is not a Party to this Agreement, or of a Party to which the denying Party does not apply this Agreement.

R22

14 Dec 91 10:29 REVDEF.D6

·7· 6 46-16-P

Attachment "B"

14.12.91

REMARKS

Revised Definitions of Terms

These remarks refer to the preceding side-by-side text of the Revised Definitions of Terms. The reference points are indicated by the placement of a remark number in the third column of the side-by-side text.

Remarks

R1: The title reflects the fact that suggested text Article I now covers only the scope of the Agreement. The definitions that were in paragraph 3 of Article I are now in the Article XXXIV, where they can more easily be compared with the other linking definitions. There appeared to be no reason to separate certain definitions from others in their placement in the Agreement.

R2: The text of the modes of supply has been reworked in order to make it clearer. This was done by:

- describing all modes from a consistent point of view;
- placing the modes in a coherent order;
- placing the elements of each mode in the same order;
- refining the elements of each mode.

The suggested text provides this clarification according to the following principles:

a) Consistent point of view: the position adopted is that of the regulator of a Party who may owe obligations to other Parties with respect to their service suppliers. This was thought to be more practical for regulators, legislators and panels than

0161

6×6-16-10

- 2 -

the opposite "rights claimed" approach. The old text is a mix
of the two approaches.

b) Order of modes: the modes are placed in an order which
reflects, in general, the ~~increasingly territorial space~~ of
the supply of a service. This corresponds to the ~~importance of
the territory to the regulator or regulatory~~ it usually
reflects his jurisdiction under international law and
therefore, to a large degree, his level of interest in the
particular mode of supply.

c) Order of elements of modes: the elements of each mode of
supply are ordered consistently as to ~~territory; persons~~ and
~~type of presence.~~ Territory is placed first for the reasons
stated above. Type of presence is place after persons because
it depends on them.

d) Choice of elements of modes: the elements used to describe the
two modes of supply where there is a supplier presence in the
territory of the Party being supplied the service are
reformulated. The person supplying the service is now referred
to consistently as the "service supplier", with the difference
between the two modes reflected in the different types of
presence: natural persons (including employees) and commercial
presence (not necessarily that of a juridical person).

Several other minor changes have been made:

- the change in the chapeau of paragraph 2 from "defined" to
"means" reflects simpler language used elsewhere in the
Agreement.

- "in" has been changed to "inside" for greater emphasis and to
contrast with the use of outside in paragraph (a).

- "any other" has been changed to "another", which is synonymous
and simpler.

0162

646-16-11

- 3 -

R3: The consumer mode of supply covers cases where the service consumer is <u>not present</u> in the other Party, as long as the service was supplied there (eg. ship repair).

R4: The "cross border" mode of supply in fact covers two distinct situations:

   a) Production and supply of the service takes place "between" two Parties. This is the communication/transportation case, where the mode of supply <u>is</u> the service.

   b) Production of the service in one Party and supply in another Party, <u>without any type of presence</u>, either commercial or of natural persons, in the Party supplied. In this case, the communication/transportation mode is being <u>used</u> to supply a service, but is not the service itself.

R5: The natural person mode of supply includes employees of service providers.

R6: The definition of "commercial presence" is left wholly to the article on Definitions.

R7: The use of the phrase "or any other form" makes the inclusive condition unnecessary. It is replaced by the standard term "means".

R8: The "governmental powers" exercised by private bodies have been defined by linking then to their source: delegation from government bodies. ~~The bracketed text was considered to be covered by this formulation.~~

R9: The term "government functions" was omitted. ~~The term should either be defined precisely, perhaps through a concise list, or dropped.~~

0163

$\int k6-16-12$

- 4 -

R10:   This new definition is intended to make redundant the usage of the term "sectors or sub-sectors" throughout the Agreement.

R11:   This is a reorganization of the existing definition. The only substantive change is the addition of the words "and services" to make it accord with paragraphs 3.2, 3.3 and 5.4 of the Telecom Annex.

R12:   The terms "natural or juridical" are not necessary here. The commercial presence is simply that of the service provider. Later definitions state that a service supplier is a person, either natural or juridical.

R13:   The suggested definition of "commercial presence" has been made more concise by the specific mention of a juridical person (already defined), obviating the need to enumerate again its various forms.

R14:   The term "natural or juridical" is not necessary here, since person is later defined as being either natural or juridical.

R15:   Same remark as preceding.

R16:   Person is defined as either natural or juridical. An obvious, but useful, link for other definitions.

R17:   A shortened reformulation with no substantive change. The reference to Article XXVIII:3(b) is not necessary, since the definition is designed simply to provide for the case where technically a Party does not have nationals, not to set up a test of whether the Party has the required degree of autonomy in external economic or

0164

6 46-16-13

- 5 -

commercial policy. These criteria would have been examined at the
time such a Party joined the GATS.

R18: A shortened reformulation with no substantive change. The
description of the relevant entities is put in the chapeau,
clarifying the conditions in each case. The condition of
"substantial business operations" is inserted to take care of the
"mail box" company.

R19: A new definition, which clarifies the criteria of ownership and
control in the definition of juridical person, and defines the
"affiliation" relationship used in the Monopolies provision.

R20: The addition of the term "juridical person" provides the link to the
definition of "affiliation".

R21: Elements of this Article were re-ordered.

R22: Paragraph (ii) specifies the criterion which may be used where a
Party wishes to show that a service provider is not of another Party.

14 Dec 91 10:27 DEFREM.7

0165

646-16-14

17.12.91

CO-CHAIRMAN'S NOTE

Annex on Telecommunications

This note to GNS participants recalls that some specific aspects of the Annex have been the subject of continuing consultations to arrive at drafting solutions. In particular, alternative language has been under consideration for paragraphs 5.3.1 through 5.3.3 and paragraphs 5.7.2 through 5.7.4 to deal with mainly technical concerns. These concerns principally relate to the attachment of equipment to networks and to the ability to require designated protocols in exceptional circumstances where the interoperability of services may be sought for reasons of public interest.

Also, in the light of the final language of certain provisions of the framework, it will be appropriate to clarify whether it is necessary to include paragraph 2.1.2 and the aspect of paragraph 5.5 related to the privacy of personal data. Paragraph 2.1.2 is related to the formulation of definitions in Article XXXIV and the issue of enforcement of positive obligations of the Agreement and the paragraph 5.5 concern is related to Article XIV.

Attached is a note on considerations proposed by some delegations on technical language for some of the Annex provisions. It also reflects concerns associated with certain other provisions upon which delegations have reserved their positions. As these issues will constitute the basis for final decisions on the contents of the text, it would be helpful if delegations would indicate if their concerns are accurately cited.

0166

646-16-15

Z-TEL2.

17.12.91

CONSIDERATIONS ON ALTERNATIVE WORDING

Annex on Telecommunications

Paragraph 5.3.1: Some delegations have proposed that the words "to purchase or lease" and "customer premises" should be deleted. Others have proposed adding "network interface" equipment.

Paragraph 5.3.2: Some delegations have proposed that additional text should be added to confirm that interconnection of private leased circuits with public networks should be "on mutually agreed terms and conditions" and with other private leased circuits "subject to a Party's domestic law and regulations".

Paragraph 5.3.3: Some delegations have proposed that the term "proprietary protocols" should be changed to "protocols of their choice" and the text should be further modified to allow a Party to require the use of international or designated protocols in exceptional circumstances where interoperability may be sought for reasons of public interest.

Paragraphs 5.7.2 and 5.7.3: Some delegations have proposed that the text of these provisions should reflect their proposals for 5.3.3.

Paragraph 5.7.4: Reflecting their proposals for 5.3.1, some delegations believe that the term "type approval" should be replaced by the term "conditions" or "requirements" and that the term "customer premises equipment" should be deleted. Others have proposed adding the term "other network interface" equipment.

Paragraph 5.2, 5.5 and 5.8: Some delegations do not believe that these provisions should be included in the text.

Z3-TEL2

0167

외 무 부

종 별 :

번 호 : GVW-2729

일 시 : 91 1219 1600

수 신 : 장 관(수신처참조)

발 신 : 주 제네바 대사

제 목 : UR/GNS 회의(9)

12.18(수) 종료된 주요국 비공식 협의결과를 하기보고함.

1. FRAMEWORK

- 제 5조(경제통합) 및 제23조(분쟁해결)중 NON-VIOLATION 조항의 최종문안에 대한 합의를 시도하였으나 합의하지 못하고 의장 판단에 맡겨지게 되었음.

- FRAMEWOKR 조문은 대부분 참가국간 합의를 이루었으나 의장 책임하에 작성될 조문은 다음과같음.

O ADDITIONAAL COMMITMENT(협정에 반영될 것으로예상)

O 분야별 협정 부적용(배제될 것으로 예상)

O 제 1조(정의 및 범위) 및 제 5조, 23조의 문안정리

- 주요 정치적 쟁점인 MFN 일탈문제는 MODALITY는 마련되었으나 구체적인 국가별일탈범위는 미결상태

2. 분야별 부속서

- 일부 이견이 남아있는 사항에 대하여는 의장이 판단하여 초안을 제출할 예정

O 괄호로 묶여있던 5,6,7항(최조임금등사회보장법 규정용,취업 허가등에 관한정보제공)은 모두 내용 자체가 삭제될 것으로예상

나. 통신부속서

- 기송부한바 있는 CHARMAN'S NOTE 를 반영하여 제출될 예정이나 '91.1중 기술적작업이 필요한상태

다. 해운 부속서

- MFN 일탈 및 해운 보조 서비스에 대한 접근보장 의무와 관련 미국 및 개도국과기타국가간 의견 대립으로 합의점을 갖지 못하였으며 현협상 상황만 기술하는 GNS 의 장 서한안만 배부될 예정임.

통상국   2차보   구주국   청와대   안기부   경기원   재무부

91.12.20   03:31 FN

외신 1과 통제관

0168

O MFN 일탈 및 INITIAL COMMITMENT 에 대한협상과 함께 '92.1 로 협상이 이월됨.

라. 항공부속서

- 12.16 협의시 합의된바 있으나 미국이 제4항의 항공설비 서비스 접근 보장, 제2 항의 TRAFFIE RIGHTS및 직접 관련 서비의 정의, 제2항과 4항의 관련등에 대하여 기술적 검토가 필요하다고 문제를 제기, '92.1중 기술적 작업이 필요한 상태

바. 금융부속서

- 12.18 오전 개최된 협의에서 금융서비스 기구 및 분쟁해결에 관해서는 각료들의 결정 초안에 합의함.

O 그러나 동일 심야회의에서 미국,일본,스위스,EC 등이 금융부속서에 규정하지 않는 점 및 동기구가 의사결정 권한을 가지지 못하는점에 대하여 불만을 제기하였으며특히 미국은 동 문제가 92.1 재론될 수 있다 함

- TWO TRACK APPROACH 에 대하여는 일부관심 국가간에 일정 조건(TRACK 선택의 자유,MFN 적용) 하에 NEGATIVE 방식으로 자유화 약속을 할 수 있다는 기본 개념에 대하여는합의를 도출함.

O 또한 금융분야 공동 의장 초안상의 NEGATIVE방식의 규정 자체는 FRAMEWORK 이나금융부속서에 첨부될 수 없으며 다만 전체 UR협상 PACKAGE의 일부가 된다는 점에 대하여 합의하였으며 동규정들이 FRAMEWORK 규정과 상충되는 부분이 있어서는 안된다는 전제하에 동규정의 내용도 별첨과 같이 수정하였음.

O 그러나 동 문서의 법적 지위에 대하여는 동 문서가 영속성을 가질수 있도록 각료들의 결저으로 채택되어야 한다는 선진국 입장과 UR에 한정하여 사용되는 것으로서 INTITAL COMMITMENT 의SUBSTANTIVE GUIDELINE 에 포함 시키자는 개도국 입장이 맞서 의장의 판단에 맡겨지게 되었음.

(각료들의 결정 또는 UNDERSTANDING 의 형태로 제시될 가능성이 큼)

O 한편 미국은 동 NEGATIVE 방식이 부속서에 규정되고 모든국가에 적용되어야 한다는 것이 자국입장이며 '92년 동 문제가 다시 제기될수도 있을 것이라고 함.

첨부: 금융분야 TWO-TRACK APPROACH 관련 문서 1부

(GVW(F)-0658).끝

(대사 박수길-국장)

주 제 네 바 대 표 부

번 호 : GVW(F) - *658*   년월일 : *1121P*   시간 : *1800*

수 신 : 장   관 *(동기. 경가원. 재무부)*

발 신 : 주 제네바대사

제 목 : *GVW面1-272P*

종 *8* 매(표지포함)

보 안 봉 제	

외신과 봉 제	

0170

Draft
18.12.91

<u>DOCUMENT</u>

1.   Participants in the Uruguay Round recognize that ~~certain~~ *interested* Parties may, *following negotiations*
take on commitments *on the basis* ~~as~~ set out below with respect to Financial Services
under the General Agreement on Trade in Services by inscribing such
commitments *by reference to this document,* in their schedules. Participants agree that this approach ~~may~~ *shall*
be applied on the following understanding: *applying provisions of this document along with conditions or qualifications, if any,*

- it is without prejudice to the right of any Party to schedule its
  commitments without reference to this document;

- commitments negotiated pursuant to this approach ~~would be applied~~ *shall apply*
  on an m.f.n. basis;

- the application of the provisions of this document ~~would~~ *shall* not
  conflict with the provisions of the Agreement;

- no presumption is created as to the degree of liberalization to
  which a Party is committing itself under the Agreement.

0171

H2-FIN3

Draft
18.12.91

STANDSTILL

Any conditions, limitations and qualificiations to the commitments
noted below shall be limited to existing non-conforming measures.

MARKET ACCESS

Monopoly Rights

1.   In addition to Article VIII of the Framework, the following shall
apply:

Each Party shall list in its schedule pertaining to financial services
existing monopoly rights and shall endeavour to eliminate them or
reduce their scope. Notwithstanding paragraph 2 of Article 1, this
paragraph applies to the activities referred to in sub-paragraph 2(c)
of Article 1.

Financial Services purchased by Public Entities

2.   Notwithstanding Article XIII of the Framework, each Party shall ensure
that financial service providers of any other Party established in its
territory are accorded most-favoured-nation treatment and national
treatment as regards the purchase or acquisition of financial services by
public entities of the Party in its territory.

Cross-border Trade

3.   Each Party shall permit non-resident providers of financial services
to provide, as a principal, as a principal through an intermediary or as an
intermediary, and under terms and conditions that accord national
treatment, the following services:

- 2 -

(a) insurance of risks relating to:

    (i) maritime shipping and commercial aviation and space launching and freight (including satellites), with such insurance to cover any or all of the following: the goods being transported, the vehicle transporting the goods and any liability arising therefrom; and

    (ii) goods in international transit;

(b) reinsurance and retrocession and the services auxiliary to insurance as referred to in sub-paragraph 1(d) of Article 7 of the Annex;

(c) provision and transfer of financial information and financial data processing as referred to in sub-paragraph 1(o) of Article 7 of the Annex and advisory and other auxiliary services, excluding intermediation, relating to banking and other financial services as referred to in sub-paragraph 1(p) of Article 7 of the Annex.

4.   Each Party shall permit its residents to purchase in the territory of another Party the financial services indicated in:

(a) sub-paragraph 3(a);

(b) sub-paragraph 3(b); and

(c) sub-paragraphs 1(e) to (p) of Article 7 of the Annex.

Commercial Presence

5.   Each Party shall grant financial service providers of any other Party the right to establish or expand within its territory, including through the acquisition of existing enterprises, a commercial presence.

0173

H2-FIN3

- 3 -

6.   A Party may impose terms, conditions and procedures for authorization of the establishment and expansion of a commercial presence in so far as they not circumvent the Party's obligation under paragraph 5 and they are consistent with the other obligations of this Agreement.

New Financial Services

7.   A Party shall permit financial service providers of other Parties established in its territory to offer in its territory any new financial service.

Transfers of Information and Processing of Information

8.   No Party shall take measures that prevent transfers of information or the processing of financial information, including transfers of data by electronic means, or that, subject to importation rules consistent with international agreements, prevent transfers of equipment, where such transfers of information, processing of financial information or transfers of equipment are necessary for the conduct of the ordinary business of a financial service provider. Nothing in this paragraph restricts the right of a Party to protect personal data, personal privacy and the confidentiality of individual records and accounts so long as such right is not used to circumvent the provisions of the Agreement.

Temporary Entry of Personnel

9.   (a)   Each Party shall permit temporary entry into its territory of the following personnel of a financial service provider of any other Party that is establishing or has established a commercial presence in the territory of the Party:

   (i)   senior managerial personnel possessing proprietary information essential to the establishment, control and operation of the services of the financial service provider; and

0174

H2-FIN3

- 4 -

(ii) specialists in the operation of the financial service provider.

(b) Each Party shall permit, subject to the availability of qualified personnel in its territory, temporary entry into its territory of the following personnel associated with a commercial presence of a financial service provider of any other Party:

   (i) specialists in computer services, telecommunication services and accounts of the financial service provider; and

   (ii) actuarial and legal specialists.

Non-discriminatory Measures

10. Each Party shall endeavour to remove or to limit any significant adverse effects on financial service providers of any other Party of:

(a) non-discriminatory measures that prevent financial service providers from offering the Party's territory, in the form determined by the Party, all the financial services permitted by the Party;

(b) non-discriminatory measures that limit the expansion of the activities of financial service providers into the entire territory of the Party;

(c) measures of a Party, when such a Party applies the same measures to the provision of both banking and securities services, and a financial service provider of any other Party concentrates its activities in the provision of securities services; and

(d) other measures that, although respecting the provisions of this Agreement, affect adversely the ability of financial service

0175

- 5 -

> providers of any other Party to operate, compete or enter the Party's market;

> provided that any action taken under this paragraph would not unfairly discriminate against financial service providers of the Party taking such action.

11. With respect to the non-discriminatory measures referred to in sub-paragraphs 10(a) and (b), a Party shall endeavour not to limit or restrict the present degree of market opportunities nor the benefits already enjoyed by financial service providers of all other Parties as a class in the territory of the Party, provided that this commitment does not result in unfair discrimination against financial service providers of the Party applying such measures.

NATIONAL TREATMENT

1. In determining the meaning of like financial services or like financial services providers, consideration shall be given ~~inter alia~~ where relevant to the regulatory and supervisory framework relating to such financial services or financial services providers.

2. Paragraph 3 of Article XVII does not require a Party to maintain treatment more favourable than that accorded to a Party's own financial service providers.

3. Under terms and conditions that accord national treatment, each Party shall grant to financial service providers of any other Party established in its territory access to payment and clearing systems operated by public entities, and to official funding and refinancing facilities available in the normal course of ordinary business. This paragraph is not intended to confer access to the Party's lender of last resort facilities.

4. When membership or participation in, or access to, any self-regulatory body, securities or futures exchange or market, clearing agency, or any

0176

H2-FIN3

- 6 -

other organization or association, is required by a Party in order for financial service providers of any other Party to provide financial services on an equal basis with financial service providers of the Party, or when the Party provides directly or indirectly such entities, privileges or advantages in providing financial services, the Party shall ensure that such entities accord national treatment to financial service providers of any other Party resident in the territory of the Party.

DEFINITIONS[1]

For the purposes of this ~~Annex~~ document

1.   A non-resident provider of financial services is a financial service provider of a Party which provides a financial service into the territory of another Party from an establishment located in the territory of another Party, regardless of whether such a financial service provider has or has not a commercial presence in the territory of the Party in which the financial service is provided.

2.   "Commercial presence" means an enterprise within a Party's territory for the provision of financial services and includes wholly- or partly-owned subsidiaries, joint ventures, partnerships, sole proprietorships, franchising operations, branches, agencies, representative offices or other organizations.

3.   A new financial service is a service of a financial nature, including services related to existing and new products or the manner in which a product is delivered, that is not provided by any financial service provider in the territory of a particular Party but which is provided in the territory of another Party.

---

[1]The definition of a juridical person is being reviewed under the Framework.

0177

H2-FIN3

경 제 기 획 원

우 427-760 / 경기도 과천시 중앙동1 정부제2청사 / 전화 503-9149 / 전송 503-9141

문서번호 봉조삼 10502- 896

시행일자 1991. 12. 18.

수신 수신처참조

참조

선결			지시	 V
접수	일자 시간	∴ ∴	결재·공람	
	번호			
처리과				
담당자	기6			

제목 UR/서비스협상관련 수정 Offer List 제출

    1. '91년 12월 15일 현재 양허표 작성방식에 대한 거의 최종적인 GATT문서가 작성되었으며 EC, 호주, 스위스등 3개국가가 수정 Offer를 제출하고, 미국, 캐나다등 주요 국가들도 조만간 수정 Offer를 제출할 예정입니다.

    2. 따라서 우리도 '92년 1월중에 수정 Offer를 GATT에 제출할 것을 목표로 추가적인 작업을 추진코자 하니 소관업종에 대한 수정 Offer를 다음의 별첨자료를 참조·작성하여 주기 바랍니다.

- 다   음 -

가. 별첨1 :「양허표 작성방식」(Scheduling of Commitments in Trade in Services)

  - 동문서는 거의 합의단계에 있는 GATT의 비공식문서이기 때문에 동 지침에 따라 업종별 양허표를 수정·보완

  - 특히 다음사항에 대하여 양허표에 기재하지 않을 경우 제한조치가 없는 것으로 간주되는 점을 유의하여 작성

    〈 시장접근(제16조) 〉

    ① 서비스공급자의 숫자(Number of service provider)에 대한 제한조치
    ② 총거래액 및 총자산(Total value of transactions/assets)에 대한 제한조치
    ③ 총영업회수 및 총산출액(Total number of service operation and total quantity of service output)에 대한 제한조치
    ④ 특정서비스분야에 고용되는 인력의 숫자(Number of employee)에 대한 제한 조치
    ⑤ 상업적주재 형태를 제한하는 조치
    ⑥ 외국인투자 지분을 제한하는 조치

0178

< 내국민대우(제17조) >

① 제도적으로 동일한 대우를 제공하지 않는 경우는 물론 사실상 경쟁조건을 침해하는 조치도 내국민대우의 차별조치로 간주됨.

나. 별첨2 : 분야별 제1차 수정 Offer시안

- 동 수정안은 그간 관계부처에서 제출한 자료를 중심으로 경제기획원 총괄대책반에서 시안으로 작성한 예시임.

- 따라서 동 수정안은 최종적인 것이 아니며 앞으로 계속 수정·보완되어야 하기 때문에 관계부처에서 심층 분석·검토하여 제2차 수정안을 작성

3. 앞으로 관계부처에서 제시할 제2차 수정안을 중심으로 UR대책 서비스 실무 소위원회등 관계부처회의를 거쳐 최종안을 확정할 예정이니 업종별 수정 Offer를 작성하여 12월 24일까지 기일엄수 경제기획원(통상조정3과)에 제출하여 주기 바랍니다.

첨부 : 1. 양허표 작성방식 1부.
　　　 2. 분야별 제1차 수정Offer시안 1부.　　끝.

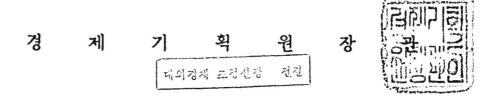

경　제　기　획　원　장

수신처 : 외무부장관, 내무부장관, 재무부장관, 법무부장관, 교육부장관, 문화부장관, 농림수산부장관, 상공부장관, 보건사회부장관, 건설부장관, 교통부장관, 노동부장관, 동자부장관, 체신부장관, 체육청소년부장관, 과학기술처장관, 환경처장관, 공보처장관, 경찰청장, 특허청장, 해운항만청장

경 제 기 획 원

우 427-760 / 경기도 과천시 중앙동1 정부제2청사 / 전화 503-9149 / 전송 503-9141

문서번호 봉조삼 10502- 713

시행일자 1991. 12. 27.

선결			지시		
접수	일자시간	91. 12. 27 :	결재·공람		
	번호	**43145**			
	처 리 과				
	담 당 자				

수신 외무부장관

참조

제목 훈령요청

---

1. GVW-2695('91.12.17)와 관련입니다.

2. UR/해운서비스관련 사무국제안에 대한 아국입장을 아래와 같이 정리하여 통보
하니 훈령 조치하여 주기 바랍니다.

- 아   래 -

- 해운서비스분야에 있어 아국정부의 기본입장은 다음과 같음.

  ○ MFN원칙은 다자화 규범의 초석으로 자유화약속에 대한 협상에 앞서 우선적
    으로 적용

  ○ UN Liner Code와 관계없이 맺어진 기존 쌍무협정에 한하여 MFN일탈허용
    (아국은 한일항로와 한소항로에 대해 '95년말까지 일탈희망)

  ○ 해운보조서비스에 대해서는 현존규제동결 및 점진적 철폐

  ○ 항만시설에 대해서는 즉각적인 접근 및 사용보장

- 금번 사무국이 제안한 단계적인 해운분야 자유화약속과 MFN원칙 적용상의
  유예기간인정은 아국의 기본입장보다 보수적이기 때문에 기본적으로 이를
  받아들일 수는 없음.

- 다만, 앞으로의 협상에서 여타서비스와의 협상연계등을 고려하여 사무국안을
  검토할 용의가 있다는 방향으로 대처하고 세부적인 검토결과는 앞으로의
  부속서 협의과정에서 제시할 것임을 표명. 끝.

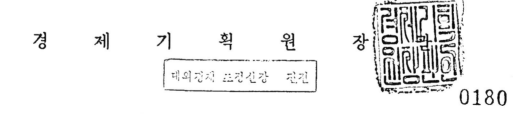

경 제 기 획 원 장

대외경제 조정실장 전결

0180

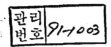

발 신 전 보

WGV-1918   911231 1222 DQ

분류번호	보존기간

번   호 :   종별 :

수   신 : 주   제네바   대사. 총영사

발   신 : 장 관 (통 기)

제   목 : UR/GNS 협상 (해운분야)

검 토 필 (1991. 12. 31.) 김

대 : GVW-2695

1. 12.30 UR/대책 실무위원회에서 결정된 해운분야의 아국 기본입장은 아래와 같음.

    ○ MFN 원칙은 다자화 규범의 초석으로 자유화 약속에 대한 협상에 앞서
       우선적으로 적용되어야 함.

    ○ 해운보조 서비스에 대해서는 현존 규제 동결 및 점진적 철폐가 필요함.

    ○ 항만시설에 대해서는 즉각적인 접근 및 사용을 보장하여야 함.

2. 따라서 아국으로서는 대호 사무국이 제안한 단계적인 해운분야 자유화 약속과
    MFN 원칙 적용상의 유예기간 인정을 받아들이기 곤란함.

3. 다만, 향후 협상에서 여타 서비스 분야와의 협상 연계등을 고려하여, 사무국안을
    검토할 용의가 있으나 세부적인 검토 결과는 앞으로의 부속서 협의 과정에서
    제시할 것이라는 입장으로 대처바람.   끝.   (통상국장 김 용 규)

보 안 통 제	ᏕᏕ

앙 고 재	91 년 12 월 31 일	통 기 과	기안자 성명		과 장	심의관	국 장		차 관	장 관	외신과통제
			조현				전결				

0181

서비스協定文案의 主要內容 및 向後 對應方案

〈 協定文案의 主要內容 〉

— 35個條文으로 구성된 서비스一般協定의 基本構造(Framework)와
MFN原側의 例外事項, 人力移動, 航空, 通信, 金融등 5개분야의
附屬書등으로 構成 (海運分野는 美國 및 開途國과 其他國家의
意見對立으로 부속서초안이 제시되지 못함)

① Framework

— Framework條文은 상대적으로 이헤대립의 정도가 약하여 대부분
합의를 이루었으나 (我國立場에 合致) 일부 異見이 있던 다음
條文은 議長 責任下에 협정초안 작성

  ○ Additional Commitment 근거조항 규정에 대하여 일부
  開途國이 반대하였으나 議長이 協定草案에 反映

  ○ EC는 분야별 협정 부적용의 포함을 계속 주장하였으나 (EC기타)
  議長이 削除

  ○ 기타 일부조문 (定義 및 範圍, 經濟統合, 紛爭解決中 Non -
  Violation)에 대하여 의장이 最終文案 作成

— 第 21 條 (讓許修正) 및 Definitions (특히 서비스 供給企業의
  定義)에 대하여는 추가 작업 필요

-1-

0182

428 우루과이라운드 서비스 협상 3

─ 다음 條文들은 UR이후 추가 협상대상으로 合意

  ○ 合理的 國內 規制의 基準, 세이프가드, 政府調達, 서비스貿易과

    環境과의 關係, 補助金

─ MFN逸脫問題는 逸脫申請方式, 協商節次, 協定發效後 再檢討方法

  등 協商 Modality에 대하여만 合意

  ○ 國家別 구체적 逸脫範圍는 '92年初 讓許協商의 일부로서

    함께 협상 예정   인허協商 過程에 사전하여된도.

② 分野別 附屬書

─ 4개 부속서 초안(我國立場에 합치)이 작성되었는 바, 航空·

  通信附屬書는 '92年初 일부 技術的 作業이 필요한 狀態

─ 金融附屬書는 美國등 일부 先進國이 불만을 가지고 있으며

  美國業界의 反應에 따라 '92年初 協商이 재개될 可能性도

  배제할 수 없는 상태

┌─────────────┐
│ 人力移動附屬書 │
└─────────────┘

  ○ 附屬書에 명문으로 規定할 것인지 여부에 대하여 論難이

    되었던 다음 事項을 議長이 모두 削除, 별문제없이 參加國

    들이 수용할 것으로 예상

    · 人力이 입국하는 國家의 勤勞關係法規 適用問題(Frame-

      work 第6條 國內規制에 해당)

    · 入國·滯在·就業등에 관한 情報提供義務(Framework

      第3條 Transparency에 해당)

-2-

0183

○ 航空運輸權 및 直接 關聯 서비스에 協定適用排除, 기타 補助 서비스에 협정규정 (MFN 포함) 적용, 航空設備 서비스에의 接近 保障에 대하여 합의

○ 航空設備서비스의 포괄범위, 航空運輸權과 直接關聯서비스와의 관계 등에 대한 기술적 追加作業 필요

通信附屬書

○ 先·開途國間 對立爭點인 원가지향 料金策定과 開途國 우대조항을 함께 議長이 削除

○ 기타 기술적 사항에 대한 追加論議 필요

金融附屬書

○ 金融서비스機構 및 紛爭解決은 他分野도 관계되는 一般的 問題 이므로 Ministerial Decision으로 규정하고 Prudential measure에 대한 紛爭解決등 특수한 事項만 金融附屬書에 반영 키로 합의

○ 美國·日本등 先進國은 金融서비스 機構가 의사결정권한 (특히 紛爭解決 관련)을 갖지 못하는 점에 대하여 불만 제기

-3-

○　Two-Track Approach를　Framework이나　附屬書에　규정하지

않고　UR協商　Package의　일부로　하는데　합의

●　동　방식의　法的地位는　議長이　일방적으로　결정하여

Understanding으로　규정

●　美國은　동　방식이　附屬書에　규정되지　못한　점에　대하여

불만제기,협상을　재개할　수도　있다고　言及

海運附屬書

○　MFN逸脫　및　海運補助서비스에　대한　접근보장의무와　관련

美國　및　開途國　對　其他國家間　의견대립으로　초안을　작성

하지　못함.

○　美國은　海運補助서비스　접근보장문제와　閉鎖同盟(Closed

Conference)問題를　연계시키고　있으며　海運分野　全體에

대한　MFN逸脫을　주장

〈評　價〉

─　현재까지　작성된　Framework　및　分野別　附屬書는　我國立場에

비추어　만족할만할　수준

○　특히　自由化　推進方式　관련　我國　및　開途國이　주장한대로

각국이　개방할　분야를　제시하고　개방시에도　조건을　添附할

수　있게　됨으로써　自由化　推進에　構造的　安全裝置가　마련됨.

─ 4 ─

○ 따라서 雙務協商에 의하여 이들의 競爭力이 脆弱한 分野가 選擇的으로 조기에 開放되는 것을 에방하고 다자간 規則에 의하여 " 利益의 均衡 " 原則下에 점진적으로 自由化를 추진하며 我國企業의 海外進出機會 확대도 가능

— 특히 海運·航空分野 (補助서비스)에 MFN등 다자간 原則이 適用됨으로써 我國 運送企業의 營業環境 改善效果

〈 向後 對應方案 〉

① 附屬書 關聯對策

— 海運分野의 MFN逸脫問題에 대해서 實利確保次元에서 對應

— 金融附屬書 論議再開時 對應論理 마련

② 서비스讓許協商對策 樹立·推進

— 92.1月下旬～3月까지 두세 차례의 集中的인 協商推進 展望

— 이를 위하여 1月中旬까지 關係部處 合同으로 다음의 作業課題를 推進

○ 修正 Offer List 作成

○ 主要國 關心分野別로 協商對應戰略 樹立

○ 相對國에 대한 2次 Request List 準備, 提出

• 旣 提出國에 대한 一部 追加 Request 作成, 提出

• 準備狀態에서 아직 提出하지 않은 一部國家에 대한 Request 提出

• 實際 進出可能性과 利益이 있는 國家 및 Request 內容 追加 發掘

○ 앞으로 서비스 兩者協商過程이 미칠 파급영향을 考慮하여 이번 協議進行內容을 소상히 言論에 弘報

— 5 —

0186

외교문서 비밀해제: 우루과이라운드2 21
우루과이라운드 서비스 협상 3

초판인쇄 2024년 03월 15일
초판발행 2024년 03월 15일

지은이 한국학술정보(주)
펴낸이 채종준
펴낸곳 한국학술정보(주)
주 소 경기도 파주시 회동길 230(문발동)
전 화 031-908-3181(대표)
팩 스 031-908-3189
홈페이지 http://ebook.kstudy.com
E-mail 출판사업부 publish@kstudy.com
등 록 제일산-115호(2000. 6. 19)

ISBN 979-11-7217-123-0 94340
      979-11-7217-102-5 94340 (set)